Socialism
and Revolution

ANDRÉ GORZ was born in Austria in 1924. While still in school he discovered the work of Jean-Paul Sartre and may be considered one of Sartre's earliest disciples. He has been a Paris journalist since the late 1940s and an editor of *Les Temps Modernes* since 1961. Gorz is author of, among other essays, *The Traitor* (New York, 1959), with a foreword by Sartre, *La Morale de l'Histoire* (1959), and *Strategy for Labor* (New York, 1967).

Socialism and Revolution

ANDRÉ GORZ

TRANSLATED BY NORMAN DENNY

Anchor Books
Anchor Press/Doubleday
Garden City, New York
1973

SOCIALISM AND REVOLUTION was originally published in France in 1967, under the title *Le Socialisme Difficile*, by Editions du Seuil, © Editions du Seuil, 1967. The Anchor Press edition is published by arrangement with Editions du Seuil.

"Sartre and Marx," in translation by Ben Brewster, appeared originally in the *New Left Review*, No. 37, May–June 1966, and is reprinted here with permission. This somewhat abridged translation has been revised and completed by the author.

Anchor Press edition: 1973
Translation by Norman Denny copyright © 1973
by Doubleday & Company, Inc.
ISBN: 0-385-04831-9
Library of Congress Catalog Card Number 74–186054

Contents

Author's Note

The various chapters of this book were written in 1965 and 1966. Although they have a unity of intent, they can be read separately and in any order.

The first essay was written in 1970 especially for the American edition. It too can be read as an independent piece in which the author brings up to date or reconsiders some of his earlier writings.

Chapter 1

IMPERIALISM

Anti-imperialist uprisings abroad have played a major role in reawakening radical consciousness in the capitalist metropoles. They have shown our system to rest on violence and not on universal values and consent. They have shown that it is not the lack of material resources, or technological "backwardness," or corrupt social systems that prevent the Third World's development, but economic, political and, whenever necessary, military imperialism that protects corrupt oligarchies against the revolt of their own people. They have shown that capitalism holds no solution to the problems of the two thirds of the world that goes hungry; that it does not represent the future of mankind; that, while it is still capable of ferociously defending old privileges, it can no longer offer a meaningful life to its own or to the world's peoples.

Because they are not deterred by our weaponry, or impressed by our material power, or ready to bargain over their rights, the "wretched of the earth" have dispelled many of our fears and illusions. They have freed many of us from the respectful awe that our fathers felt for the leaders, laws and institutions of our Empires. They have made us aware that our economic system and our standards are neither the only nor the best possible ones. They have given us the courage to question our civilization more radically than ever before. And they also have made us feel ashamed and guilty.

I wonder whether it is not a Christian feeling of guilt,

rather than revolutionary fervor, that has led many of us, mainly students, to the conclusion that our own needs, frustrations and crippled lives are not really very important compared to the Third World's atrocious misery; that it would be indecent for us to desire anything more for ourselves; that, not being engaged on the main front of the battle against capitalism, the reasons why we too should want to fight it have little relevance; that, having built our wealth and power on the deprivation of others, our turn has come to deprive ourselves.

Feelings like these give rise to theories that need to be discussed: the theory, for instance, that our washing machines and TV sets are paid for at least in part by the toil of the Third World masses; the theory that all classes in the capitalist metropoles share in the fruits of the Third World's exploitation, and therefore would be poorer after imperialism's defeat. These theories, in turn, lead to the supposition that imperialism has to be defeated from the outside, by the onslaught of the Third World's masses, and that the working class in the metropoles cannot be expected to play a major role in the destruction of capitalism.

All these theories contain a measure of truth, inasmuch as they reflect the disgust that we can't help feeling when faced with the real situation. Theories, however, should not merely express feelings; they should enable us to grasp the situation, to bring it under control and to change it. In a situation of guilt, shame and helplessness, theory, to be true, must enable us to conceive of actions by means of which we could abolish the reasons for our shame and guilt. In this respect, the approach taken by the more extreme or mystical "Third Worldists" is self-defeating and must be challenged.

As long as we work on the assumption that all classes in the metropoles have a material stake in imperialism, we must also assume that the anti-imperialist and anti-capitalist struggle rests on merely the ethical and intellectual motivations of only a small minority. Our behavior and methods will of course mirror this assumption. And we will then find it impossible ever to build up sustained mass support.

If, on the other hand, we work on the assumption that all people, except a small minority, could win a better life and higher standards of civilization by the overthrow of capitalism, then anti-imperialist militancy in the metropoles will appeal to the needs and interests of large masses. It may then be possible to work towards a revolutionary alliance of the metropoles' working class and the Third World's peoples, each shouldering the other's struggle and depending upon the other's victory. It may even be possible then for the richest nations' workers to want more out of life without feeling ashamed and guilty.

But is such an assumption legitimate? Can it be proven that living standards need not deteriorate in the metropoles after imperialism is defeated? Can it further be proven that the peoples of the developed countries could actually live much better without in the least depriving their Third World brothers? Let us have a closer look at these questions.

(1) The looting of the Third World's natural resources has been a major source of capital accumulation in the metropoles. It is not only responsible for the Third World's "poverty"; it has "underdeveloped" the latter by forcing upon it political, social and economic patterns that make development impossible.

The mechanism of looting is well known: mineral and agricultural resources are exploited by or for the sake of international monopolies and paid to the producing countries at a price that allows neither the reconstitution or reproduction of their assets, nor sufficient profits to promote accelerated growth. Profits are made mainly (or even solely) by imperialist monopolies who reinvest them in such a way as to secure their own growth, power and control over world resources.

Though plundering is all-important to the imperialist monopolies themselves, it has ceased to be a main and

vital source of capital accumulation to the metropoles'
economy as a whole. Two key figures illustrate this asser-
tion: imports from the Third World presently represent no
more than 2.3 per cent of the industrialized capitalist
world's GNP.[1] Were the Third World to gain autonomy
and were the price of mineral resources to reach three
times its present level, the "loss" to the imperialist nations
would still amount to no more than 5 per cent of their
GNP, or one year's growth.

Such a "loss" would certainly not be a serious blow to
the living standards and economy of industrialized nations:
they are used to wasting, sterilizing or destroying a much
larger proportion of their GNP. A 5 per cent "loss" could
be compensated for almost immediately if it coincided with
the overthrow of capitalism.

Unrestricted access to cheap mineral resources may
prove less vital than has been thought. The search for alternative sources of raw materials (such as the oceans and
the seabed), for substitutes and for new technologies may
even make for unprecedented economic growth and scientific advances.[2] Although it would never accept such a
situation unless it were compelled to by defeat, capitalism
may prove capable of adjusting to it. This capacity to adjust has filled its bitterest and most outspoken enemies with
awe.

(2) Traditional methods of imperialist looting are now
overshadowed by subtler and more complex methods of
exploitation. The industrialized capitalist world no longer
draws its economic power and superior level of development mainly from imperialist domination. It is rather the
superior development of productive forces that made im-

[1] According to the UN annual statistical abstract (1968) and
to GATT's *International Trade* (1966), these imports represented $25.8 billion in 1965, compared to the industrialized
capitalist world's GNP of 1,100 billion dollars.

[2] See Charles Bettelheim's Preface to Arghiri Emmanuel's
L'Echange inégal (Paris: Maspéro, 1969), reproduced in
Monthly Review, June 1970.

perialist domination possible and then further increased the imperialist nations' advance at the expense of the Third World's underdevelopment. The main source of the capitalist nations' wealth and power is their powerful industrial base, abundance of skilled manual and intellectual labor, high level of productivity and accompanying high rate of exploitation of the domestic labor force.

It is therefore unscientific to assert that the American working class is a direct beneficiary of imperialist exploitation; it is rather the tool that makes possible imperialist domination; it forges the chains of the Third World at the same time as its own. The profits accruing to American corporations from their huge investments in foreign industries (which by 1966 amounted to some $45 billion) are not shared by American workers. Schematically, the mechanism of foreign investment can be described as follows:

The American home market no longer offers monopolies sufficient opportunities for profitable investment. Were they to reinvest all of their profits at home, they would, in a way, compete against themselves. They could make full use of their additional capacities and sell their additional production only by lowering their prices. But by doing this, they would undermine future profits. The administration of their home market as well as the logic of profit maximization drive them to look for investment opportunities abroad, in countries where the market keeps expanding and where high rates of return can be attained.

Paradoxically, Third World countries are not the main outlets for the investment of surplus capital. They may offer extremely high rates of return (30 per cent in South and East Asia), but they offer only very limited investment opportunities. Their domestic market is narrow since their population's purchasing power is extremely low. Imperialist investment cannot promote the rapid expansion of their market since the most profitable new industries do not employ much native labor. On the contrary, in countries like Brazil, imperialist investment in new industries

creates fewer jobs than it does away with by ruining old
domestic industries; it thereby further narrows the domestic market.[3] The production of these new industries therefore must be geared mainly to export markets. The Third
World's cheap labor must produce for the wealthy metropoles commodities it cannot buy and does not need.

It is hard to see what benefits the workers in the metropole draw from this process. They may get cheaper commodities eventually. But they will also find it harder to
keep or get jobs, since commodities produced for the
American market, at great profit, by the American corporations' Third World subsidiaries, represent the substitution of cheap Asian labor for American labor at twenty to
thirty dollars a day. Monopolies may even find it profitable
to close down some of their plants at home, thereby producing regional underdevelopment, and to build new factories abroad. By doing this, their aim is not to promote
growth in the underdeveloped countries (much more
would be needed to achieve this) nor to make life cheaper
and easier for the American worker. Their aim is to
achieve higher profits by keeping wages down; they hire
Third World labor to help them wage a class struggle
against American workers.

What use is made of the corporations' imperialist profits?
Can it be argued at least that the high profits corporations
earn overseas are spent in a way that is beneficial to the
American people as a whole? As we have seen, these profits cannot be wholly reinvested in the Third World since
markets there are too narrow for additional commodity
production; nor will they be wholly reinvested in the metropole itself, where virtual saturation of the market and
high labor costs tend to depress profit rates. A sizable pro-

[3] Among the more accessible writings on the subject, see
Eduardo Galeano, "The denationalization of Brazilian indus-
try," in *Monthly Review,* December 1969; Ernesto Laclau, "The
Argentinian contest," in *New Left Review,* July–August 1970;
Jamil Rodriguez, "Avant-garde armée et masses," in *Les Temps
Modernes,* March 1971.

portion of the profits derived from American operations in the Third World is therefore channeled into already developed countries such as Canada and Western Europe, where markets keep expanding but where the need for American investment is highly questionable.[4] It is hard to see what advantage this is to the American people.

The American working class has the very dubious privilege of sustaining by its labor a huge military establishment, costing 8 to 10 per cent of the American GNP, whose purpose is to make the world safe for American capital. American workers generate the surplus capital that is being exported and the surplus capital that is being destroyed, with great profit for the corporations, by plant closures and by military production. The same capitalist logic which prevents the economic and social development of the Third World prevents the utilization of the metropole's huge economic surplus for purposes that are necessary but not profitable in financial terms: doing away with disease, slums, unemployment, ghettos, malnutrition, illiteracy, pollution, inequality, stupefying and subhuman work in the metropole itself. . . . Therefore, while we certainly are guilty of the overt and covert crimes inherent in imperialist exploitation and oppression, it cannot be said that these crimes are committed in the interest and for the good of our peoples. Imperialism does not loot the Third World so as to make its own people thrive in happiness. It rather breeds underdevelopment not only abroad but at home as well, turning cities into slums, simultaneously producing affluence and new types of poverty, academic sophistication and new types of illiteracy and ignorance, technical

[4] During the years 1959–65, American corporations have taken out of Third World countries $9.2 billion more than they have invested there. During the same period, American corporations have invested in Western Europe and Canada $5.2 billion more than they took out of these countries. About 60 per cent of the profits taken out of the Third World were thus channeled into "first world" countries.

perfection and mutilated human beings working efficiently for sterile and destructive purposes.

True, it may be argued that corporations would pay lower wages if their profit rates weren't bolstered by exploiting the rest of the world. But what conclusion are we to draw from this? That we need to have imperialism so as to have high corporate profits and high corporate wages? Or rather that we had better get rid of imperialism, corporations and capitalism altogether because the type of growth they promote and the type of commodities they offer are now generating worse, not better living conditions for the people, whatever their wages? What sense have high profit rates or high rates of capital accumulation when more than a quarter of productive capacities remain unused, when the economic surplus amounts (according to Baran and Sweezy's evaluation) to 40 per cent of the GNP, and when there is already an overabundance of everything that can be produced at a profit, but an increasingly acute scarcity of all the rest? High profit rates have become an obstacle to economic and social development everywhere and so has capitalism as a system. The main contradiction does not lie between the needs of the Third World and the needs of our people, but between the logic of capital and the needs of people everywhere.

In short, we may be worse off if imperialism is defeated but capitalism manages to survive in its strongholds; but we shall be better off if the defeat of imperialist domination abroad and of capitalism at home go hand in hand. The first event need not necessarily lead to the second. Though monopoly capitalism is inherently imperialist, though it will never relinquish its imperial positions of power unless it is forced to do so, it may prove able to survive even in hostile surroundings by resorting, if necessary, to barbarian forms of domination. It has happened before. Capitalism does not collapse unless it is swept away by revolution from within.

OUTCASTS

Revolutions are made not to get more (or, of course, less) of what we already have, but to get something altogether different which will put an end to conditions that are felt to be unbearable. Though a wide spectrum of social forces may concur in the making of a revolution and be ideologically and politically unified in its process, revolution can be carried out only by a class whose position in the social process of production carries some effective power that can be built up through class struggle into the conquest of power *tout court*. Let us examine more closely how these two axioms apply to the present situation in the advanced capitalist world.

It is widely held that the most unbearable condition is that of the most oppressed and poorest sectors of the working class. This assumption is morally and ideologically correct, although it may be questioned on factual and political grounds. It is ideologically correct because the truth of a society lies with those it oppresses and reduces to subhuman misery: the most oppressed sector of the population—the foreign or non-white workers, the unemployed, the aged, the physically disabled, the small farmers, the adolescents, etc.—reveals all other sectors of the population as privileged and the whole society as resting on injustice, selfishness and inequality. Social change would be meaningless if one of its foremost aims were not to wipe out poverty and oppression, that is, if the task of building a new society were not viewed through the eyes of all those to whom everything is denied under the present order.

It would be erroneous to assume that the more than 20 per cent of the population that, in the capitalist countries, lives in subhuman conditions, is "marginal" to the economy or, as is sometimes stated, only "pockets of misery" "left over" from the past which will be absorbed through further economic growth. While some of the poorest strata

—the aged, the disabled—may be called marginal in so far as their existence is in no way functional to society as a whole, the same does not hold true for other sectors of the poor. Highly developed capitalist societies need a mass of outcasts that can be burdened with the kind of work the rest of the population considers too degrading to be acceptable. In all the capitalist countries (including Sweden and Switzerland) at least 15 per cent (and up to 35 per cent in Switzerland) of the industrial labor force is drawn from the less developed areas of the world. This "foreign" labor force is denied all political and most civil rights, is held in complete subjection, housed in barracks or shantytowns, exposed to police persecution, forbidden to organize and prevented from bargaining over the price at which it will sell its labor. In this respect, the situation in the United States is not exceptional; it is exceptional only in so far as the non-white labor force is legally entitled to equal rights (which it is denied in fact).

The existence of this mass of outcasts facilitates the rest of the population's promotion to more skilled and better paid jobs and diminishes the political weight of the working class. Most important, it enables the system to subtract a significant proportion of the labor force from the prevailing laws of the labor market and thus to deny it the *historic price* of its labor.[5] This historic price would be ex-

[5] In Marxist terminology, the historic price of labor is the wages that enable a laborer to reproduce his labor power (i.e., his and his family's life) in the historic conditions of the society he lives in. For all practical purposes, the historic price of labor amounts to the wages that are necessary to live according to the normal standards of a given civilization. In an advanced capitalist country, this means that a worker's wages must enable him to house, heat, feed, dress his family normally, to keep clean and healthy, to educate his children, to buy the standard household goods and means of transportation, to get the amount of rest, relaxation and medical care that are necessary to maintain or restore his physical and nervous balance, etc. As Marx forcefully pointed out, human needs (including basic biological needs) are never purely individual or biologi-

tremely high for all the exhausting, unhealthy, dirty and dangerous jobs society cannot dispense with—in the steelworks, the chemical industry, public works, mines, laundries, etc. To make these jobs acceptable to a normally educated citizen of an advanced country, he or she would have to be granted wages, social benefits, housing conditions and shorter working hours that would offer a fair compensation for the individual and social disadvantages that are attached to the nature of these jobs. The corresponding historic wage would probably be as high as an engineer's, accountant's or professor's salary. It would be considerably higher than that paid presently for jobs that are reputedly skilled, but that—because of their desirability, convenience and social "status"—are much more sought after than the jobs of foundry worker, garbage collector or bricklayer.

In other words, paying manual labor at its historic price would be incompatible with the present wage scale and income distribution. It would also be incompatible with the present scale of social values and the social hierarchy of capitalist society. The hierarchy, that is, the scale of values and income distribution on which capitalist civilization and bourgeois domination rest, can be maintained only as long as capitalism has at its disposal a mass of outcasts denied

---

cal, but always also social and historic, since their satisfaction has to be pursued within a historic and civilizational context and with the means available therein: in New York, one can't live on boiled rye and coconuts, although it might be rational and healthy in a different civilization. Poverty cannot be measured by any universally valid meter. Poverty is not the impossibility or difficulty of subsisting (keeping alive biologically); it is the impossibility of living up to the standards of normal life in a given society and enjoying the socially available opportunities, facilities and possibilities of this society. One can subsist quite well without teeth, and the wealthy merchants and aristocrats of the sixteenth century used to lose theirs. But because dentistry nowadays is socially available (i.e., *potentially* available to everyone) a person who can't have his or her teeth seen to is denied a social possibility and is poor.

the normal benefits of its civilization and excluded from its labor market.

It is important to point out in this regard that foreign or non-white labor is not exploited by the fact that other workers have access to benefits denied to it. Nor are the wages of other laborers reduced by the existence of the outcasts' cheap labor power. But the absence of such a cheap labor force would make the present patterns of distribution and consumption impossible: were the mass of social outcasts to disappear or to withhold their labor, capitalism would be obliged to pay all its labor at its historic price,[6] which it would be unable to do without disrupting the system's economic and social balance, its hierarchical structure and civilization.

It may therefore be said that the whole setup of our civilization rests on an artificial basis: the exploitation of a labor force that cannot bargain over the price of its labor or live up to the normal standards of the society it serves. The liberation of this labor force and its integration into capitalist society would be incompatible with the functioning and the ideology of the system; it would mean granting the "lowest" manual workers the highest wages and redistributing income according to unheard-of criteria. It is inconceivable that any capitalist government would take such measures; should it attempt to, it is hard to see whence it could draw the strength to make them stick.

The liberation of the most oppressed can be achieved only by the oppressed themselves, and requires a social and cultural revolution. The issue is not how to give the outcasts access to middle-class standards of living and values, since these imply contempt and rejection of manual labor. It is not the class of the outcasts that is to be "upgraded" and "integrated"; it is the whole social pattern that is to be disintegrated and rebuilt on a new basis: on the evaluation of work according to its social usefulness;

[6] Unless, of course, it could resort to generalized forced labor.

on the rotation of the most unpleasant tasks over the whole population; on the abolition of the social division between manual and non-manual work; on the subordination of the purposes of production and of work processes to human needs as defined by free collective debate. Obviously, the natural subject of revolution is, first of all, the most oppressed sector of the working class because its liberation depends upon total subversion at all levels of the present order.

This, however, does not mean that the most oppressed sector can and must be the main bearer of revolutionary ideology, its actual vanguard, with the other sectors of the working population content to follow and to support it. Nor does it mean that the most oppressed sector of the working class is the most readily available social base for radical mass action. It clearly is not, since the very essence of oppression is to deny the oppressed the material and intellectual means of questioning the ruling class's domination, that is, the social order and ideology. Not only has the dominated class no access to the dominant class's culture; this culture, were it to become accessible to the oppressed, would be of no use to them in grasping and fighting the nature of their oppression. Domination produces an ideology that justifies domination as natural and necessary and makes non-acceptance of it a crime. The deeper the oppression, the greater the inability of the oppressed to think of themselves as possible subjects and agents of their own liberation and to create a consciousness of their own.

It is this situation that has led reactionaries to talk of "happy slaves" and to deny that the oppressed are aware of their oppression or desire to become free. The truth is that this awareness exists; but it does not have the means (which are ideological and cultural) to assert itself. And an awareness that cannot assert itself through words and actions is "repressed," much as all of us are by the pervasive social image we have of ourselves, our possibilities, our lives and our futures. This image is borne by the very language we use to account for all that happens, which obliterates (or "censors") what can't be accounted for with the usual words; it is sustained by the familiar objects around us, which always reflect this same kind of relationship with the rest of the world; this image, in short, is our prefabricated and alienated identity as defined by our place in a society that never ceases to designate us in a certain way, to pervade us with its ideology. We are so deeply conditioned by it that we have no words to say and to think what we really want or do not want. There are only two ways to break out of this ideological captivity: by subversive actions and by finding words that subvert the dominant language. Each leads to the other: subversive language leads to subversive behavior and actions; and subversive action to outbursts of words, to the invention of a liberated language of our own, a language to express our needs and desires.

Violence is the first and necessary step by which the oppressed refuse their oppression and assert themselves as potential subjects and agents of history. But bursts of violence, although they express a total and immediate rejection of the established order and its discourse, are only a substitute for their destruction through effective action. Effective action, which requires a method and an overall view of ends and means, may grow out of the new sensibility that violent revolts set free. But explosive violence is only the first, albeit an indispensable step towards it.

STUDENTS

For the most oppressed sector of the working class to break through the barriers of ideological captivity and repression, the credibility of the dominant ideology must already have been weakened and the established order undermined. This, as we have seen, has been done by the armed anti-imperialist struggle in the Third World and mainly in Vietnam.[7] But the ideological effects of this weakening do not immediately reach down into the most oppressed sector of the capitalist nations' population. In all capitalist countries, the sector that has been most immediately sensitive to these effects and has gradually made them felt by the rest of the people has been the students. Their protest movement did not, however, make them a revolutionary vanguard. Its role was more subtle: by attacking the dominant ideology in the very centers where it is traditionally produced, the student vanguards brought its discredit into the open and encouraged other groups to reject established values and to wage violent actions against the institutional authorities. There is, of course, a whole complex of reasons why students should be the most readily available sector for ideological subversion and open revolt.[8] Without going into too much detail, it is worthwhile examining the most important ones. They point to a key contradiction of highly developed capitalism: the system's inability to satisfy new non-material needs which it cannot help generating.

In previous times universities were to a large extent training centers for the children of the bourgeoisie, whom they impregnated with bourgeois culture and values. They prepared them for the positions of privilege and power to which they were predestined by birth. The cultural bias of the whole school system was such as to bar promotion and access to institutions of higher learning to those who did not have the "right" family background.[9] All this no

[7] Some Marxists rightly consider the Vietnamese people and other armed liberation movements to be the real world revolutionary vanguard. See for example Göran Therborn, "From Petrograd to Saigon," *New Left Review*, March–April 1968.

[8] I have attempted to analyze these reasons in "Mai et la suite," *Les Temps Modernes*, August–September 1968.

[9] For a theoretical analysis of the school's function in reproducing the social system, see Pierre Bourdieu and Jean-Claude Passeron, *La Reproduction* (Les Editions de Minuit, 1970).

longer holds true. The development of means of production has intellectualized work and increased the need for intellectual labor. On the average, the knowledge required at any given moment by any available job is not greater than in the past; most of the time it is more specialized and narrower. But the required knowledge changes at a quickening pace as scientific and technological innovation accelerates. Therefore the acquisition of a predetermined skill and knowledge is no longer a sufficient preparation for available jobs: the main quality required by industry, business and administration is "adaptability," i.e., the ability to acquire new knowledge, new skills, to change. As a consequence, good training must go beyond the teaching of skills; it must rest on an education giving students a measure of self-reliance and the ability to keep learning by themselves. But, as we shall see, the capabilities education fosters are frustrated by the capitalist division of labor.

Moreover, more students are being trained than will be needed. This inflation of students is due not only to industry's desire to have a reserve army of intellectual labor to draw from. More fundamentally, it is a result of the rising cultural level of the overall population. The cultural barriers that prevented the children of all but the "upper" classes from entering universities are breaking down. The biased system of preselection of students has proved faulty. And as a significant proportion of each generation of adolescents "invades" the colleges and universities, an old myth is exposed: the myth that higher learning is an open door to social promotion.

The link between academic degrees and social promotion could be maintained only as long as higher learning, though theoretically open to all "capable of it," was in practice restricted to a small minority. The traditional struggle of liberals (and, in Europe, of socialists and communists) for the "democratization" of the educational system, turned out to be a fallacy when, in the nineteen-sixties, an ever growing proportion of adolescents won access to universities only to be eliminated in the course of their studies by new and arbitrary mechanisms of selection, or else to end up either actually or intellectually underemployed. Initially, the struggle waged by Western European students against these new mechanisms of elimination bore the clear imprint of petit bourgeois ideology: they were fighting for the universal right to study, i.e., for the right to win social promotion through learning. Gradually they became aware that the demand was self-contradictory: if all are to be allowed to study, it is obvious that all cannot be socially promoted.

The demand that all are to be allowed and enabled to study makes sense only if the right to study is divorced from the right to social privilege. Therefore, the right to study became a demand *per se:* it could be claimed only on the ground of free access to "culture." The acquisition of culture was held to be an end in itself that could confer no privilege whatsoever: it should be considered normal that university graduates worked with their hands and that workers went to a university. The cultural battle thus turned into a battle against social barriers, against cultural inequality, against the social and technical division of labor, against the separation of intellectual from manual work. This struggle, however, could make sense only if the nature of culture itself was questioned and its class characteristics attacked.

If studying was to become open to all as an end in itself, its methods and contents had to be redefined. Since degrees could secure neither higher incomes nor rewarding and meaningful work, students had no reason to put up with any kind of regimentation at school or with traditional academic standards and methods. Studying had to become an end in itself, which means: it had to hold some intrinsic interest and had to be related to what were felt to be the real issues. Learning could become worthwhile only if one could learn how to shape one's life differently and how to shape a different world.

This rebellion, which exploded after years of maturation

(1967 in West Germany and Italy, 1968 in France, not to speak of the sustained student guerrilla movement in Japan and in the United States) drew some inspiration from the Chinese Cultural Revolution. The students' "insurrection" was bound to reach down sooner or later into the factories and offices. People who had rebelled against regimentation at school could hardly be expected to accept regimentation at work. Nor were they likely to accept meaningless and stupefying jobs after they had rejected meaningless and stultifying teaching. They were no longer prepared to become cogs and cadres in the capitalist machine. Their rejection of a hierarchically biased educational system was bound to lead to the rejection of the hierarchical division of labor and of capitalist relations of production generally.

New subversive questions tended to crop up: why couldn't work be organized in such a way as to allow the free display of creative faculties? Why shouldn't productive work and learning go hand in hand? Was not prolonged schooling a form of "forced unproductive labor" aiming to make unemployment less conspicuous? Since production no longer had any use for a significant proportion of the available labor force, why not spread the socially necessary work over the whole population, thereby reducing the working week to twenty or thirty hours? Would it not be possible then to grant all students the right to work and, conversely, to grant all workers the right to study for as long and as often as they wish? Would not such a system free students and workers from their respective cultural ghettos, provided both the educational system and the production technology were radically reshaped? By establishing a permanent link between education ("schools") and work (all kinds of work) could not work be made enjoyable and enriching, and learning rewarding and productive? Would it not be possible then continually to enrich jobs (all jobs) so that all workers (or rather groups and teams of workers) might perform tasks that become increasingly complex and diversified as their knowledge and experience widen?[10]

These kinds of questions were at first brought up by students only and were regarded as a form of intellectual subversion. But as rebellion spread from the universities to high schools, technical and professional schools, and further to factories, where young workers would no longer stand for idiotic discipline, hierarchization and repetitiveness of work, students reached the conclusion that the universities were not a fit ground for putting their subversive insights into practice. Though the universities are essential to the system to reproduce its social relations—i.e., an elite capable of perpetuating them—they are not essential at any given moment to the process of material production: their going on strike, while it may shock the population at large into becoming aware of the extent and the depth of the crisis, does not paralyze the system or jeopardize its daily functioning. Because the students are not yet integrated into the social process of production and have no actual position in it, they have no power over it. Therefore, politically speaking, there is no such thing as "student power." The power of the imperialist state can be attacked and weakened ideologically but not materially by student insurrections. The same goes for the social division of labor: it can be effectively attacked and jeopardized only by those who are submitted to it in the centers of material production. Thus the task revolutionary student groups felt confronted with was to help carry ideological subversion into the factories and offices, where their "spiritual weapons" would combine with and contribute to forging the "material weapons" of revolution. Their own struggle could continue and expand only if it reached beyond the universities.

[10] For a practical discussion of most of these questions, see Antonio Lettieri, "L'Usine et l'école," in *Les Temps Modernes* August–September 1971. Lettieri belongs to the national secretariat of Italy's metal workers' union FIOM-CGIL.

All revolutionary student groups in the advanced capitalist world have sooner or later come to this conclusion. To put it into practice—which is no easy matter—they have had to stop considering themselves specifically student organizations and movements. They have had to become groups of political agitators and militants whose vision encompasses the whole of society; their work within the universities has had to become only one aspect of their militancy; students' problems have had to be approached from and situated within an overall view of the crisis of capitalist society and capitalist division of labor. Indeed, the function of the school and of the educational system generally in reproducing this division of labor can be questioned effectively only if students gain concrete insight into how the capitalist system uses the educational system in building and perpetuating the hierarchical structure of the labor force; and if, conversely, the labor force is led to understand, on the ground of its own concrete experience, that its own struggle against hierarchical barriers and submission in work can ultimately succeed only if the present educational system is torn down and replaced by something completely different.[11]

[11] This system is presently common to the capitalist and the so-called socialist societies of Europe (including Russia). Only China and, in theory at least, Cuba have taken a completely different approach to education by refusing the separation of manual and intellectual work, of practical and theoretical training and, as a consequence, the separation of the school from real life. The basic idea—which also has been forcefully set forth by Ivan Illich, the director of CIDOC at Cuernavaca (Mexico) and, independently, by the Italian group of *Il Manifesto*—is to do away with the school as an institution of learning and training divorced from social production and creation, and consequently to do away also with the division between those who are to teach, those who are taught and those who are neither taught nor teaching. The existence of a professional staff of teachers who monopolize once and forever the transmission of knowledge and skills they have neither acquired

WORKERS

The linkup between students and workers presupposes that the working class is not really reconciled with the system and that the traditional demands for higher wages do not mean that it can be bought into submission. These "quantitative" demands are, rather, a confused way of voicing deeper aspirations and discontents, which may explode if there is awareness of what the struggle is really about—what (besides the degradation of purchasing power) makes the condition of the working class unbearable. In this respect, some of the motives of the students' and working class's rebellion can be shown to be fundamentally similar.

As already stated, the capitalist development of the means of production increasingly requires intellectual and potentially creative faculties. But while rapid technological innovation calls for a high degree of adaptability, versatility and insight, the present division of labor does not allow for the creative unfolding of human faculties within work at any given moment and in any given job. Workers are expected to be versatile but to accept narrow specialization; they are expected to adjust to new situations and to be creative and at the same time to perform dull repetitive work and be submissive to the hierarchy. The required faculties are thus permanently underemployed and frustrated. And this frustration is the inevitable consequence not of a necessary division of labor, but of the division of labor that is functional to capitalism.[12] It is a distinctive

---

through practical experience nor are capable of putting into practice, is considered a tremendous waste of energy and of potential talent and a most counterproductive method of "education."

[12] According to Marxist terminology, the *relations of production* are the way in which *labor power* (i.e., human energy)

characteristic of capitalism to organize the work process in
such a way as to predetermine the task and competence
of each worker, whether blue- or white-collar. The
parceling-out of the task, the definition of narrowly specialized responsibilities, the resulting fragmentation of work
all aim not only at increasing each worker's productivity
and efficiency; they also (and mainly) keep the responsibility and initiative that are required from him within pre-
set limits so as to allow permanent control from above, and
ultimately to keep the power of decision making concentrated at the top of a hierarchical pyramid. The division of
labor is at one and the same time an organization of the
production process and a technique of power. It is functional to maximizing productivity only in so far as the
search for this maximization does not run counter to

---

is combined with the *means of production* to give rise to the
process of production.

The latter brings into play the *forces of production* that are
available at a given historical level of development, namely:
natural resources (raw materials, non-human energy, land),
labor power, means of production incorporating technology and
science.

Under capitalism, the forces of production are combined in
such a way as to produce the maximum increase in capital
(the maximum profit). This search for profit maximization entails a particular way of evaluating the respective importance
of the forces of production: for instance, man-made means of
production (so-called "capital goods") are held to be more
important than the physical and psychic health of workers
(sellers of labor power) or than the preservation of the environmental whole wherefrom natural resources are drawn.

The forces of production therefore cannot be seen in isolation
from the relations of production: under a different economic
system, in which profit maximization would not be the main
goal, the forces of production would not be assessed in the same
way as regards their respective importance; therefore, the means
of production, technology and work process would be shaped
differently too.

keeping power concentrated and labor in disciplined subjection.[13]

This pattern, which has been traditionally applied to manual labor, has been extended to intellectual or white-collar labor in such fields as information, communications, administration, research, etc. The planning, co-ordination, marketing, physical and financial management of the big corporations' production have been rationalized in the same way as the production process itself. Administrative personnel has been divided into dozens of sharply defined specializations, and the responsibility of each employee has been given narrow limits and rigidly predetermined aims so as to break the power of decision making into minute interlocking fragments and to prevent the workers from gaining the kind of overall view and insight that might enable them to question the policy of top management.[14]

The resulting estrangement and hierarchical oppression becomes all the more frustrating as the development of the forces of production goes hand in hand with the development of potentially creative human faculties. The process of production and of valorization of capital cannot help requiring an increasing proportion of intellectual, scientific, imaginative and creative work. Hence the "danger" that the human faculties that are brought into play will become

[13] See "Division du travail et technique du pouvoir," an acute anonymous analysis, in *Les Temps Modernes,* April 1970.

For a concrete description as to how the concern for keeping power concentrated and personnel under control may interfere with the quality of service (or with the use value of products) and with the rationality of the work process, see Elinor Langer, "Working for the New York Telephone Company," *New York Review of Books,* March 12 and March 26, 1970.

[14] The building of huge national and international corporations cannot be explained simply by the so-called economies of scale. It is motivated essentially by financial considerations of capital valorization and market domination, and not by technical and economic considerations, as is well documented by the development of conglomerates.

aware of their autonomous and creative nature, demand to pursue their own ends and self-realization, and refuse to be the disciplined and venal servants of capital and of the division of labor on which its domination rests.[15] Capital thus cannot perpetuate its domination unless the individual's need for autonomy and creativeness is repressed and diverted towards substitute activities and satisfactions, which capitalism readily offers and stimulates.

The repressed needs are not, however, altogether suppressed. They persist, although the possibility of expressing themselves is denied to them by the falsification, misinterpretation and commercialization of the language and the

[15] Cf. Marx, *Grundrisse*, p. 505 of the German edition. Taking issue with Adam Smith, who can see work only as a "curse," Marx writes: "It does not dawn on A. Smith that the individual, 'in his normal state of health, activity, dexterity and skill' also needs a normal portion of work. It is true that the measure of work seems to be predetermined from outside by the purpose that is to be fulfilled and the obstacles that are to be overcome. But it does not dawn on A. Smith that the activity of overcoming obstacles is in itself an exercise in freedom—and that moreover the external purposes, once they cease to be presented as a natural necessity, are purposes set by the individual himself—i.e., self-realization, objectivation of the subject, i.e., real freedom whose action is work.

"However, he is right in so far as under its historic forms of slave work, of serfdom, of wage labor, work always appears repulsive, always presents itself as forced labor. . . . This goes . . . for work which has not yet created the objective and subjective conditions for its being attractive, self-realization of the individual—which does not mean pure fun, as Fourier naïvely thought. Really free work, as, for instance, composing music, is at the same time a most profoundly serious, most intense effort.

"The work of material production can acquire this character only if (1) its social character is asserted, (2) it has a scientific character and is at the same time work in common, effort by man not as a natural force that has been trained in a certain way, but as a subject that appears in the process of production as the activity which regulates all natural forces."

objects (literature, songs, work of art, subversive behavior) through which they seek to assert themselves. Their persistence was well demonstrated in France in May 1968, when the key demand was for the free unfolding of creative faculties and rejection of the values and patterns of capitalist civilization. It is remarkable that these themes of the French May were rooted in a deep and hitherto unexplored anti-capitalist sensibility that belonged equally to intellectual and to manual workers. The first (mainly technical and scientific personnel and office workers) did not as a rule prove to be the driving force of subversion:[16] they were drawn into the battle by the revolt of students and young manual workers and were won over to egalitarian demands (equal wage increases for all and, in some places, equal wages for all) and to the rejection of the authoritarian and hierarchical structure of industry. Left to themselves, technical, scientific and managerial employees were capable only of questioning the rationality of top management's policy and the competence of directors; they were not (except in individual cases) prepared to question ideologically the overall rationality of the capitalist division of labor. Their sense of frustration and alienation, their feeling that their own capabilities were being underemployed and misused led them to demand local self-management, and thereby to reject both private ownership and the centralized power structure, but not the capitalist division of labor.

The demands of young manual workers tended to be more radical: they were aimed at the abolition of all power from above (including state power) by the establishment of workers' councils to control production and eliminate the separation of workers from the means of production. The driving motive behind these demands was the feeling that the monotony of the work, its harassing speed, its

---

[16] Except locally, where there was a tradition of white- and blue-collar solidarity, and in some research centers where political radicalization had started years before.

minute specialization and fragmentation, the systems of job
evaluation and wage differentiation were not functional to
the process of production as such, but were arbitrary and
despotic devices to keep workers in subjection and to destroy the initiative, inventiveness, autonomy, creativeness
and skill that—however unskilled the job—they realized they
possessed.[17] While in the higher echelons (including the
union bureaucracies) demands for self-management, for
nationalization and for labor democracy are aimed mainly
at throwing out the despotic representatives of capital and
taking over the "government" of the units of production,
in the lower echelons the mere substitution of bosses and
top managers by representatives of labor and the state was
held to be just another way of perpetuating the oppressive
organization of work and the hierarchical division of labor.
What they therefore demanded was not a change in top
management and a different way of running the units of
production, but a change in the actual process of production—i.e., in the organization of work and the technological basis of the work process—so as to do away with
stupefying, frustrating and harassing working conditions.

Indeed, so long as the technological basis of the work
process is not radically changed, the technical division of
labor that it requires will necessarily perpetuate—or revive
—the social division of labor that is characteristic of capitalism. This is precisely what happened in Russia and in
Eastern and Central Europe, where the capitalist bosses

[17] They possess these faculties for the simple reason that
they are required by the work process: though each job may be
quite simple at any given moment, the functioning of the factory
actually rests on the workers' ability to hold a variety of simple
jobs, to change from one machine to another, to adapt to
changing work speeds, techniques and cycles. Were they not
capable of doing more complex work than they are asked to
do at any given moment, and were they not taking the initiative, the factory would grind to a stop. This was demonstrated
in a spectacular way by workers of the huge Fiat plant at
Turin in the summer of 1969.

were wiped out to be reborn as a "state bourgeoisie," i.e.,
a class of technocrats and bureaucrats who control the
means of production and exploit the labor force though
they do not individually dispose of the surplus (or
profit).[18]

POWER

The explosion of the French May; the Italian "creeping
May," which, from the summer of 1967 onwards, has produced an uninterrupted chain of skillful and often violent
mass strikes for better wages and workers' control; the
wildcat strikes that have embarrassed labor unions in the
rest of Europe and in North America, are proof of the
persistence or rebirth of class consciousness and of a revolutionary potential which has been lying dormant in the
working class of the advanced capitalist countries. The fact
that there is "revolutionary potential" does not, however,
mean that revolution is "ripe" or is "maturing" spontaneously within the masses. It means only that the working
class has old and new motives for not being reconciled
with capitalist exploitation and that in favorable circumstances these motives lead to action. Outbreaks of violent
mass insubordination, though they may be construed as
signs of a pre-revolutionary or (as in France) of a pre-
insurrectional situation, endanger the survival of capitalism only if the seizure of power becomes an open issue in
the course of mass action. And this in turn can happen
only if mass action is led and organized in such a way as to
build up within the factories and cities organs of direct
popular power, such as workers' councils and citizens'
councils. These organs of "dual power" become effective
in taking power and in destroying the capitalist state when

[18] For a theoretical discussion of this subject, see Charles
Bettelheim, *Calcul économique et formes de propriété* (Paris:
Maspéro, 1970).

they are co-ordinated organizationally and unified ideologically by an overall political vision and a credible political leadership. Co-ordination and political-ideological vision and leadership must not be superimposed from above
or imported from outside: if they are to lead to the building of popular power and a new state, they must be internal to the mass struggles themselves, so as not to create
from the outset a new social division between those who
lead and those who are led, between the workers and their
"spokesmen," between the masses and the vanguard, between state power and the people.[19]

It is the actual process of revolutionary mass struggle
and change that teaches the masses self-organization instead of subjection to power. To change minds and out-
looks, to liberate the energies and imaginations that will
look for new solutions and new political forms in keeping
with liberated needs, there must be revolutionary action.
Neither the needs nor the solutions can be blue-printed by
a vanguard party. Hence the need for spontaneity in all
genuine mass movements.

Conversely, the capacity to anticipate the possibility of
new solutions—new social and economic relations and a
new way of life—is a necessary element in mobilizing and
liberating repressed aspirations and energies. Hence the
tendency to voluntaristic and elitist forms of "vanguard-

[19] The history, structure and ideology of the Bolshevik Party
—conceived as a vanguard separated from the masses, as an
elite who had to bring to the mass of ignorant people the
truth whose sole depositary it believed itself to be—can be held
to contain the matrix of later deviations and degenerations.
Conflicts between Bolshevik leaders and workers' councils
(soviets) broke out both in 1905 and in 1917. On this subject
and on the rejection by part of the European revolutionary
movement of the Bolshevik "model," see the debate between
Rossana Rossanda and Jean-Paul Sartre in *Les Temps Modernes,* January 1970; Lisa Foa's and Massimo Salvadori's
articles in *Il Manifesto,* January 1970; the debate between
Adriano Sofri and Romano Luperini in *Les Temps Modernes,*
October 1969.

ism" which, when organizationally separated from the immediate struggles and aspirations of the masses, always degenerate into dogmatic, bureaucratic political machines or sects. One of the intrinsic difficulties of revolutionary leadership and education is that they can be entrusted to neither an "enlightened" and self-appointed vanguard, nor the spontaneity of the masses, who are never "ready" or "prepared" for revolution: revolution, in this respect, is always "premature."

Presently, the problem of building a revolutionary movement and organization is further complicated by the degeneration of labor unions and parties. Historically, unions developed out of the workers' need for self-defense and self-organization. As long as they were genuine organs of self-organization, they tended to be quite radical.[20] The turning point came when they were recognized as and considered themselves to be the sole lawful representatives of the working class within the capitalist system. As permanent institutions holding legal rights and responsibilities, labor unions developed into permanently structured—and therefore hierarchical and bureaucratic—organizations to administrate the "interests" of the working class through juridically defined forms of bargaining and action. Such institutionalized organizations cannot, of course, be expected to jeopardize their self-interest (i.e., their institutional power and the position and status of their leaders within the capitalist state) by stimulating or defending aspirations and demands that run counter to the logic and power structure of the capitalist system. Thus demands that are not negotiable and have no chance of being accepted by capitalist managers, were eliminated from the outset. Labor unions saw it as their function to translate all de-

[20] The present tendency of many "leftists" to discredit labor unions generally as subservient to capitalism is an oversimplification. Unions that spring from the "base" as instruments of self-defense and self-organization can rapidly become breeding grounds of revolutionary consciousness, as was well illustrated by the "Revolutionary Union Movement" of Detroit (DRUM).

mands that sprang up (or threatened to spring up) from
the rank and file into propositions that would be acceptable
to the representatives of capital. Their objective function
thus became ideological and political mediation: they
acted as mediators between the capitalist and the working
classes, and thereby strengthened the system. By repressing
unnegotiable demands that did not fit within the system's
logic and promoting demands that were or could become
compatible with the functioning of capitalism, labor unions
helped to integrate the working class into capitalist society.
The subversion of the ideology and practice of institutionalized trade unionism is therefore essential to the building
up of a revolutionary movement.

Similar considerations apply to the traditional working-
class parties. Inasmuch as they aim at being voted into
power, i.e., at exercising governmental responsibilities
within the framework of the bourgeois state, they must
present themselves as orderly and respectable forces, capable of controlling the masses rather than helping them
to self-determination and self-rule, to confront and destroy
the bourgeois state. Thus, whatever their intentions, these
parties in effect stifle the aspirations and potentially revolutionary motives that have led recently to outbreaks of mass
violence, new forms of mass action and insubordination,
and to the widespread feeling that capitalist development
and civilization are in the throes of a crisis.

The key issue, therefore, is not getting working-class
parties into power; it is the building up of a genuine power
of popular self-determination and self-government in opposition to centralized state power, which is the supreme
instrument of bourgeois domination by which the social
division of labor is perpetuated. Indeed, the question of
winning power is practically meaningless unless a certain
number of things have been done or have happened to
liberate repressed needs and aspirations, promote the capacity of popular self-rule and effectively raise the issue of
alternative power. This approach—which was supported by
Marx in *The Civil War in France*, by Rosa Luxemburg

and recently by various groups to the left of the European Communist parties—has become alien to the traditional working-class parties. To the extent to which they are intent on winning power, either through the constitutional process or by a coup, and to running the state as a centralized instrument of government from above, they do not question either the existence of the state as a separate sphere holding the monopoly of power, or the division of society into a practically powerless mass of people on the one hand and professional politicians, bureaucrats and holders of power on the other. The concept of politics as the exclusive sphere of politicians and the concept of democracy as a process of delegating power and choosing those who are to exercise it is thus perpetuated by the very political parties that claim to "represent" the interests of the working class and to fight for its liberation.

The first prerequisite for building a revolutionary movement is not the creation of a new party organization—however "pure" and "genuinely revolutionary" its program and ideology—but rousing the workers to fight for things that are within their reach and can be realized by their own direct actions: namely, working conditions in the factories.[21] Self-determination of the purposes and methods of the struggle; self-management of strikes and/or production[22] through permanent debate in open assemblies; the setting up of strike committees at the shop and factory

[21] These include work speeds, wage differentials, the evaluation of skills and jobs, health and sanitary conditions, transportation to and from work, breaks, working hours, industrial organization, the right of assembly on the spot, etc.

[22] One of the most significant experiences in this respect was the strike of the Pirelli workers at Turin (later imitated by workers of the Fiat plant) who, at the beginning of 1969, refused to work according to the rules that had been "scientifically" set, and ran the whole complex factory of 5,000 workers clockwise, at work speeds they themselves had determined, thus short-circuiting the plant's chain of command. See "Une grève exemplaire," *Les Temps Modernes,* April 1969.

level, whose elected members are answerable to the general assembly of workers and may be recalled at any time —all are liberating experiences that reveal to the working class its capacity for self-rule and for mastering and modifying the work process, and that prepare it to refuse domination by management and by the state as well as by party and union bureaucracies.

These experiences, of course, have a revolutionary potential only as long as they are "spontaneous," i.e., self-organized from below. They lose their revolutionary character when workers' committees become institutionalized forms of "representation," recognized by factory management and by the state and coexisting with capital. Such coexistence may be inevitable during a limited period of time, during which it will take the form of a trial of strength. But if this trial is not rapidly won; if the positions of power won by the working class in the factories are not used to launch new offensives to break the power of capital on all the other levels of social life, workers' committees inevitably degenerate into new organs of mediation: they become local agencies of the labor unions,[23]

[23] This is precisely what happened in Italy during the spring and summer of 1970. During the previous year's unprecedented wave of mass strikes, the metal workers, despite their unions' reluctance, had won the right to elect directly shop and line delegates who would keep working with their comrades, be revokable at any time, answerable only to the workers' assembly and whose job it would be to register complaints about work speeds and working conditions. These delegates were meant to keep the union and management under permanent pressure and to facilitate both effective control from below and immediate action whenever demands remained unsatisfied. Though in principle the delegates were to be independent from the local union leaders, the latter progressively manipulated them into accepting the union's line as defined by its top leadership. To withstand this manipulation, a clear political concept would have been necessary as to how the new power of workers' councils and assemblies could be used strategically to build up the political power of the working class.

"representing" the rank and file and voicing its demands in regular meetings with the representatives of management. Bargaining takes the place of collective debate and mobilization. In the ensuing exchanges between workers' representatives and management, the overall logic of capitalism will inevitably prevail, since it will not be fought in the name of an opposite overall logic (the logic of social appropriation and social management of the means and process of production),[24] but only in the name of particular local demands.

The development of autonomous self-organized actions from below to win direct power over the process of production can therefore grow into a lasting revolutionary movement only if it is accompanied by the building up of political consciousness and organization. In other words, the instrument for winning political power[25]—i.e., the power to change society as a whole—or "party" must be

[24] The capitalist logic rests upon maximum valorization of capital in each economic unit (i.e., on the so-called law of profit maximization). The pursuit of maximum profit can be subjected to certain limitations by pressures from without (e.g., the employer's obligation to pay the labor force a legal minimum wage; not to ruin in too short a time the workers' health; not to destroy completely the natural environment, etc.); but these limits are extrinsic to the logic of capital and do not substantially infringe upon it. A completely different logic or combination of exigencies can be imagined to rule the social process of production: e.g., maximum social usefulness of products; maximum free time; maximum development of personal faculties and voluntary co-operation within and outside work; maximum preservation of environmental balance and/or natural resources, etc., which would call for a completely different pattern of consumption and technology and, of course, for a planned economy and a planned price system.

[25] This instrument is usually referred to as "the party." We shall keep to this appellation, though the form this instrument may take can be quite different from traditional party organizations, which should by no means be considered a necessary and lasting form.

built up "from within" self-organized actions and movements and not from without as their external leadership:
the party is to be the means of the working class's own
conquest of power and not a new machine for exercising
power *on behalf* of the working class. Without a revolutionary party that stimulates effective self-expression from
below and offers a unifying political perspective to autonomous and "spontaneous" struggles, there can be no lasting
revolutionary movement; conversely, without a movement
that draws its vitality from the imagination and inventiveness of the masses, the party, however powerful its organization, is doomed to become a force of repression and
domination and to waste its energies in internecine struggles and conspiratorial tactics. This was one of the lessons
taught once more by the French May.

MAY—OR THE LIMITS OF SPONTANEITY

A revolutionary movement always feeds itself on the
radical and total rejection of the existing social order and
all its possible improvements. But it can move forward, assert itself and bite into the existing order only if, in its
progress, it evolves the outlines of a new kind of society,
the instruments of its construction, functioning and future
development.

The specific function of a revolutionary party is to construct the bridges, to define the "mediations" or intermediary objectives, which will guide the rejection of the
crumbling order on to building a new society. Lacking such
mediations and incapable of moving beyond the moment of
the rejection, the movement will tend to be an end in itself:
nothing more than an outbreak of liberating violence. It
will explosively assert all the possibilities that are ordinarily
denied us and the desires that are repressed by the social
division of labor; but these desires and possibilities, since
they are embodied in no objective undertaking coming to
grips with reality, will consume themselves in subjective

exuberance, in imaginary objects and acts (slogans, images, rituals). And then the agony of the movement begins.

What is at issue here is not—as "realists" and "sober and responsible people" would like us to believe—to condemn the explosive, libertarian and imaginative nature of the May Movement. What is at issue is the incapacity of the political and trade-union machines to guide the audacity and imagination which the movement had released towards actions which could not subsequently have been nullified, and towards goals which, once attained, would have effected irreversible changes in the social system and set in motion the process of its dislocation.

The anarchic and extreme leftist character of the May uprising, which the French Communist Party and the CGT have condemned as a "political crime," was in fact the reflection of the total political bankruptcy of the organizations claiming to represent the working class. Once these organizations had shown themselves to be incapable of understanding and translating into political action the deep impulses underlying the movement, the latter could only proceed without them and against them, while vigorously refusing to let itself be dragged back into the customary line of submissive and respectful corporative demands.

It was the spontaneity of the movement that enabled it so rapidly to acquire a frankly revolutionary *form*—supremacy of rank and file assemblies; liquidation (at least at the critical points) of all hierarchy, bureaucratic rigidity and delegation of powers and responsibilities; self-determination from below; incipient "cultural revolution" by the overthrow, through the occupation of factories and through free assemblies, of social and professional barriers; challenging of all forms of inequality and of the hierarchic division of labor, etc.

But it was also this spontaneity that prevented it from defining goals and organs which would have given it unity of purpose and the strategic capacity to co-ordinate immediate demands and local action in a broad perspective and general political offensive. The lack of these organs of co-ordination, mediation and political synthesis was a weakness constantly felt by the movement's local exponents. Because of this the movement could not avoid becoming fragmented into a multiplicity of local actions out of step with one another. Worse, it gradually became a multiplicity of corporative actions—on the part of architects, doctors, journalists, scientific researchers, etc.—incapable of finding a language or perspective common to their own struggles and those of the students and workers.

It is very easy to argue from this that the uprising was revolutionary in form while remaining corporative and trade-unionist in substance, and that therefore it was not "truly" revolutionary. The truth is that the pattern of events in May and June disclosed the *possibility* of a revolutionary approach and at the same time its rejection by the predominant organizations. The gap between the radical nature of the forms of industrial action and the narrowness of their declared goals had been constantly apparent before May. It revealed the extent to which political work and leadership had fallen behind political sensibility: young workers possessed neither the knowledge nor the means to give their spontaneous demands political or even trade-union expression.

The ambivalence of the May Movement has to be understood in the same way—as the inability of any spontaneous movement alone to define the goals expressing its deeper intention, which would enable it to organize its action in time and space. Did the millions of strikers wish simply to secure higher pay, or did they want to overthrow the Gaullist regime and even the capitalist system? The question was meaningless: they used wage demands to express a revolutionary aspiration, and the reverse. But at the peak of the movement no wage increase could satisfy them, not because they asked *more* but because the form and dynamic of their action had taught them that they could obtain, and should therefore demand, *something dif-*

ferent, and that this "something different" was not calcu-
lable or realizable within the framework of the system.

"Tell us exactly what you want," exclaimed the bourgeois liberals to the refractory students and workers. But
how were they to put it into words? The revolt itself was
the only language they possessed, and it was not a language
that could be translated into speeches. In order to say what
they wanted they would have had to regroup, to organize,
to analyze the situation and to decide in common *what
they were in a position to want:* in other words, how the
diversity of specific actions and demands might be merged
in a program of radical change while still preserving their
autonomy. Only a revolutionary party immersed in the
movement could effect this synthesis and translate it into
policy, devise a strategy and set in motion a process of
revolutionary change.

No such party existed. But even if it had, it could not
have brought about the socialist revolution overnight. The
setting in motion of a revolutionary process does not mean
the immediate destruction of the bourgeois power system,
but the creation of deep rifts within it. It means transforming the balance of social forces as they exist at the height
of the movement into a necessarily unstable association of
political forces, and preparing, thanks to the autonomy and
dynamism generated by the movement itself, for victory in
the new trial of strength which will emerge after the fall of
the regime and the setting up of a provisional government.

To a revolutionary party capable of thinking in terms
of transitional strategy there would have been nothing
alarming in the formula of a provisional "union of the
left" government (as proposed on May 26, 1968, by
Mitterrand and Mendès-France). This would have given it
a chance to consolidate—even by dubious means—the popular victory over the Gaullist regime and, the struggle having reached this point, to embark upon the next stage. The
question of a "common program" was not of decisive importance because any program hastily agreed to by the
various political machines would have been rapidly over-

taken by the radicalism and vigor of the mass movement. Moreover there was nothing to prevent a revolutionary party from itself favoring the outflanking from below of a program devised by the traditional political machines. The party needed only to operate on a dual front: on the one hand it could exert political and programmatic pressure upon the reformist leaders (leaders without troops) conducting the provisional government; and on the other it could help the driving forces of the movement—in action committees, in the factories and communities, student and teacher committees, radical committees of doctors, architects, journalists—to formulate and co-ordinate their own reform plans *and to put them into effect without delay,* wherever possible, by seizing power on the local or professional level. The community self-management of information media, public services, large housing projects, hospitals, research centers, educational and cultural establishments and certain large industrial enterprises was possible and could gain ground. In the public services particularly, self-management could introduce the principle of non-payment as did the public transport workers at Nantes.

Provided it was *inside* the movement without pretending to control it from above, the party could both participate with other party leaderships in the provisional government and at the same time serve as a liaison for the convocation of a national congress of committees holding local power. Even more, the co-ordinated action and *independent* program formulation of popular power assemblies (organs of dual power quite comparable to the soviets) should have appeared to the party an essential condition of its participation in the provisional government. Indeed, only the outflanking thrust from the base could lend it sufficient power to impose on its "partners" in government the more advanced points in its program.

All this implies a dialectical conception (very different from that of the French Communist Party) of the relationship between the party and the masses, between the program and the movement, and between political and governmental action. It implies that the party would rely upon the independent dynamism of the movement, that it would not seek to control or direct it, and also that it would not seek to control the provisional government but would aim to submit it to the pressure of the movement at large. In short, it was necessary for the party to be so far merged with the movement as to be able to represent it at government level without being repudiated, and for the movement to be so far independent and uncontrollable from above that the party could not possibly be asked to break or restrain it, or impose on it any discipline or restrictions.

The fact, unacceptable in any other circumstances, that a provisional government, presided over in theory by Mitterrand and Mendès-France, would have aimed at breaking up the movement and bringing it back within the bounds of neocapitalist reformism would not, in the revolutionary situation of May 1968, have confronted a mass revolutionary party with any insuperable problems. It did not justify the French Communist Party in rejecting the provisional solution proposed to it. A *provisional* reformist government, formed and compelled to act *in the heat of the moment,* had far less chance of implementing a centrist, neocapitalist policy than the non-provisional, popular front government which the FCP had been advocating with the heterogeneous array of reformist and centrist factions with which it had sought to establish a "minimum common program."

Had a popular front government been elected *in a calm and orderly fashion,* this minimum program would at once have come up against the implacable resistance of the bourgeoisie; the government coalition, whatever its programmatic pact, would have fallen apart the minute it tried to break this resistance. The program, having no popular impetus behind it, would in all likelihood have been watered down, spread over a period of time, and finally shelved entirely.

On the contrary, had the Gaullist regime been over-

thrown and replaced by a provisional government under
the thrust of a popular uprising, this would have represented, however moderate the *intentions* of the new government, an irreparable rupture of the political and economic balance. The rigidity of the French capitalist system,
and the conservative defeatism of the bourgeoisie would
not have allowed the reformists sufficient space for maneuver for them to be able to stabilize the situation. A new
crisis and trial of strength, more rugged than the first,
would have occurred within weeks or months; and the
working class would have been far better equipped than
under a popular front government to repel the reactionary counter-offensive, get rid of the centrists and enforce
an undisguisedly socialist regime.

Why, then, were the Communists, when confronted by
a popular uprising, so dismayed by the centrist tendencies
of those very factions with which for years they had been
seeking an alliance? Did not the May uprising offer an
ideal opportunity for a revolutionary mass party to corner
its reluctant allies, letting them take over in a revolutionary
situation they could not possibly master and preparing
thereby the second stage of the revolution?

The answer is that the revolutionary process, the chain
reaction which the collapse of the Gaullist regime would
have provoked, was precisely what the French Communist
Party feared. They were afraid of coming into power by
way of an extra-legal process which threatened to shatter
the capitalist state apparatus—this apparatus they had always planned to use in its existing form for the gradual and
orderly transition to socialism. This being so, the party
preferred to break the movement and to prolong the life
of the regime.[26]

[26] See Lucio Magri's remarkable analysis in *Considerazioni
sui Fatti di Maggio* (Bari: De Donato, 1968):

"Mitterrand and Mendès proposed to set up a transitional
government based on a very wide spread of forces—from the
student movement to the liberals—within which the supporters
of a policy of stabilization under democratic-bourgeois hegem-

Thus the May crisis posed in practical terms for the first time the prospect of revolution in the West; and it disclosed the fact that neither the French Communist Party nor any other political force was prepared to face this prospect. The transition to socialism suddenly became an immediate issue; but there was no organized force capable of determining the nature of the transitional society, the distribution of power within it or its economic, cultural and international policies. Capitalism had suddenly raised the curtain on what lay beyond it, but no one knew how to

---

ony would compete with those advocating a policy of socialist transformation. The Communists considered that both policies might have extremely dangerous consequences. Above all they feared that, however unwillingly, they might find themselves the accomplices of a left-center, neocapitalist, pro-American policy. They feared it not because the policy had any real chance of success (How could the weakened central parties hope to succeed against the thrust of a popular movement?), but because in order to resist it they would have had to place themselves in direct opposition to the capitalist system, form a block with the other forces of the extreme left and appeal to the masses. The Mitterrand proposals offered two alternatives only: stabilization under a moderate hegemony or revolutionary radicalism; the Party would be caught in the clash between the two and in either event would pay the price. The acceptance of the offer would therefore have entailed, not a tactical decision but a change of strategy. . . .

"It can obviously be objected that the Communists would have been confronted by the same dilemma after the popular front electoral victory they had been working for for years, and that the economic crisis and disruption of political parties would very rapidly have forced upon them the same choice between centrism and the transition to socialism. But the necessity of this choice is precisely what the Communists have always denied (hiding behind the smokescreen of their anti-monopolist program). If it were ever forced upon them, they intended to meet it from a position of power within the government, free of the burdensome pressures of an uncontrolled mass movement. Such are the contradictions of popular frontism; but Communist policy has for years been based on those contradictions."

reach that beyond. It terrified the very men who professed
to be leading the people. And so they did nothing.

The May movement finally collapsed for lack of any
political interpretation. And the machines calling themselves the French parties of the left collapsed politically
because they did not know how to interpret the movement.

THE MATURITY OF REVOLUTION

Bourgeois democracy entered its death throes forty years
ago. Only the setting remains, a parliament without power,
electoral diversions, a multiplicity of bourgeois parties competing for the same clientele and proposing, more or less
consistently, to pursue the same policies. What it comes to
is that the political function of parliament is obsolete.

Essentially this function was to reconcile the conflicting
interests of different sections of the bourgeoisie and petit
bourgeoisie. Parliament was the place where these interests
could find expression and be composed in the light of
public compromises, of changing electoral majorities, of
the dislocation and relocation of hegemonic groups capable
of representing a class interest which embraced the diverse
interests of the bourgeoisie and was acceptable to their
allies as the expression of the "national interest."

But this kind of political-ideological mediation is no
longer possible. The interests of the different sections of
the bourgeoisie and petit bourgeoisie are no longer merely
disparate, they are divergent. And the dominant sector of
the ruling class, the monopolist bourgeoisie, can no longer
allow its positive interests to be subjected to the arbitration
of non-monopolist sectors, or to the chances of public debate and governmental instability. The interests of monopoly capital cannot be made a matter of public negotiation
and discussion. Long-term planning of investment and of
technological innovation, advance assessment of costs, the
gaining of new commercial strongpoints abroad and the
protection of those already existing—all this calls for po-

litical and monetary stability, "social peace," and rationalization of administration, internal trading, agricultural and trade-union discipline. The competitive power of the monopoly groups depends on these things, and it must not be imperiled by the shifts and changes of a parliament in which the representation of non-monopoly interests is numerically preponderant. Parliament must therefore be divested of its powers; the executive and administration must be granted wider powers, and their decisions, taken in conjunction with corporate capital, must be excluded from public debate.

The death of bourgeois democracy is therefore not due to the class struggle, but to the concentration of political power necessitated by capitalist concentration. It is due to the impossibility of carrying out a policy suited to the requirements of large-scale capital within the traditional framework of bourgeois democracy. The bourgeoisie have to secure the enforcement of this policy by other means.

They have to abolish the state as an organ of political compromise, and take it over as an organ of administration and direct management of the economy. They have to discredit political debate and politicians as anachronisms and insist that the "real" problems are no longer political but require economic and technological solutions, to which politics must be subordinated. In other words, for the monopolist bourgeoisie, there is no longer any room for political debate because henceforth no policy is feasible except their own, of which the imperatives are not debatable. As Jean-Jacques Servan-Schreiber has superbly put it, the debate is confined to the matter of .5 per cent more or less annual GNP growth. The depolitization of politics is the ideological weapon of corporate capital.

Therefore the only viable capitalist state is a strong, technocratic, stable structure which for continuous political debate substitutes direct co-operation between the executive and those class organizations, themselves depoliticized, which are modestly termed "socio-professional organizations." It is no accident that this scheme of things is com-

mon to the Mendès-ists, the Gaullists and the Defferre-ists
in France, to the British, German and Scandinavian social
democrats and to the Italian left-center. They may differ
in manner but not in essence, which is that only one type
of state and one kind of politics suits the needs of monopoly capitalism. Once it is accepted that this is the only
possible economic system, then "democratic" debate can
concern itself only with the best way of running the state
and operating the policy.

But the fact that a strong, technocratic state may be
the only one to suit monopoly capitalism and arm it
against recurrent crisis affords no automatic guarantee that
this kind of state will be equal to the task of imposing its
rulings on the non-monopolist strata of the bourgeoisie
and on the working class. All that is certain is that no
other type of capitalist state can function efficiently. In
the same way, the fact that the only viable capitalist policy
is that of the monopolist bourgeoisie affords no guarantee
that the corporate bourgeoisie will be *capable* of defining
its policy and enforcing it. Here again there is only one
certainty, namely, that the non-monopolist bourgeoisie will
be incapable of enforcing a policy of its own, or even of
having one.

This is what clearly emerges from the history of the
Fifth Republic in France,[27] which, all things considered,
is a history of failure. Monopolist bourgeoisie has shown
itself to be incapable of basing its factual dominance on
a political hegemony which would make this dominance
lasting—that is to say, acceptable to the whole or a large
part of the other classes. It has not found a social basis
for its policy of capitalist rationalization to operate on.

This social basis, in the older capitalist countries, cannot
encompass all of the possessing classes. As we have shown,
the policy of monopolist rationalization must inevitably
attack the parasitic strata (rentiers, pre-industrial and even

[27] Also from that of Mendès-ism and Defferre-ism, of Wil-
sonism in England, and of the Italian left-center.

pre-capitalist strata) of the bourgeoisie, the petit bourgeoisie and the peasantry; it affects small and medium-
sized businesses, small shopkeepers and farmers, real estate
speculators and the closed professions. The corporate bourgeoisie can assert its domination over the possessing classes
as a whole only if, discarding their political unity (the
"conservative block"), it succeeds in uniting under its control the "driving forces" as opposed to the "dead weight"
of society. For this it needs the political support of the
"cadres," industrial proprietors and other "modernists";
and since these in themselves do not carry enough weight,
it must also find allies in the labor movements who, for the
sake of progress and rationalization, will induce the working class to accept a policy of "concertation," participation
and wage regulation.

A policy of monopolist rationalization cannot succeed
in the absence of this kind of "modernist block" of capitalist reform. And the block must necessarily extend in two
directions: towards ownership and industrial "cadres" on
the one hand, and towards labor on the other. If the monopolist bourgeoisie cannot win over traditional business
to its policy—which means in practice dominating business-
men's organizations—it has no chance of persuading the
"cadres" and the labor unions to adopt an attitude of
"participation" and to enter into a "dialogue between
social partners." And if the labor unions remain unper-
suadable, or go over to the offensive, the corporate bourgeoisie has no chance of detaching the traditional manu-
facturers from the "conservative block" and thus
constructing a social basis sufficient for its purpose.

Gaullism failed in both directions, and its failure was no
accident.[28] Modernist corporate capital has never been
able to establish its hegemony over the smaller industrialist
who, after 150 years of class warfare in France, has come
to regard the labor movement as a mortal enemy and the

[28] Wilson in Britain, and the Italian left-center, did very little better.

maintenance of the "conservative block" as the essential basis of his power. This alone was enough to condemn the Gaullist plan to failure. Being committed to preserve the political unity of all the possessing classes, the policy of capitalist rationalization was obliged to come to terms with those same pre-industrial and parasitic interests which it should have eliminated. In consequence it had to inflict the cost of capitalist rationalization, reduced to fragmented and erratic measures, solely on the working class. Its attempts to conciliate at least a section of the labor movement thus lost all credibility.[29]

The failure of monopolist rationalization in France under a right-wing government led the modernists to conclude that it might succeed under a "left-wing" government. They argued that since monopoly capital had been unable to establish control over the rest of the business sector from within, it would have to do so from outside, by allying itself with the labor movement. This was the policy of the Mendès-ists, the Defferre-ists and the social democrats. But is the working class really disposed to accept an alliance with corporate capital against the pre-monopolist bourgeoisie? Is it amenable to a *modern right-wing*[30] policy of which the proclaimed goal is to preserve

[29] The defeat of De Gaulle on April 27, 1969, confirms this. Following the concessions secured by the working class in May 1968, the cost of capitalist rationalization, now a matter of extreme urgency, had necessarily to be borne by the pre-industrial strata (small shopkeepers and peasantry for the most part), while the revival of the policy of "concertation" (rebaptized "participation") with the workers' organizations was foredoomed to failure. Still traumatized by the working class uprising, French ownership (CNPF) dared not accept the political risks which, in their view and now more than ever, the breakup of the "conservative block" entailed. Allying themselves with the PME (small and medium-sized enterprises) and the hard-hit sections of the petit bourgeoisie, they connived the overthrow of De Gaulle in the hope that his successors would be able to restore the political unity of all owners.

[30] Termed "modern socialism" by the technocratic bodies.

capitalism by rationalizing it on American lines? Has it no
requirements other than those which a more efficient capitalism may one day satisfy—a day which must of necessity
be preceded by a period of austerity and labor discipline?

The reply, of course, depends to a large extent on the
working-class parties. But for these to come out in favor
of class collaboration does not necessarily mean that the
workers will follow them. They followed no one in France
in May–June 1968. They did not follow Wilson in Britain
or Nenni in Italy. The fact that the capitalist system is
compelled to seek working-class support does not yet enable it either to ask for that support or to get it. That
the policy of the corporate bourgeoisie is essential to the
survival of capitalism is not enough to make that policy
feasible. Nor is it enough that the old form of capitalism
is obliged, in the face of repeated political, social and
economic crises, each hastening its decline, to transform
itself into monopoly capitalism for the transformation to
be socially and politically practicable.[31] In fact, it is not
practicable in a number of European capitalist countries.

[31] Wherever it has occurred, this transformation has been in-
separable from a prolonged crisis, profoundly shaking the social structure and creating a pre-revolutionary situation. There
was the crisis in the United States from 1929 to 1941; the crisis
in Germany from 1918 to 1934, completed in 1948 by a monetary reform which swept the reviving non-monopolist bourgeoisie from the economic scene. There was also a sanguinary and
dramatic transitional process in Japan, which despite its unique
nature, was not altogether dissimilar from the German process.
In Holland it was the devastation of World War II followed by
military defeat in Indonesia which caused the elimination and
reconversion of the pre-industrial bourgeoisie. The Swedish
transformation also possessed original qualities that make it
comparable with that in Japan. An agrarian country, it
completed its long-delayed bourgeois revolution in the early
nineteen-thirties, following a violent social crisis and, under the
leadership of the laborites, recommenced industrialization under
a state monopoly-capitalist regime.

The crisis in reformism and the crisis in the capitalist system are one and the same.

It is at this point, when the survival of the system depends on its ability to reform itself but the ruling class lacks the political power to do so, that the working class has its historic chance of achieving supremacy. It may miss the opportunity from lack of political preparation. But it can seize it if there is a revolutionary party capable of defining the "socialist alternative": of defining it both theoretically and in practical terms as a task of *immediate urgency*.

For between the strong state capable of applying, by force if necessary, the measures required by monopoly capital, and the revolutionary changeover to socialism there is no middle way. There can only be a series of short-lived compromises and crises. No third force exists, between the monopolist bourgeoisie and the working class, capable of acquiring political hegemony; there is only the political impotence of the social forces of obstruction, i.e., old and new parasitic strata, pre-industrial and pre-capitalist segments of the bourgeoisie and the petit bourgeoisie. For the most part these strata are vestigial remains. Capitalism must eliminate them, and so must socialism, although not in the same way. Economically, their power is nil. Politically they have only as much power as the two potentially dominant classes allow them while using them as pawns in the class struggle. Of themselves these "middle strata" are incapable of having any policy: history has passed them by. They are the party of refusal, of fear, of meaningless, makeshift compromise; they are the "center," prompt to join the stronger camp in order to influence and paralyze its policy from within. Far from representing the "middle of the road," they merely represent a sum of corporative interests and nostalgias marking the inexorable decline of the system and its economic, political, technological and cultural subjection to American imperialism and that of its more powerful allies. The "Europeanism" of the central parties accepts this subjection in

advance. The conservative defeatism of the French bourgeoisie is an historical constant: they accept foreign domination and colonization when their power and class
privileges can be safeguarded by no other means.

Only two blocks can correspond to the alternatives of
monopolist rationalization and socialist revolution:

—the modernist block, which seeks through its technocratic ideology to disguise the domination of the monopolist bourgeoisie by stressing the importance and "power"
of cadres and technicians, the "participation" of the unions
in capitalist management and their "compensatory" role;[32]

—or the socialist block, which seeks to detach scientific
workers, technicians and intellectuals from the bourgeois-
technocratic ideology, not by flattering their corporate interests but by laying stress upon the specific and potentially
anti-capitalist exigencies of scientific, technical and intellectual work, for which only communism can ensure true
social valorization and cultural fulfillment.[33]

[32] See J. K. Galbraith's ideological *tour de force, The New
Industrial State,* in which he succeeds in making monopoly capital's power disappear into the "technostructure."

[33] "The common ground between technicians and wage earners, at the present stage of capitalist development . . . is not
due directly to the economic exploitation of the technician, but
to the contradiction, essentially 'political,' between the free development of the technician's professional, creative work and
the profit system—that is to say, the subordination of the content and quality of his work to the needs of capitalist relations
of production.

"The first stage in the liberation of the technician, the first
shot in his battle with capitalism (although obviously not the
last) must be action on his part to secure the continuous expansion of his professional knowledge and therefore his professional liberty, and also a leading position in the process of
production . . . His struggle—in factories, in schools and in the
community—must be for the continuous development of productive forces and of a science independent of what capital
considers worthwhile; a struggle which will abolish the myth
that it is in the interest of corporate capital to foster techno-

Outside these two approaches there is nothing but crisis, paralysis and defeat for the working class. The political union between the latter and the non-monopolist strata is simply a matter of electoral arithmetic and the absolute negation of any political strategy. A union of this kind, based on the juxtaposition of sectional interests, with only "anti-monopolism" as a common denominator, can never produce a politically or ideologically commanding block.[34] The notion of an "advanced" but non-socialist democracy, which would abolish the power of the monopolies without abolishing capitalism, has neither economic nor political substance. Modern capitalism must either be monopolist or cease to exist. There is no such thing as anti-monopolist reform; there is only anti-capitalist reform, which is synonymous with revolution.

And revolution cannot be brought about by adding up votes or by any union of non-monopolist elements based on a minimum program. It has to be brought about by the creation of an anti-capitalist block, by mass struggle for reforms which will set the revolutionary process in motion, by defining a socialist alternative to the monopolist policy of rationalization and the kind of society this

---

logical development in directions which suit the needs of the community as a whole." Bruno Trentin, "Les doctrines néo-capitalistes et l'idéologie des forces dominantes," in *Les Temps Modernes*, September–October 1962, p. 672.

[34] "A more thorough study of the problem of alliances should lead the workers' movement to formulate in clearer and more independent terms a policy which will not confine itself to pointing out the community of interests between itself and the non-monopolist producers, but will offer them a genuine alternative to the monopolist expansion-process, into which they are now trying to integrate themselves, or within which they hope to survive . . . Such a policy should take the more fruitful line of formulating new structural objectives . . . proposing to these producers new forms of organization, association and liaison with state intervention and the organs of a decentralized democracy." Bruno Trentin, op. cit.

demands. In all these respects a revolutionary party is indispensable.

FUNCTIONS OF A REVOLUTIONARY PARTY

(a) Theoretical work.

The problem of a revolutionary strategy cannot even be raised without a constantly revised analysis of the evolution and contradictions of the capitalist system at every level; the points of weakness through which it may be breached and discredited; the relative positions of anticapitalist forces and movements within the productive process; the situation of the national · bourgeoisie in the capitalist system of world relations; the adaptation or non-adaptation of institutional structures, etc.

But this analysis cannot be confined to the national field or even to the capitalist system. The acuteness of the crisis at present assailing world capitalism is, in fact, largely concealed by the no less acute crises which those European states that claim to be socialist are also undergoing. Neither system can any longer surmount, by means of internal reform, the problems to which its own development has given rise. Neither system offers a solution to the other's problems. At the best, each system can only invoke the other's crisis as an excuse for its own.

In these circumstances a revolutionary program can have credibility only if the party representing it is equally critical in its theoretical analysis of both systems' defects. Soviet Marxism has long since given up any close analysis of capitalist contradictions. Having in arbitrary and propagandist terms proclaimed the general crisis of capitalism, it dropped the subject for reasons of internal and international policy. A vast field of research has thus been ignored or surrendered to bourgeois political economists. Among matters deserving of attention the following may be cited:

—a study of the theory of imperialism which would, in particular, examine the redistribution of neo-colonial over-profits within the imperialist camp, and their importance to the dominant national economies;[35]

—the connection between the crisis in the international monetary system and the pillage of the "Third World," principally through unequal exchanges;

—the crisis in state intervention, capitalist planning and neo-capitalist reformism which in Europe has led to the intensification of international competition, with the following consequences: increased inflexibility and vulnerability of economic equilibria and management policies; dena-tionalization of decision-making centers; reduced power of intervention on the part of national states; aggravation of regional imbalances; general tendency to sacrifice social and cultural investment to profitability;

—the sterilization of an increasing part of the economic surplus on which the American anti-crisis policy is based; acceleration of scientific and technological innovation as a by-product of this sterilization; the resultant increasing gap between the *possible* use of scientific and technological resources (abolition of poverty, squalor, ugliness, igno-rance and degrading forms of work) and their *actual* use (armaments, space exploration, color television, specialized repressive and counter-guerrilla military formations);[36]

[35] For the United States see Harry Magdoff, "The Age of Imperialism" in *Monthly Review,* June, September, November 1968.

[36] Cf. Herbert Marcuse, *One Dimensional Man* and *Essay on Liberation.* In fact the critique must bear not only with the use made of scientific and technological resources but with the structure of these resources. Scientific and technological devel-opment is not an entirely autonomous and ideologically neu-tral process. It reflects in its general tendencies (the questions it raises and those it leaves aside) the demands made upon the research potential by governments as well as by corporate groups. Thus it is conditioned by the prevailing ideology—that is to say, by the ruling class's idea of the purpose and social function of science—and governed by the social relations of

—the insoluble contradiction between the American internal anti-crisis policy and the supremacy of the dollar as a means of international payment and external domination, etc.

The fact that, despite the gravity of its contradictions and its state of crisis, the capitalist system is still not discredited, but can on the contrary boast of its achievements without fear of ridicule, is directly due to the shortcomings of Marxist theory in the West. To the vote-catching machines that have replaced left-wing parties, the study and popularization of Marxism appears a time-wasting luxury. Theory, they feel, does not attract votes: it raises awkward questions which are better left unasked if tomorrow we are to find ourselves presiding over the capitalist state. The effect of this disinterest in research is that, failing any thoroughgoing criticism of the system, only short-term issues can be raised, capable of solution within the system. The issue of superseding capitalism is left aside, and the credibility of the system is thereby reinforced and its permanence affirmed.

It is certainly true that votes cannot be won overnight by theoretical work. But the strength of a revolutionary party does not depend in the first instance on the number of votes it can command. It depends on the party's ability

production. The result of this is that the unequal development of disciplines leads to a distortion that partly sterilizes scientific progress as a whole. The very rapid progress in electronics, synthetics, metallurgy and nuclear physics, for example, is offset by far slower progress in preventive medicine, psychiatry, pedagogy and ecology, and also in those intermediate disciplines that allow the spread of knowledge and its social valorization. Generally speaking, the techniques for the dissemination of knowledge are falling increasingly behind the techniques for the acquisition of new knowledge, theoretical synthesis is falling behind highly technical specialized research, and the application of science to the problems of social and economic development (the major problem of this century) is falling behind its use for military and commercial purposes.

to propound the basic historical problems of the time, to define them in clear terms, and to indicate, better than any other party, the direction in which basic solutions may be found and the form of action that is called for.

Clearly, no limits can be placed on a study of this kind. It must not shrink from investigating those states which claim to be socialist. The reasons for their state of crisis and bureaucratic malformation must be unsparingly examined. The theory of the state must be redefined and it must be shown that bureaucratic centralization, state control of parties and of culture, and the disciplining of trade unions are not an inherent part of socialism. The study must explain how planning can be both democratic and centralized, how it can master the problems of quality and technological change and operate in conjunction with worker self-management. It must illustrate the conditions and means whereby the open market, market relations and inequalities of income can be abolished; and to the capitalist pattern of life it must oppose a pattern that is qualitatively superior.

The number of questions that have gone unanswered, and indeed unasked, is one of the chief causes of the political weakness of the socialist and revolutionary movement in the advanced capitalist countries. Life within those countries is not so unendurable that the exploited classes are prepared to run great risks in order to free themselves from bourgeois domination. They will be won over to the revolutionary struggle only if the revolutionary party can show (even by its own behavior) that individual and collective liberation is not contrary to rationality but the necessary condition of a higher type of rationality.

Revolution in the West depends upon an unprecedented critical and theoretical effort at rethinking socialism, getting rid of old taboos and new anathemas, and fertilizing Marxist research with the positive and negative lessons to be learned from revolutionary experience in Europe, Latin America and Asia.

(*b*) *Ideological synthesis of sectional contradictions and demands, taking into account their specific nature and autonomy.*

This function is essential to the ideological hegemony which the revolutionary party must achieve in order to construct a revolutionary block of anti-capitalist forces which will wrest power from the dominant block after dislocating it. And the word "block" here does not mean simply an alliance between classes or strata exploited by the bourgeoisie. The weakness of the traditional type of alliance is that it consists of separate group interests and sectional grievances that are merely added together and turned into a list of demands that never amount, in their sum total, to a comprehensive critique of the existing order and to a unifying vision of the struggles to be waged for its supersession.

The absence of a revolutionary party entails a multiplicity of demands and struggles for limited goals remaining within the bounds of the system, with no organic link between them and no unifying purpose. The potentially anticapitalist forces fight parallel and successive battles, which, from a false conception of the "concrete," remain entirely abstract. They lack the theoretical capacity to aim beyond the immediately obvious reasons for the discontent, at the true underlying reasons (ultimately the capitalist relations of production) and to challenge neo-capitalist ideology, in its logic and set of values, with a higher conception of rationality, civilization and culture—a conception in which sectional demands will be critically assessed in their peculiarity, transcended and replaced within a comprehensive vision.

Both before and during the May Movement, no group was capable of translating into a comprehensive anticapitalist vision the various criticisms of capitalist rationality that were more or less clearly expressed by the most advanced elements, technically and culturally, in French society. What emerged from these criticisms, which were generally fragmented and corporative, was that creativity was being stifled by parasitic structures, bureaucratic inertia and hereditary privilege. Architecture and town planning were paralyzed by speculative development, bureaucratic centralization and professional elitism; scientific research was sterilized by private ownership of the means of production, commercial secrecy, managerial routines and industrial and financial Malthusianism; the practice of medicine was reduced—in the absence of any policy of preventive medicine, hygiene, urban improvement and safeguards for the health of the workers—to the level of just another profitable career or, at best, to acts of private charity; "education for all" was a myth unless the concept, goals, methods and conditions of teaching were subverted. The motive forces of the economy were hampered in their development by, on the one hand, private ownership and vendettas between owning dynasties and, on the other, the weight imposed on them by the hypertrophy of "service" activities and the archaic state of other branches, etc. In a nutshell, it is impossible to be fully a doctor, an architect, a sociologist, a teacher or an engineer under the capitalist system.

Anti-capitalist contestation has steadily gained ground among those sections of the population upon which the development of the capitalist system, its productivity, and *its ability to reproduce itself* and impose its ideology, depend. These strata are wondering more and more openly whether the reforms necessary for further social and economic progress are compatible with the political power of the French bourgeoisie. But although their contestation is objectively anti-capitalist, it is not yet explicitly socialist. It is ruining the hegemony of the bourgeois ideology, but without rejecting the reformist illusion or strengthening the ideological hegemony of the working class. For this last step cannot be accomplished without the ideological mediation of a revolutionary party.

The party must not make *concessions* to the corporatist

interests of the "middle strata." It must demonstrate, on the contrary, that the contradiction giving rise to the resistance of intellectual workers is nothing else than the contradiction between the forces of production and the capitalist relations of production. It must prove to the intellectual workers that the true valorization of their work can be achieved only through the emancipation of all work and the abolishing of capitalist power. It must show that only a socialist society is capable of releasing the full sum of creative energy which capitalism stifles, leaves untapped, sterilizes or trivializes. In so doing the party, far from opening its ranks to the "right," will strengthen its ideological and political hold on all the non-capitalist strata, including the working class. Indeed, its ability to achieve ideological and political hegemony will depend on its ability to unite with the working class and win over to socialism all those strata that are linked with the most highly developed forces of production and creative activities.

The importance of evolving a socialist "model" now becomes clear. The intellectual workers, however opposed they may feel to capitalism, will break with the capitalist ideology only if they can see socialism as a superior form of rationality. Nothing but a clearly defined socialist pattern, as opposed to the pattern of capitalist development, can demonstrate the irrationality, the waste, the squandering of energy and the needless suffering which the latter entails.

But the formulation of a socialist pattern must not be conceived simply as an academic exercise or a projection of technocratic counter-plans. It must be the ideological subversive weapon of a *revolutionary practice* which squarely unfolds itself beyond the capitalist logic in both its actions and its ultimate aims.

Here, too, the radicalism of the student movement is a positive contribution. The students have, for one thing, placed themselves outside the system by refusing to accept as impossible what indeed is impossible within the system's framework. But since it is sectional, and not a class van-

guard, the student movement cannot lay claim to the ideological and political hegemony needed for the creation of
an anti-capitalist block. It can only present itself as the
theoretical and practical expression, at a specific level, of
the contradiction between the capitalist relations of production and the forces of production; on this level it can
become a thorn in the flesh of political society and the
bourgeois state, and by its radical actions and positions
keep the latter in a state of perpetual crisis, while at the
same time demonstrating to the workers the possibility and
necessity of radical struggle on all levels.

In this sense its contribution to the general crisis of the
system may be decisive and lasting, but only provided it is
integrated in the broad strategy of the class struggle as
one of its specific, autonomous components. It is because
this integration has been denied it that the student movement is tempted to put itself forward permanently as a
substitute for a revolutionary party and working class vanguard, clearly with no hope of success. Left to themselves
the students cannot go beyond their sectional limitations
except in words, by abstractly calling upon a mythical
working class to perform a mythical revolution. Only a
revolutionary party, gathering together all the threads of
the anti-capitalist struggle in a project of radical transformation of all levels of social existence, can enable the
student movement to transcend its limitations and become
part of a mass revolutionary movement.

(c) *Education and political leadership.*

The function of the party is to express the permanent
nature of the struggle and its objectives, even in periods
of reflux. It foreshadows the workers' state and demonstrates to the working class its ability to become the ruling
class. It embodies the presence of socialism under capitalism as the latter's positive negation. It ensures the survival
of the movement, and of revolutionary consciousness,
during fallow periods when the balance of forces rules out

decisive action. But to fulfill these tasks the party must appear both as a memory and as the prefiguration of struggles more advanced than those which are possible at any given moment. It must present itself to every worker as a guarantee that everything that can be done will be done, in no matter what circumstances, to break the enemy front and emancipate the working class. Not that the party should centrally direct any local or sectional conflict; its function is rather to situate separate encounters in the framework of the struggle as a whole, and to explain how short-term, localized demands can really transcend the particular interest of a local group and be linked with a strategy of intermediate objectives. In this sense, far from putting itself forward as the defender of a predetermined political line to which all social struggles must at any price be subordinated, the party, by its complete mobility, must be capable of recognizing new and more advanced aspirations and of feeding them back to the people by relating them to a comprehensive program of revolutionary change.

The political function of this program is to render credible, by its consistence, goals for which the working class will fight wholeheartedly only if the means of attaining them have been clearly outlined. For example, the demand in the French automobile industry in 1968, for a minimum monthly wage of 1000 frs. looked unconvincing to a great many of the workers, although it came from the grass roots—"they'll get it back by raising prices and by speed-up." But such a demand, although in isolation it sounds like trade-union demagoguery, acquires a revolutionary significance if it is embodied in a program of radical change which will establish the conditions necessary for its fulfillment.

What kind of economic, social and industrial policy, what form of planning and distribution, will enable low salaries to be very substantially raised without increasing unemployment, without inflation, and without weakening the overall efficiency of the economy? The problem is typical of those that will arise during the transitional period, since it calls into question the relations of production, the market relations, the structure of the working population, the educational system, the pattern of consumption, etc. Hence its educational value. And it is a question that the program must answer. If the party is unable to supply the answer and convert it into positive goals; if, fortified with the answer, it cannot point out the line of attack, in political and mass action terms, on the measures whereby capitalism seeks to reabsorb wage increases, then discouragement and skepticism will overtake the masses, and it will be as though they had asked for the impossible. To disrupt the system without being able to exploit the ensuing crisis for the benefit of the working class is to let victory be turned into defeat.

In the same way, to administer a temporary shock to bourgeois power without winning positions from which the struggle can be continued and the bourgeois establishment overthrown is finally to strengthen the bourgeoisie by enabling it to repair the breaches in its own fashion.

Which brings us to the fourth function of the party.

(d) *The conquest of power and transformation of the state.*

A separate study would be needed to show how the administrative and political centralization of power has weighed upon political life in France, inciting popular movements to turn to the central authority for the solution of any and every problem, and causing political parties to present themselves, above all, as the potential managers of a supposedly omnipotent state. The effect of centralization in France has been to produce a statist distortion of ideology and political life at every social level. Control of the state apparatus is held to be the sole requisite of social and political change. Popular demonstrations are regarded either as protests calling upon the central authority to redress the grievances of a particular section of the community or, at best, as public manifestation enabling the opposition parties to advertise their claim to run the state.

This statist or centralist mentality is one of the main obstacles to the birth and dissemination of a revolutionary consciousness. It relegates mass action to a subordinate position and operates against the education and emancipation of the masses through self-determination of methods and goals and democratic life at the base. This to a large extent explains the weakness of the French political parties, their salesman-customer relationship with the electorate, and the crushing weight of their leading figures and central bureaucracies.

But this centralist, bureaucratic distortion, although it is more marked in France, is not peculiar to the French parties. The strengthening of the central authority and the weakening of peripheral power centers and local government is essential to monopoly capital rule. It is natural, therefore, that all those political parties that aim at controlling the state apparatus and modern capitalist society but not at changing them, should model their own structure on that of the state as it exists. A revolutionary party, on the other hand, is distinguished by its assault, both theoretical and practical, on the authoritarian, centralist nature of the state as an expression of bourgeois monopolist rule; and by its ability to destroy the illusion that this degree of centralization is unavoidable in a modern industrial state, whether capitalist or socialist. The destruction of this myth entails in the first place that the party should not behave as—and should not be considered as—a machine for winning power for itself and for its leaders. It must be viewed not as the *holder* of future power but as the *instrument* whereby all the power will be transferred to the people and exercised by themselves. Not the winning of state power but the destruction of the state as a separate center of power ruling the people, is the revolutionary goal.

This goal must of course reflect itself permanently in the party's life style and way of exercising leadership. The party must be above all a center of permanent debate and direct democracy; it must encourage collective self-determination and self-rule everywhere; it must not be a mere organization specializing in politics and political leadership, but also a place where people come together to experience a different life, to work out practically and theoretically the politics of life. The meanings of "politics" and "party" must themselves be subverted. They must be seen as being nothing but the conscious collective practice of liberation.

This approach has been set forth with particular clarity in Europe by Lotta Continua, an organization of undogmatic Italian Maoists. Their tentative program, "Let Us Take the City," says:

> Our struggle must make it quite clear to all that our life, which capitalists make us curse, can be beautiful; that the program of proletarian struggle is not a "better life" but a totally different one; that the organization of the proletarians is not simply part of their lives as they are—something whereby certain benefits can be attained—but that it is the only way to overcome the material and moral misery of everyday life, its loneliness, unhappiness, hopelessness.
>
> Class struggle must destroy politics as a separate specialized activity; which means that we must overcome within ourselves all forms of specialization, elitism and bureaucracy. We must change our language, our methods of working, stop measuring our advances by the number of closed meetings we hold, and unite ourselves with the masses where they are: in the streets, the neighborhoods, the cafés, the homes. Popular assemblies, street demonstrations, pickets on the marketplaces, day care centers where proletarian children are no longer regimented, meeting places where proletarians discuss, write leaflets, finance the instruments of their information and organization, meet friends, boys or girls, have fun in a way that is not commercially perverted and exploited—all these are the tools of our work. Our rejection of professionalism and false politization must be reflected also in our way of breaking the law: unlawfulness, revolutionary violence and its organization are not the prerogatives of a pathetically weak and self-sacrificial military vanguard task force; they must be part of the masses' own experience.

Our task, in the present phase, is not to invent "islands of proletarian revolt" but to fuse the various dimensions of on-going revolts in a comprehensive program, a comprehensive organization.[37]

This approach has important implications for the way in which an organization or a party is to be built. First of all, *when* is the organization to be built? If its existence is decided by some leadership group who first define a doctrine and program and then co-opt people who agree with it, the organization will never belong to the masses: they will belong to it. The cornerstone of future bureaucracy, dogmatism and sectarianism will thereby have been laid. A genuinely revolutionary organization can be built only *after* the need to organize has been experienced by people engaged in mass struggles. The role of the initial leadership group is not to organize people first so as to get them struggling later, but first to spark them into action and help them self-organize so as to expand and co-ordinate their actions. The proper moment for building an organization is when mass action is developing.

The choice of the proper moment is important also in regard to the question of *who* is to build the organization. Ideally, the answer should be: the masses themselves; all those who are submitted to daily oppression, exploitation, violence, arbitrariness, and therefore can liberate themselves only by resorting to collective counter-violence. In practice, however, those who are aware of their oppression and want to fight are initially a minority. They do not know each other, are isolated by institutionalized repression, cannot communicate or get together and evaluate their strength. Therefore, an initial vanguard group is needed that could bring together all those who might wish to engage in active struggle. This initial group—the "external vanguard"—is usually made up of students and people with some political education. Through leafleting

[37] "Prendiamoci la città" (Let Us Take the City). French translation in *Les Temps Modernes*, October 1971.

and agitating in the neighborhoods, slums, ghettos and at factory gates, they set out to establish by trial and error what themes, goals, language and demands correspond best to the potential militants' aspirations and sensibility. The initial function of the "external vanguard" is to offer potential militants something they can relate to and around which they can gather: namely, people who can help them to establish contacts, write and print leaflets, find meeting places and regular opportunities for discussing and exchanging experiences. The "external vanguard," as Lotta Continua sees it, is but the catalyser of an internal vanguard.

Once this first stage has been reached—which may require months of continuous exploratory work—new militants and potential leaders will join the initial group. They will not be co-opted into it but, on the contrary, will gather around it because it offers them the opportunity to speak their mind and to do and learn what they feel the urge of doing and learning. They will not become leaders and members of a vanguard because some central committee has appointed them to some office and pre-established responsibility, but because they will have proved on the spot their ability to spark people into action, to make them speak up, to suggest during discussions what everyone feels to be the right thing, to say during debates what everyone would have liked to say if only he could have thought of it.

When active nuclei spring up in the factories and communities, the second stage of organizing can begin. To expand further and give continuity to its actions, the vanguard groups—which by now are no longer merely external—need to acquire some definite identity. They need to relate their slogans and specific themes to a doctrine and tentative program, to a tentative comprehensive concept of the kind of society and life they aim at and of the ways, means and strategy of fighting for it. Without such a clear political identity, the group can have neither continuity nor credibility; it can only agitate, pull off actions here and there, but the overall meaning of its actions remains blurred and the group cannot capitalize on them. It just stands for itself and represents no more than what it does here and now. Acquiring a political identity is the only way to break out of immediacy: the group must be seen as representing much more than itself, it must relate to past movements of liberation and to the struggles abroad, its actions must be seen as aiming at much more than can be achieved presently. Hence the importance of a comprehensive philosophy and program.

Though a set of basic principles must guide the group's work from the outset, its comprehensive philosophy and program cannot be blueprinted once and forever. Nor can they be worked out by specialists and intellectuals. Though intellectuals are definitely needed, it must be a fundamental principle of the revolutionary organization that they cannot perform useful work in isolation and are entitled to no special authority or privilege. Their research and formulations have to proceed in permanent contact and interchange with the people; their work can be valid only if its essentials can be conveyed to, discussed and controlled by everyone. As Edoarda Masi says:

> Nowadays, there is no longer any need for the intellectual type of professional revolutionaries specializing in and entrusted with the working out of theory and the direction of political practice. On the contrary: they are dangerous because they represent the worst example of intellectual professionalism in a field where its abolition is urgent. In the bourgeois system, the working out of political theory and even the functions of representation (for instance, parliamentary work) have become professions. The activities which are monopolized by these professionals must be taken over by the people as a whole.

Revolutionary leaders, however, are indispensable. To be true leaders, they must be submitted to the permanent control of the masses and be revocable. They must not become professionals: professionalism implies a specific competence, the specialized knowledge of things which cannot be known or controlled by all the others. At any moment, theory and practice must be presented as being totally understandable to all, so that everyone may decide in complete freedom and responsibility.[38]

This approach is of decisive importance in shaping within the revolutionary movement the kind of egalitarian and non-hierarchic relations which are to be a key feature of a liberated society. For intellectuals, it means breaking out of their isolation and giving up the privileges attached to superior knowledge; in exchange, they will gain the possibility of being equals among equals and of helping others to gain the insights they need to liberate themselves and to master collectively problems which are the concern of all. For the movement, it means that the holders of superior knowledge are in no way entitled to hold superior power. If, as is presently the case, decisions continue to be taken by those whose specialization it is to know, technocracy and elitism will not be overcome. Superior knowledge does not entail superior rights but the duty to make knowledge accessible to those who do not possess it and to submit whatever insights it permits to the evaluation and verdict of the "laymen." Decisions based on considerations that cannot be conveyed to and understood by all those who are concerned, cannot be politically "correct," however "right" and "justified" they may be in the eyes of the specialists. There can be only one correct line: the line of revolutionary mass democracy, that is, a line that leads people to organize their own liberation and to rule themselves collectively.

For all these reasons, building a party is a *process* and not something that can be decided by the "founders." As Lotta Continua says: "One does not 'found' a party. The party comes into being little by little as the vanguards gain the ability to have the movement advance towards communism and to give it one unified political direction from

[38] Edoarda Masi, "Sur l'auto-contestation des intellectuels" (On the Self-contestation of Intellectuals), in *Les Temps Modernes*, February 1971.

within its struggles. This ability must grow from within the development of class struggle by taking on increasingly general tasks; there is not a given moment when one could say: here we are, from now on the party exists."

This approach is in sharp contrast to the present proliferation of self-appointed vanguard parties. It rests on the conviction that "the masses are organized when they are capable of directing their struggle" and that an organization should not be larger than the actions it can wage and the practical tasks it can tackle. When an organization is bigger than is required by what it does and can do, it is bound to become an end in itself, a bureaucracy, an institution struggling for its self-perpetuation. It then degenerates rapidly and becomes an obstacle to liberation. Therefore, a revolutionary organization cannot be measured by the number of its members; it must not grow faster than is warranted by its ability to act. In periods of reflux, rather than clinging to inflated structures and stiffening them, it must shrink, keep a minimum of permanent structures, so as to be capable of arising anew when the expansion of the movement again becomes possible.

Chapter 2

Unions and Politics*

* Expanded text of a lecture delivered in February 1966 at the Mexican National School of Political and Social Sciences under the heading: "The European Labor Movement and the Crisis of Representative Democracy."

THE CRISIS OF REPRESENTATIVE DEMOCRACY

Representative democracy in every industrially advanced country is in a state of profound crisis. But we have been accustomed for so long to accept democracy in the form of its outward appearances and parliamentary institutions that its decay often does not become apparent to us until those institutions have been either brushed aside or reduced to a purely decorative role. The changes we then perceive, however, have been maturing for a long time. The authoritarian power which emerges from the ruins of parliamentarianism was in fact already in existence, in a diffused form, before it found the men to give it expression. What characterizes the modern forms of authoritarianism is not primarily an absence of elected assemblies or free elections.

The characteristics of a modern authoritarian regime are, first, the restriction of policy making to an oligarchy which as a rule is closely connected with the leading economic groups. Second, and as a result of this, the lack of influence of elected assemblies, traditional political parties, workers' organizations and local or regional governing bodies on the central organisms that evolve broad policy decisions and put them into effect. Finally, the decline of the political parties, which continue to operate too exclusively on the electoral and parliamentary level: that is to say, on a level where it is no longer possible for them to shape or represent or give effect to the will of the people in basic matters.

There is no country today, in Western Europe or on the American continent, where elected assemblies any longer represent a democratically evolved vision of society or of general interest. There is no nation where major decisions are not made by committees of experts sheltered from publicity, and where parliamentary debates are anything more than ineffective ceremonies.

The process of economic, technical and financial concentration in all advanced capitalist countries has meant that decisions affecting the community as a whole are in the hands of a small number of capitalist groups. In all these countries, without exception, the function of the state is to bring the development and functioning of these groups into line with the general interest: but this also implies the reverse, *that the general interest shall be made to conform to the requirements of these groups*—that is to say, to the interests and logic of corporate capital. The smooth functioning of these dominant privately owned groups, which is considered indispensable to the health of the national economy, must be sustained by corrective and co-ordinating action on the part of the state: by subsidies and incentives in the form of state contracts, both civil and military, low-interest loans favoring private enterprise, tax concessions and so on.

The indirect social and economic costs which the growth of these groups entails—education, public health, city planning and urban development necessitated by the geographical concentration of industry, etc.—must be borne by the state if the machine is not to grind to a halt. The material and social conditions of private growth must be financed out of public funds. The public facilities and services which the state considers desirable for the equilibrium and proper functioning of the system as a whole must themselves be made attractive in capitalist terms: that is to say, they must, by means of state assistance and subsidy, be rendered as profitable as undertakings in the private sector.

This permanent and unavoidable state involvement which characterizes state monopoly capitalism is accom-

panied by a process of "concertation" and close interpene-
tration of public and private management and a constant
expansion of the operations of bureaucracy. The decisions
which determine the basis and framework of policy become the exclusive preserve of an elite composed partly of
the representatives of industrial and financial capital, and
partly of high government officials, most of whom themselves come from the same social background and schools
as the economic oligarchy.

Elected assemblies are thus sidetracked. Basic policy decisions are reached by small commissions outside democratic control, and this for two reasons. In the first place,
public assemblies are by their nature unsuited to play a
part in the process of "concertation"; and, secondly, the
facts on which the decisions have to be based are largely
withheld on the grounds of commercial and national
security.

It makes little difference whether this decay of representative institutions takes the form of Gaullism, Wilson-
ism, Italian left-centerism, the so-called Great Society or
Scandinavian social democracy. These various regimes are
all characterized by the same governmental and bureaucratic centralization of power, the same absence of democracy in the functioning of the dominant parties and the
shaping of policy decisions, and the same tendency to use
the trade unions merely as a bureaucratic conveyer for
passing on decisions centrally arrived at; in a word, by the
same tendency to substitute the manipulation and conditioning of the fragmented masses for the power of the
people to group together in order to determine and exercise their collective will.

It would be quite useless to attempt to reverse this process by any form of legislation restoring to parliaments the
powers which in practice they have lost. Any serious attempt to re-establish democracy must start with the realization that representative democracy has always been, and
must necessarily be, a mythical substitute of government
by the people. We can get a rough idea of its limitations

and restrictions by listing the things which, according to capitalist thinking, cannot be influenced by democratic decision making. The latter, cannot bring the nature or general direction of industrial production into line with the needs of the masses; it cannot determine the technical and social division of labor, or the investment policies of private monopolies or of the state, or the use made of the economic surplus. . . . So what remains? Only those matters that come under the heading of individual and social liberty.

These are by no means negligible. By summarily dismissing them as "bourgeois mystification" Stalinism has deepened the divisions in the Western labor movement and contributed to the discrediting of socialism within a section of the salaried class in the capitalist countries. But what matters here is that this individual liberty is in no way extended, deepened or rendered more substantial by capitalist development. On the contrary, it tends to be robbed of its cultural, social, economic and political content. Democratic life in the capitalist world, far from expanding with the rise in production and the standard of living, has been emptied of its substance and is in a state of crisis causing the disaffection of the masses with regard to institutions and political forms which they feel are being manipulated behind the scenes by forces outside their control.

There are theorists of capitalism who consider, with Seymour Martin Lipset, that this is probably the best way. They take the view that the participation of the masses, the social management of society, is undesirable. Centralized, bureaucratic administration and technocracy on a national scale are to be preferred. For one thing, they allow the individual greater freedom to pursue his private leisure occupations, since he is relieved by the power elite of the tasks and responsibilities which, in a self-managed society, absorb the time and energy of its citizens. Moreover, central administration by a competent elite is more efficient.

Since the problems to be solved are in any event more technical than political, to bring them within the field of politics is to add to the difficulty of their solution.

What matters, in short, is to provide an efficient administration and a rational ordering of affairs so as to achieve the maximum development of production, consumption, comfort and leisure. The claims and requirements of the workers are to be confined within this field and thus may be satisfied, eventually, by the growth of the national product. All "social categories" must work together to increase the size of the pie of which everyone will have his share; and when, thanks to scientific and technical progress, a state of affluence prevails, every individual will be free to seek his own personal fulfillment through consumption and leisure.

It is in confrontation with this "American" vision of progress, wealth and "authoritarian democracy," and no longer against the older forms of poverty and dictatorship, that the socialist workers' movement now has to define its position, not only in Europe but also in North America, in certain South American countries and in Japan. In the name of what, and on what basis?

To answer the question by a refutation, supported by facts, of the myths relating to the "civilization of affluence and leisure" is comparatively easy; nor is it difficult to demonstrate the hollowness of that concept of civilization in purely ideological terms. Critical analysis of this kind is no doubt essential; but such criticism must remain theoretical and in practice ineffective if it is not embodied in the economic and political struggle of a dominated class that is capable of becoming dominant.

Can the workers' movements in the advanced countries still give expression *in practical terms* to this criticism of the premises and consequences of progress on capitalist lines? Or, as some Marxist theorists already believe, are they reconciled to integration in an authoritarian system which will render exploitation acceptable and alienation comfortable?

The writings of Herbert Marcuse afford a useful point of departure for the study of these questions. In *One Dimensional Man* in particular he demonstrates at the outset the absurdity of the principle underlying all consumer theories, of which the slogan might be "consume and shut up." The principle is that the emancipation of men *as individuals* can result from a process perpetuating and intensifying their *collective* enslavement; and that quantitative growth will, at a given moment, become automatically transformed into qualitative improvement. The evolution of all advanced capitalist societies proves the opposite.

So long as industrial research and development is dictated by purely quantitative standards, and so long as the whole ideology and ethics of a society is governed by productivism, it is impossible for quantity to be transformed into quality or for the growth of power, wealth and individual comfort to transcend the realm of necessity toward the realm of liberty. This liberation can take place only if it is consciously and methodically brought about by the concerted action of men and women—in the first place, by the class directly involved in the process of production; that is to say, the people who in their daily lives are confronted by questions which are ignored by economic thinking: What purpose does production serve? What are we to work for and how? How are we to live and what for?

If any lesson is to be learned from the present situation in the United States or Sweden, for example, it is the following. Political economy in general, which is the study of the efficient use of limited resources, and capitalist logic in particular, which seeks to achieve maximum efficiency in micro-economic terms, is incapable of putting an end to the rule of scarcity. Even when the technical conditions for the elimination of scarcity have been virtually established, as is the case in the United States, and when it is technically possible, in Marcuse's expression, to "pacify existence" by abolishing degrading and fragmented manual labor, and to foster the growth and free activity of the individual—even in this situation capitalist economy has shown itself to be incapable of realizing its own potentialities. This is because use value, free time, the unfolding of human faculties, creation, the meaning of life and the richness of human relationships—all these are *extra-economic* riches and values. It is because the development and realization of these riches can be achieved only by the subordination of economics to ethics, and therefore calls for the overthrow of the primacy of economic considerations, the subversion of basic approaches, and the creation of a new economy and a new form of state.

Here we find an interesting point of convergence between Marx on the one hand and such non-Marxist American economists as Galbraith or Piel on the other. Galbraith shows that advanced capitalism, far from abolishing scarcity, deliberately perpetuates it and unconsciously reproduces it on new levels. I shall return to this. There are passages in Galbraith closely akin to the celebrated argument in which Marx foresees automation and shows that capitalism is incapable of taking advantage of it.[1]

However, this contradiction in the capitalist system between the liberating potentialities of the forces of produc-

---

[1] *Grundrisse der Kritik der politischen Oekonomie.*

"When work in its immediate form has ceased to be the main source of riches, the time spent on work ceases, and should cease, to be the measure of wealth, and exchange value the measure of use value . . . The free development of individuals and not merely the reduction of labor time necessary to produce a surplus; the reduction to a minimum of the socially necessary labor time . . . [these become the goal] . . . with a corresponding development of individuals in artistic, scientific and other ways, thanks to the additional free time and the facilities which have been created for all.

"But capitalism rejects the idea of reducing working hours to a minimum since it regards the time spent on work as the sole measure and source of wealth. Accordingly it reduces the labor time in its necessary form to increase it in its superfluous form, thus presenting superfluity to an increasing extent as a condition of the necessary."

tion and the use made of them by the capitalists, can become an issue only if a class exists which is actively fighting for the *individual and collective* liberation of men in a
society ruled by *extra-economic* criteria. If the full development of the forces of production has not been preceded
and conditioned by a long period of anti-capitalist struggle conducted with a sense of the true purposes of work
and life; if the working class has not during this period
developed a hegemonic capacity, an intellectual and political vanguard and a comprehensive concept of post-
capitalist society—then, not only will the full development
of the forces of production be unaccompanied by liberation, but the contradiction between virtual abundance and
the persistence of scarcity, struggle for life and cultural
impoverishment, will go *unperceived,* as will the contradiction between the liberating potentialities of technology
and the increasingly authoritarian organization of society.

It is at this point that I take issue with Herbert Marcuse.
To say, in effect, that a contradiction *may not* or *will not*
be perceived is quite different from saying that it is not
perceptible. If a contradiction exists, it must of necessity
enter at some level into the experience of the masses. The
problem, then, is to make the unperceived perceptible.

Marcuse seems to question the very possibility of achieving this. Using America as an example he demonstrates
admirably how advanced capitalism contrives to suppress
and blindfold the urge for liberation by its systematic conditioning of the individual in his consumption, his needs
and his thinking. He shows how the powers of technology
and wealth are used by monopoly capitalism to render
alienation tolerable and even prevent it from becoming
conscious; and to prevent the growth of a comprehensive
economic, cultural and political vision by means of which
capitalist civilization may be challenged as a whole, in its
ideological premises, its values and its practices.

Marcuse's analysis has the merit that it refutes the revolutionary catastrophism, that is, the belief that as the contradictions in capitalism become deeper, so will awareness

of them inevitably deepen. It confirms Lenin's saying that "without revolutionary theory there can be no revolutionary action"—that without awareness of the contradictions these may never come into the open, and that modern state capitalism can paper over the cracks and make it more difficult for them to be seen.

But from this assessment of the present situation in the United States, which certainly has relevant aspects for other capitalist countries, Marcuse goes on to draw rather hasty general conclusions regarding the near impossibility of preserving or creating a truly revolutionary movement within the framework of advanced capitalism. I believe on the contrary that the present crisis in Western socialism and the workers' movement is due to the fact that they have fallen behind in their thinking, and that this lapse, which may be only temporary, is due to a wide variety of historical causes. It appears to me that the present position of the workers' movement in the United States cannot be considered wholly representative of any general tendency, since American society differs in many respects from most other capitalist societies.

The United States is, in the first place, a colonial society born of immigrants to an undeveloped country. This has meant, in most of the states, the absence of local civilization and culture, and the absence (except in New England and the Deep South) of hereditary social stratifications. It has led to the predominance in every sphere, but particularly in agriculture and the exploitation of natural resources, of what may be termed the *mining approach*— that is to say, a ruthless attitude to the natural environment which, being perceived as conquered territory, has been exploited without much thought of preserving it as a living environment, a *culture*. From this has resulted, among other things, an extreme mobility of labor, no great concern for making the best use of the land and its resources, and the "immediatism" which characterizes all societies of colonial origin, whereby rapid consumption and the production of expendable or rapidly perishable goods takes precedence over the creation of and attachment to the more "lasting values," which in Europe and some parts of Latin America are rooted in that ancient stone- and earth-based culture which the United States has never known.

Secondly, American society is deeply pervaded with puritanism and, like all Protestant societies, comparatively impermeable to Marxist thinking—less so, certainly, than societies of a Catholic (or Buddhist) persuasion, inclined to search for the sense of history, to eschatological thinking. If we add the American isolationist tendency where other countries are concerned—that is to say, a kind of provincialism and a deep-rooted inclination of all classes to unite against the enemy abroad—we have the main historical reasons (there are, of course, many others) for the weak class-consciousness and autonomy of the American labor movement, for its corporatism and lack of internationalism. That is why the attempt to interpret other advanced capitalist countries in the light of the American example may be dangerous.

The speed with which the Americanization of other capitalist societies is being brought about cannot be explained solely by the *internal* repetition, in Western Europe and Japan, of the social, economic and political processes which have governed the formation of American industrial society. This transformation is also being caused by the strong *external* pressure exercised by American policies and the American economy. Had it not been for the Cold War, the economic and military aid programs and, more recently, the need to compete with the big American trusts on both the home and export markets, Western Europe and Japan would not have evolved in the same fashion. The urge to produce *similar products* on the same scale as the United States, and thereby to create a comparable consumer market, is due (particularly in the rapidity with which it has developed) as much to the economic and commercial hegemony of the United States as to any process of internal evolution.

THE DEADLOCK OF TRADITIONAL UNIONISM

What is true, however, is that the European labor movements, with very few exceptions, have been taken aback by
this process. They were insufficiently prepared to take positive action on the level where the change of capitalist
society was being brought about and where Western civilization was being shaped. With a very few local exceptions
the European workers' movement as a whole has opposed
the *effects* of capitalist development but has not raised the
level of the struggle to the point of demanding that development should be along other lines. The movement has
questioned the effects of economic growth and the unfair
distribution of the proceeds, but has seldom concerned
itself with the quality and purposes of this growth. In consequence the workers' opposition for the most part has
been conducted within the framework of, and subordinate
to, the capitalist system. It has not fostered a political
awareness and strategy designed to demonstrate the necessity of socialism not merely as a theoretical addition to
everyday demands but as their true meaning and intention.

So long as working-class demands were prompted by
poverty—that is to say, by the impossibility of gaining a
sufficient livelihood—they embodied within themselves a
radical rejection of capitalist society. At that stage the
formulation, in advanced terms, of a noncapitalist concept
of society was not needed. Food, equality and freedom
were clearly visible goals, and all were in themselves revolutionary.

But from the moment when capitalism is able to allow
the workers some degree, however limited, of rights and
liberties, enabling them to earn a basic livelihood and even
a modest surplus, the need to secure a better way of life
ceases to call for revolutionary change. If this better way
of life is expressed in purely quantitative terms, capitalism
can absorb it. And if, at a moment peculiarly favorable

to the workers, their demands lead to a crisis in capitalism
(as happened in France in 1957–58 and in Italy in 1962–
63) this crisis will be resolved to their detriment by an
economic and political counter-offensive on the part of the
owners *unless* the following precondition has been fulfilled.
If the workers are to take advantage of the situation, their
demands must be put forward within the context of a
political strategy; they must hold in reserve an alternative
policy for the long term as well as the short term; they
must have built a political block capable of assuming
power. It is this wider aspect, this comprehensive approach
raising working-class demands to a higher plane and attracting the support of other strata of society, which has
hitherto been lacking.

Wherever, as with the British, American and German
trade unions, the workers' demands have been restricted
to wage demands, they have ended by strengthening the
capitalist system. Unless it forms part of a political strategy,
the fight for higher wages simply calls for a redistribution
of the national income within the capitalist structure. From
this one of two things must follow. Either the wage increase is such as to threaten the equilibrium of the system, in which event the owners, supported by the state,
engage the unions in a trial of strength which they are
the more certain to win since the workers' case is not
conceived in terms of the struggle for a new kind of state
and a new economy; or else the increase demanded can
be absorbed by the system. In the latter event the unions
will merely have obtained what the system is able to con-
cede—an increase of purchasing power for which ownership will compensate itself by increased productivity and
intensification of work, thereby preserving and possibly increasing its margin of profit.

The trade-union struggle on normal lines cannot change
the nature of the system, the balance of forces within it,
or the condition of the working class. Traditional trade
unionism implicitly accepts the principle that the workers
are to remain subordinate—an exploited class, oppressed

and alienated in their work. It confines itself to demanding higher individual purchasing power and at the same time greater leisure—in other words, *non-work,* in compensation for the fact that where his work is concerned the worker is a *non-man.*

In every advanced capitalist country trade unionism of this kind is in a state of crisis. It is encountering strong pressure on the part of the state and the owners to limit and pre-define, by means of an incomes policy, the degree of wage increase that can be allowed. This pressure expresses an increased inflexibility in the system, due to the following:

1. The speed of technological developments, and the consequent necessity of increasing and planning capital investment;

2. the increasing burden of fixed capital, notably in the heavy industries, as opposed to circulating capital;

3. the increasing importance of amortization, provisions and financial costs, leading to a greater rigidity in management policies;

4. the intensity of international competition between overequipped concerns.

On the level of private enterprise these factors are already compelling capital to plan in advance the cost of labor in the context of a medium or long-term program. The union therefore cannot enter into wage negotiations with any particular concern without taking into account not only the concern's managerial policy, which determines its wage policy, but also the *kind of economic or political development* that this policy favors. It can be effective in contesting managerial policy only if it acts: (1) in full knowledge of the facts; (2) at the moment when that policy is being decided; (3) with the intention of modifying it by imposing constrictions on capital; (4) on the basis of a different pattern of development embracing different branches of the industry and the economy as a whole.

For this growing inflexibility is not confined to individual enterprises but is equally apparent on the level of the economic structure as a whole. The expansion of the consumer industries, which is the motive force of European economic growth, can only be maintained by the public financing of the infrastructures that make possible this expansion: in particular, roads for the use of the private motorist, housing for the rural masses attracted by industry to the already overcrowded industrial centers, general education and vocational training for the increasing number of adolescents and adults required by industry, and scientific and technical research, 70 per cent of which is state-financed in the United States and in France.

The rising cost of economic growth affects both the direct and the indirect—that is to say, social—cost of monopolistic expansion. Apart from structural modifications relating to the orientation and mechanism of growth, the equilibrium of the system allows only a narrow margin for maneuver. The concern of all modern capitalist states during this period is to guarantee private monopolies sufficient profit to enable them to continue expanding while at the same time covering the social cost of private expansion, as far as possible—but generally to an insufficient extent—out of public funds.

A twofold pressure, both public and private, tends therefore to restrict and predetermine wage increases, and this pressure takes the form of a twofold attack, by the state on the one hand and the owners on the other, on the trade union's bargaining power. The attack assumes a variety of forms: taxation, the freezing of public salaries and wages, intransigence on the part of the owners, layoffs in order to create a pool of unemployed and the further exploitation of the workers by more stringent working conditions, lower skill ratings, reduction of bonuses and so on.

Under these circumstances any improvement in the workers' condition, whether qualitative or quantitative, is impossible unless the unions attack not only management but the whole system within which it operates, as the CGIL

in Italy and the FGTB in the French-speaking part of
Belgium have been the first to understand. For the
working-class movement is faced by these alternatives:
either it must accept the logic of the system and conform
to its discipline, bargaining only for such marginal improvements as the system may allow, or it must fight for
its autonomy. But the latter can be preserved only if the
logic and mechanism of capitalist accumulation are con-
tested *and if a different policy and development pattern,
a different form of state and balance of forces, are advocated on the political level and imposed by the power
of the masses.*

The European workers' movement has now reached a
decisive phase. Even the workers' most immediate demands
can no longer succeed without challenging the economic
policy and the mechanism of capital accumulation; but this
challenge by itself can effect nothing unless it goes beyond
the field of protest to propose positive changes entailing
the transformation of the economy and of society.[2]

In other words, even current trade-union demands relating to wages, hours and working conditions imply an

[2] "The growing incompatibility between union autonomy
and the stability of the system has confronted all trade unions
and working-class parties with an essentially political task which
is now one of particular urgency: namely, the formulation of
an alternative to national economic policies; a political alternative of which the purpose will be to implement new mechanisms
of accumulation based on a radical reform of the economic
structure and on a democratic system of policy making, and
which will prove itself capable of reorienting public and private capital investment on a basis of selective priorities. That
is to say, a new policy of economic development reconciling
union autonomy with guaranteed full employment and the rapid
expansion of those consumptions and collective investments
which are of primary importance to the working masses."
Bruno Trentin, "Present Tendencies in Class Struggle," in
Tendenze del capitalismo europeo, (Rome: Editori Riuniti,
1966); French translation in *Les Temps Modernes*, February
1967.

objective attack on the inflexibility of the system and the logic on which it is based. They can effect a breach in it, and arm themselves against its formidable resilience, only if the objective political and economic implications of the attack are subjectively reflected in a conscious and coherent political purpose.[3] If the workers' movement is too slow in devising a political-economic alternative, broadening the demands of the working class and offering them a prospect of success, there is a real danger that the whole union movement will fall into decay. Why go on fighting if the resistance of the system proves insurmountable, if strikes fail to secure the smallest result, and if, to prove the fruitlessness of head-on collision and the advantages of compromise, the state and the owners finally make marginal concessions against the inadequacy of which the unions have struggled in vain?

We are at present in a period of transition when the drive for higher wages and improved conditions is still alive but is yielding diminishing returns, when the workers' organizations still vigorously refuse to bow to the system, but when the leadership of those organizations is already divided on the subject of whether it is possible to escape a state of subordination, to preserve their freedom of action and to raise the workers' struggle from the purely economic to the political level.

The fundamental question at this moment is whether the demands arising from the rank and file, and the workers' reasons for rejecting their subordination to, and integration

[3] "Old and new working-class demands can no longer be satisfied by bargaining at the level of the individual enterprise or branch of industry; today, even more than in the past, the framing of traditional demands in a wider context—that of economic policy, of politics *tout court*—is called for . . . In order to preserve their autonomy and to carry on their fight for full employment, the trade unions in all European countries will be compelled to engage in a wider battle for the transformation—limited or wholesale—of the mechanism of economic development." Bruno Trentin, op. cit.

within, the existing system, afford a sufficient basis, subjective as well as objective, for an effective anti-capitalist
political struggle. The question is to know whether the
workers' day-to-day demands do not really go beyond their
ostensible content—wages and employment—or whether in
fact they are symptomatic of something far deeper although
still largely unexpressed: their refusal to accept their present condition in the factory and in capitalist society, which
will become manifest when more advanced goals and wider
horizons are proposed to them.

There can be no empirical answer to the question.
Sociological research and opinion polls conducted in cold
blood are wholly misleading. The question can only be
answered in action—by the formulation of theory and its
testing in practice, through active conflict, in order to bring
to light the deeper motives, the new and radical antagonisms, underlying the traditional but still living workers'
movement.

Clearly the test can be conducted only on a large scale
and over a comparatively long period. But it is also clear
that if the arduous task is to be undertaken at all it must
be from a conviction that it is worth the trouble: in other
words, that despite the workers' improved standard of living, they still find their condition unacceptable for a variety
of reasons, some old and some relatively new; that these
reasons can be merged in an anti-capitalist strategy; and
that in this way it may be possible to release a revolutionary
potential which, in the absence of such a strategy, can
only remain latent.

NEW FIELDS OF CONFLICT

The conviction that the task is worthwhile is what I am
seeking to affirm: namely, the belief that there is no overwhelming reason why the working class should be integrated within the present system, and that a change of
emphasis and direction is occurring in the class struggle of

which wage bargainings on the traditional pattern often
take little account. We may take as our point of departure
the fact that the drive for higher pay, the refusal to accept
a wages policy, the stubborn defense of trade-union autonomy against attempts to subordinate it to the system,
is no less vigorous, and sometimes more so, in the higher-
paid industries and branches of industry than among the
ranks of the lower-paid workers. This fact cannot be accounted for solely by the growth of unsatisfied consumer
demand on the part of the more highly paid. It appears to
me to be due rather to the following causes:

1. The worker, no matter what his pay, feels that no
price, however high, will compensate him for the time, the
freedom and the life he sacrifices to an employer, public
or private, who dictates the entire nature and conditions
of his work.

2. Wage claims are the most immediately effective form
of protest against the *social subordination* of the worker:
against non-recognition, in the factory and in society, of
the responsible, creative and personal factors inherent even
in relatively unskilled work.[4]

[4] Both points have been admirably illustrated by a workman
in the Olivetti Company: "As production increases, thanks directly or indirectly to the efforts of the worker, so does his state
of subordination increase, the oppressive pressure exerted upon
him by management and the decisions it makes. On the technical level the worker is obliged to make an increasing number
of important decisions. In theory these are things that should
generally be decided in the offices, but in practice it is the
worker who decides them.

"This means that the worker plays an important part in the
productive process. But it is precisely through this that he becomes aware of his subordinate state—either because his true
function is not acknowledged in his work rating or (and this is
even more important) because in making essential decisions he
comes up against a string of obstacles and provokes disputes for
which he is not responsible but which he cannot avoid.

"On top of all this . . . it must be borne in mind that he is
only relatively well paid; above all, that his wages do not com-

It is in terms of these factors, which are ignored by the upholders of the "consumer theory," who believe that the working class will vanish and be absorbed into the middle classes when it has attained a certain standard of living, that we must look for the fundamental and permanent causes of class antagonism: namely, the persistence of exploitation whatever the wages; the subordination of the workers, individually and collectively, within the capitalist relations of production; and the specific *intolerability* of the workers' condition.

I shall confine myself to giving a few instances of this, some old and some relatively new.

1. At the Point of Production

a. The despotic or military hierarchy in the factory. Civil liberties—speech, assembly, press, etc.—are suspended when the worker enters the factory premises. Repressive, judicial and economic power are concentrated in the same hands. Civil law is not equipped to prevent arbitrary or illegal acts on the part of management, even when notice of these is given.

b. The discretionary powers of management over working conditions (skill ratings, speeds, overtime, etc.), over the organization of work and the terms of its payment and evaluation.

c. The contradiction between the passive obedience and the technical initiative required of the worker; and between his technical responsibility, which is often great, and his absolute powerlessness to influence production policy in its technical and economic orientations.

d. The crisis of the rating system caused by technological innovation, which leads to the destruction of *individual*

---

pensate the worker for his importance to the productive process, and that only an effective say in the conditions under which he works can reflect that importance." Mario Carrara, "L'Inchièsta operaia alla Olivetti nel 1961," in *Quaderni Rossi,* No. 5.

skills and to the requirement of higher *social* qualifications in most new semi-skilled jobs.

e. The disparity between the general level of education and technical responsibility required of an increasing number of workers, and the underemployment of their abilities in monotonous and fragmented tasks.

f. The crippling of the worker, even before he goes to a job, by a hurried and inadequate "training" which affords him no opportunity to grasp the productive process as a whole and from the outset limits his intellectual autonomy.

2. At the Overall Economic Level

a. Job insecurity and unemployment.

b. The technical and geographical concentration of industry which—through plant closures, layoffs and retirement of highly skilled workers and professionals, and abandonment or neglect of entire regions—leads to the wastage or sterilization of human energies as well as to the displacement of populations and overcrowding of already congested and ill-equipped centers.

c. The bottleneck of public services and amenities in industrial centers—transportation, housing, cultural and medical facilities, etc.—which raises the cost of living, adds to the fatigue of labor and causes deterioration in the general living condition of the workers even when real incomes are rising. Those inadequacies can be remedied only by public investment, and it is impossible to raise sufficient public funds without attacking the mechanisms of capital accumulation by public management of the economy.

In listing these points I have arbitrarily separated the workers' condition in the factory from their condition in society. I have done so in order to illustrate to what extent the two conditions overlap and influence each other, to what extent the workers' situation in the factory is in itself a social situation, and to what degree the circumstances of his life outside the factory are determined by his life within it.

That is why it is impossible to divorce the labor struggle for better wages and working conditions from the broader political and economic struggle embracing, for example, education, city planning, social services, regional development and so on—all problems to which no lasting solution can be found except in terms of an anti-capitalist policy.

Yet, clearly, it is from the point of production that the struggle must necessarily begin. For (1) it is at the point of production that the workers undergo most directly the despotism of capital, and have the direct experience of their social subordination; (2) it is here that capital, by methods of division of labor which, often without technical necessity, are methods of domination, sets out to produce decomposed, molecularized, humiliated men, whom it can then dominate in society; (3) finally, and especially, it is only here that the workers exist as a group, as a real *collective force* capable of collective action which can just as well modify their condition in its most immediately intolerable aspects as force the class enemy to confront them.

The decline of militancy and weakening of the working class as a political force are closely bound up with the difficulty the class organizations experience in promoting and pursuing the struggle at the place where it must start, *the place of work*. Speeches about the absolutism of capital, the destruction of democracy and the authoritarian nature of the corporate state can become fully meaningful only if they refer to the vast dehumanizing process to which all workers in the major corporations are subject. Conversely, talk about economic and political democracy, the fight against monopolies and the reshaping of the state, must remain abstract unless it is sustained by active struggle on the factory floor against managerial despotism.

Though from a theoretical point of view there can be no liberation of the workers until the state in its present form, and the capitalist relations of production have been abolished, in *practice* their abolition will become a plausible goal if it comes alive as the meaning which daily actions and demands lead up to. To gather momentum, action cannot from the outset be directed against the total structure that is finally responsible for intolerable conditions; it must proceed from attacks on the "consequences" to reach back to the ultimate "cause." The workers are not *at first* interested in overall political-economic changes which, eventually, may also change their daily lives. It is by acting upon their present work situation that they will develop an interest in issues and struggles affecting society as a whole. Unless it is bound up with the struggle for worker control in the factory, the fight for democracy is in serious danger of remaining an abstraction.

The fact is that the working class has been ceaselessly mystified in the name of democracy. The conquest of democratic rights and liberties has never penetrated beyond the factory gates or in any way changed the oppression and exploitation of the proletariat. To enter the factory is to find oneself in an authoritarian and absolutist society as rigidly hierarchic as the army, with its own private police force, where the working life and activities of the workers, as well as the nature of the goods produced, are governed by unilateral decisions based on criteria which the ruling stratum does not allow to be discussed. Even in countries such as Sweden, where a workers' party is in power, the working class may have its constitutional rights suspended if it does not bow to arbitration. In the day-to-day life of industry the workers have to do what they are told and remain powerless toward the means of production, employment policy, organization of work or anything else.

In short, from the worker's point of view democracy is a farce. It will be worth fighting for only if it is brought down to earth from the realm of institutional make-believe and made to express the workers' positive power to shape their own working life, and their collective power over the means and goals of production. It is through the struggle for "industrial democracy," as the British call it—that is to say, the workers' power of control, of management and self-management, rising from the shop floor to the corporation and the industry until it embraces the economy as a whole—that the working class learns to know the value and necessity of socialism and thus grows up to become the ruling class.

The struggle for the emancipation of the proletariat cannot, of course, be won at the factory level; it has to transcend itself into an overall action and political vision involving society as a whole. But to reach this higher level, it has to start at the lower, the basic level; it cannot be built from the top down. Either the protagonists of democratization will be the masses or there will be no democratization—nothing but technocratic reforms.

The remarkable fact, when the matter is considered in this light, is that wherever the labor movement has concentrated on achieving worker power on the shop floor, its efforts have generally been rewarded not only by an immediate increase of militancy but also by a growth of political awareness, *provided political vanguards were available at shop-floor level to raise the political issues which rank-and-file action involved.*

The importance of this proviso is clearly illustrated by recent events in West Germany and in Britain, where, for lack of a political relay, thrusts of working-class combativeness have either subsided or degenerated into the defense of sectional interests, or else attempted to supplant inadequate parties by creating political arms of their own.

A few years ago, for example, the workers at a large German automobile factory were considered to be hostile to unionization. The number of trade unionists inscribed on the books of I. G. Metall amounted to only about 1 per cent of the total labor force. The leaders attributed this to high wages and American-type personnel management. Eventually a new union organizer, determined to get to the bottom of the matter, went around the shops talking to the men. Nearly all had grievances. Accordingly he circulated a printed questionnaire asking the men for their opinion of conditions in the factory. There was an impressive number of replies. These were analyzed, major grievances were listed under appropriate headings and a report was published in the factory union journal. The stir it caused was so great that there was nearly a strike. As generally happens in West Germany, however, this was averted by the intervention of the union, both at management level and on the factory floor.

The workers' grievances were principally concerned with speeds and organization of work, its monotony and the nervous fatigue it engendered; also with the relations between workers and foremen, foremen and engineers, etc. Negotiations with management resulted, at least temporarily, in certain improvements, and it was left at that.

The matter might have been carried much further. The workers' grievances constituted a typical basis for demands for workers' control—that is to say, for the workers to have a collective power in shaping working conditions: speed, composition of teams, workshop organization, skill ratings and so on. The broad tendency would have been to enrich fragmented tasks, to establish a system of rotation for the less gratifying jobs and to subordinate production technology (and the technical division of labor) to the needs of the workers—in a word, the *optimization* of working conditions.

This optimization consists essentially in the diversification and enlargement of jobs so as to enable the individual worker to make broader use of his faculties, instead of merely using one of them, which leads to nervous exhaustion and eventually to permanent psychic mutilation. Clearly, if it is to be translated into concrete demands, optimization requires that the union, in consultation with its own experts and in permanent contact with the rank and file, will evolve alternative schemes of work organization to be put forward in opposition to those of the management, not merely in isolated cases, but whenever (and preferably before) technical innovations are introduced. And this implies a state of permanent conflict, since the goal, the radical transformation of the workers' condition, transcends any partial concession that may be secured.

In many cases the demand for optimization will be in conflict with the principle of maximum output, and workers' control will give rise to a new set of issues. For example, can a given series of improvements be made compatible with higher productivity? What technical adjustments would be required for this to be the case? How long would they take? How much would they cost? Is it true that management can adopt them only to the detriment of wage increases or even of the existing wage levels?

There is one way only to get an answer to these questions: let the company open its books. What are the profits? How are they used? Could they not be used differently? Is there no waste or inefficiency at management levels? Are organization, productive capacity and output in line with the needs of the people? And so on.

In a word, workers' control of the *technical division of labor* must lead inexorably to a demand for workers' control of management, that is to say, it implies a challenge to the *social division of labor*.

When this level is attained the movement can progress no further in the purely plant level. It must go beyond it. No solution to the conflict can be found in worker participation in management, which would merely give the workers a stake in the logic of capitalism. They would very soon be confronted by the following dilemma: either optimization of working conditions or wage increases, but not both. And if the union refused to accept these as alternatives, the management would threaten to close down the business. Here we come to the root of the capitalist system: if capital cannot get what it considers a sufficient reward, it goes on strike. Against this strike threat the local union is helpless unless it can raise the conflict to the political-economic level, where it can be shown that the apparent impasse is due to the system and is not an impossibility in itself.

IMPORTANCE OF A MASS PARTY

Thus, by following up the logic of rank-and-file demands, we find ourselves brought back to the political dimension of the class struggle. These, being uncompromis-
ingly defended by the embattled militants—as is the case,
for example, in Britain—may for a time frustrate attempts
to integrate the union into the system. But in themselves
they have only a limited effectiveness. Unless they are informed by an overall concept of the social and political
implications of "work optimization," they are bound to
degenerate into sectional struggles in which management
can play one trade or skill against another. By reorganization, layoffs and the offer of selective advantages, management will seek either to rid itself of workers who, because
of their technical importance, are in a position to enforce
the demand for workers' control, or else to appease them
with offers of bonuses (which may later be revoked),
improved working conditions, profit sharing and "human
relations." And the workers will fall into the trap because
their specific demands are not linked to a "global alternative" embracing a new pattern of production and consumption, of life and development.

The formulation of this "global alternative" is essential
in order to refute the managerial thesis, often very plausible
so long as one remains within the bounds of micro-
economic argument. At plant level, where the margin is
often small, demands embracing both optimization and
wages may indeed find themselves restricted within very
narrow limits.

There is no way of passing beyond these limits except
by the socialization of profits (or surplus). But this must
not be taken to mean that the mere distribution of surplus
will enable the problems of quantity and quality to be in-
stantly solved. The advantage of the socialization of
profits, and therefore of the function of investment and

accumulation, lies rather in the fact that it paves the way
for a new development policy, on selective and qualitative
lines, allowing for needs and aspirations hitherto suppressed under capitalism, so that individual consumer demands—and therefore individual earnings—will be profoundly modified.

The consumer needs of the individual are not given by
nature: they are very largely determined by the market
and above all by the way of working, by the individual's
relation to his work. The needs of "affluent" consumption created by advanced capitalism are not wholly artificial. To a very great extent they are the needs of the
crippled and frustrated worker who, being unable to find
any interest or personal satisfaction in his work, falls easy
prey during his leisure hours to the merchants of distraction and creature comfort, *private* compensations for the
traumas inflicted on him by the social process.

So long as work continues to be destructive of the individual, a constraint and oppression which he is obliged
to endure, the field of non-work will be the field of escape,
distraction and passive enjoyment. In Bruno Trentin's
words, "The alienated consumer is the individual whose
consumer needs reflect his alienation as an agent of production."

What has been called "mass civilization" or "the consumer society" can and must be reinterpreted in terms of
the capitalist relations of production. The essential fact is
that factory and office workers are engaged in the productive process as isolated individuals, *molecules,* submitted to
the social and technical division of labor, and with no say
in the why or how of the process of which they are a part.
It is this molecularization, and the powerlessness it en-
genders, that create what is called the "mass individual"—
that is to say, the individual who is not himself either in
his work or in his consumption, who has no influence over
his environment or over society and sees both from the
outside, as a spectator and a consumer; and whose only
thought is to dig himself a hole sheltered from the social

100   SOCIALISM AND REVOLUTION

world where he will be "at home." This is the aspiration which "affluent" capitalism claims to satisfy, having first promoted it.

Empirical sociology is wholly misleading when it "discovers" this aspiration as a fact of nature or a free choice. The truth is that all desires are conditioned by the possibility of their fulfillment, in other words, by the general social conditions in which they arise. Apart from intellectuals and militants, the individual wants what he has a hope of getting in existing circumstances and does not look for what he can get only in altered circumstances. The worker in a capitalist society wants a car, or a better car, and is prepared to work longer hours in order to acquire it. The car comes higher on his list of priorities than a larger dwelling in a pleasanter neighborhood, better schools for his children or other social facilities.

But one cannot base any theory of human nature on this list of priorities: what they reveal is the social environment. We are dealing with a society in which the automobile is already established, and which organizes its transport and urban systems in terms of motoring, treating every individual as a potential motorist. Moreover, the car affords the worker a means of escape from the slums or the dinginess of his suburb. The acquisition of a car is within his reach, provided he keeps his job, while, on the other hand, better housing, schools and social facilities are things about which, as an individual, he can do little or nothing. They are not within his reach. Accordingly, there is not much point in asking for them individually. They can move within his reach only if he agitates for them, not as an individual but as a member of a group formed for the express purpose of changing social relationships and subjecting the entire way of life and of working to the common will of the people.

Questions of optimum production in terms of use value, of the techniques employed and of living and working conditions, cannot even be *raised* except by the *grouped* producers of a given branch or sector; and the question of the optimum pattern of life and consumption can only be raised by individuals grouped in places of production, habitation and culture, on the level of the community, the region and the nation. And clearly to raise the question is to query the standards and logic of a system based on maximum profit at the micro-economic level of private enterprise—standards leading to distortion, imbalance, waste and the priority of the superfluous over the necessary, futility over culture, which have been exposed in the United States by writers of such widely differing views as Baran, Marcuse, Galbraith, Packard and the Committee of the Triple Revolution.

If we define liberty as the power of the individual to shape the conditions in which he lives and to change those conditions according to his needs and his desire for self-fulfillment and self-transcendence, we are bound to recognize that liberty as defined by bourgeois democracy is a myth. And if we define liberty as the power of social individuals over their social existence, then we must see that capitalist democracy is devoid of content. The only places where liberty and democracy, by these definitions, can be exercised or conquered are the political parties and unions, *insofar* as these are designed for common action based on the common existence and experience of working and living communities. Therefore the formation of democratic parties and unions—that is to say, of groupings having political and social goals, whose activities are sustained by the formulation in common of a common project embracing the entirety of their common existence—is possible only if they organize individuals in the places where they live together and where their common interests are a matter of direct experience: namely, places of work, habitation and education. There can be no democracy that does not proceed from direct participatory democracy, that is to say, from democratic power effectively exercised by assemblies and councils in the factories, agricultural co-operatives, communities, etc.

But the process of capital accumulation and concentration in itself entails the destruction of local groups and communities, therefore of basic democracy and finally of the whole democratic process, considered as the development of a common endeavor. The whole pattern of Western progress is based on a bourgeois revolution of which we are here concerned with one fundamental aspect: namely, the separation of civil society and the state, paralleled by the dissociation of the private and the social individual. In other words, in the bourgeois concept of democracy the individual is free to pursue his *private* aims and interests within the framework of existing and resulting conditions; but he is not free to change those conditions in response to *common* goals and needs. The bourgeois revolution has institutionalized individual liberties, but at the cost of restricting freedom to the sphere of individual choices.

The tasks exceeding that sphere devolve upon the state, of which the historic function is to perpetuate conditions permitting the exercise of private enterprise. By the same token the state is bound to prevent groups of individuals from exercising a decisive influence on general conditions and making them conform to their collective will. In this respect both the labor unions and the private ownership cartels are under suspicion, but whereas the latter are difficult to fight, being linked by secret agreements, the former can easily be dealt with since they derive their strength from open mass action. In the United States, legislative proposals have even gone so far as to assimilate labor unions with monopolies and to restrict union rights which might disrupt competition on the labor market.

Briefly, in a society based on the dispersal and separation of individuals, the state monopolizes the sovereignty of the "people" and is constantly concerned with breaking up groups formed for the purpose of winning that sovereignty for the benefit of the grouped individuals. The state claims to be the sole representative of the general interest as opposed to particular interests, while in fact it endeavors to particularize all interests in order to be their only mediator. But its mediating functions are exercised within the framework of monopoly capitalism and therefore in the interests of the latter. For practical purposes the state follows in the wake of the major capitalist groups, seeking to render economically viable and socially tolerable decisions arrived at in private which affect the life of the community as a whole. It co-ordinates its public policies with the decisions of those groups, ruling in partnership with them, in what Perroux has called "close symbiosis," and furnishing private interests with a political platform and ideological rationale which appears to bring them into line with the general interest.

Thus, while civil society is molecularized into a pullulation of abstract individuals, its unity and universality are embodied in an external state which is no less an abstraction where the "citizen" is concerned. Unifying and integrating the citizens is a specialized, external political-ideological function over which the citizen himself as a rule has only a formal influence—i.e., practically none. The liberty of the citizen consists in his right to vote from time to time, to choose between newspapers generally controlled by monopolies, to listen to radio and television controlled by the same monopolies when they are not run by the state, and to choose between the varieties of branded goods competing for his custom. The citizen is free in matters of secondary importance and powerless in matters that count. He has no say in the organization, orientation and priorities of production; in the creation of employment; in the organization, content and methods of education; in the geographical distribution of investments, their amount, etc. All these decisions affecting the meaning and quality of society come within the sphere of the ruling capitalist groups and the state that serves their general interests; they are made in response to financial and commercial considerations unrelated, in any major sense, to any kind of economic, social or human optimum.

Faced by the concentration of economic power in the hands of a small circle of administrators, often personally

related, and by a state whose business is politically and
ideologically to reconcile monopoly interests with those of
society as a whole, it would be astonishing if the forms
and institutions of bourgeois democracy were able to avoid
running into crises and becoming discredited. The crucial
decisions are not, and indeed never have been, publicly
debated in elected assemblies, but are reached in the centers of power. Moreover, elected assemblies are wholly
unfitted to express any kind of "popular" will insofar as
they are created by the mere adding up of the miscella-
neous votes cast in the name of sectional, local or national
interests by dispersed and bewildered voters under the influence of publicity-oriented electoral campaigns.

A parliament can have true representative value and
reflect the popular mind only if it is composed of mass
parties deriving their authority from collective action and
continuous public debate on policy; and if those parties
have a comprehensive view of society, a grasp of its contradictions and the means of overcoming these and moving
on to a culture yet to be created. It is only in such parties
that a common will can be born of people grouped together
on the basis of their common goals—and "common goals"
must be understood to mean, not the sum of separate,
similar aims but a common perspective that can be attained only by all acting together. The popular will can find
itself only in parties such as this, not in ballot boxes or in
elected assemblies where a miscellany of separate individual purposes are mechanically added together; but in
parties that are centers of true democracy, in which a
comprehensive concept of man and the society to be built
emerges from constant debate and the exchange and conflict of experience.

To say this is clearly to argue that the crisis and decadence of democracy in the advanced capitalist countries
is, first and foremost, the crisis and decadence of the political parties. To ask whether this decadence is a consequence or a cause seems to me beside the point: it is both.
The political parties have declined to the extent that they

have made their first objective the exercise of power within the framework of the state and the existing system, which confines within very narrow limits the amount of political discretion left to the holders of power. Political competition, in these conditions, does not bring into play opposed concepts of policy and of the state but is simply concerned with different ways of implementing the same basic policy determined in advance by the existing balance of forces and social relations.

It will be argued in reply that this decadence of the political parties, which is primarily a decadence of the anticapitalist parties, is due to the impossibility of overthrowing a modern capitalist state by revolutionary means, to the weakening of class barriers and the class struggle, and to the disappearance of the radicalism which working-class poverty is supposed—wrongly—to have engendered. I do not accept any of this. I do not believe that the decadence of so many workers' parties is to be accounted for solely by the impossibility of revolution. On the contrary, I think the workers' parties are themselves largely responsible for the apparent impossibility, which arises out of their crisis no less than it causes it. We need first to understand the reasons for this crisis. They go back to the Stalin era and to the Cold War, which for a long time paralyzed thinking on such matters as the new type of party that was required, alienation and new needs, and on the new forms of struggle and democracy which had to be opposed to the authoritarian state of monopoly capitalism.

Thinking of this kind has been pursued only on the fringe of the capitalist world by comparatively youthful Marxist parties. Its broad tendency, in opposition to the authoritarian and totalitarian tendencies of capitalism and socialism, and to mass "civilization" and mass "democracy," is to construct centers of direct democracy which, on the plan of the early soviets, will pave the way for large local and regional autonomies, and for the self-management of production and exchange by the associated producers of urban and rural communities. The pattern of monopolist development is to be countered by a campaign for an "articulated" and decentralized democracy rooted in such basic communities as co-operatives, communes, factories, and cities, with their horizontal and vertical linkages. The political battle is to be dislodged from its parliamentary and electoral rut and removed to the places where people work and live together, where they can have a direct bearing on their condition, where their needs and conflicts with existing society arise, and where they feel the need for liberation and for a collective power which is incompatible with the present structure of the state.

Lelio Basso has written:

The type of party with which we are familiar has generally been formed to meet the requirements of the parliamentary struggle or the traditional revolutionary struggle on Russian or Chinese lines. But a party seeking to guide the proletariat in a campaign with revolutionary objectives, to be carried on every day at every level of society, must necessarily have a different structure. It must realize in the first place that its efforts cannot be confined to the political sphere envisaged by bourgeois society, that is to say, to parliament (however important this may be as a reflection of the struggles taking place within the country) but must pervade the whole fabric of social relations. Only thus can it organize and guide the masses, who are not merely voting abstractions but human beings involved in definite social relations and moved by definite reasons and circumstances.

Representative democracy is not capable of expressing, let alone of fulfilling, the aims of people who, in response to their positive needs, constantly create new structures, new forms of association, new institutions. The political parties, as presently organized, remain as a rule outside this many-sided reality. Although they may secure a large measure of support for the general principles they advocate, they are not always successful in co-ordinating and guiding the conflicts arising from diversified centers of social life between which there are few links. It is therefore urgently necessary that the parties should adapt themselves to the real course of evolution and appeal to the real man—in the place where his

urge to struggle is born and his hostile awareness of bourgeois reality is formed—in such a way as to make him feel
that he is sharing the party life; also, that the party should
relate its political strategy and campaigning more closely to
the firsthand experience of the workers.

In other words, it must sustain to the utmost the impulse
rising from the base to the top, take constant note of experience at the grass roots, encourage initiative among the masses,
and make use of this experience and initiative to remedy the
lack of democratic power fostered by bourgeois institutions,
and to favor the growth of the organism required for this
kind of struggle . . .

It goes without saying that this line of action calls for a
type of organization which will penetrate into all the centers
of social life, in order to interpret their most deep-seated demands, convert them into battle potential, and prevent the
party from becoming isolated and operating in a void.

For that is the danger that threatens us today. A danger already apparent in the weak attendance at meetings; in the
diminishing number of militants and the declining circulation of party newspapers; in the growing indifference to the
political parties which—in France, for example—is manifest in
the proliferation of clubs concerned with narrow sectional
interests where these are sufficiently dynamic; and, more generally, in what is commonly called depolitization, which is
probably the expression, not of indifference to politics as such
but to the manner of its practice.[5]

5 "The Prospects of the European Left," in *Tendenze del
Capitalismo europeo* (Rome, 1966). French translation in *Les
Temps Modernes,* February 1967.

Chapter 3

Students and Workers*

* Communication to the conference organized by the Gramsci Institute in July 1965 on "Tendencies of European Capitalism" and published in *Tendenze del Capitalismo europeo* (Rome, 1966) and in the *International Socialist Journal*, No. 10, August 1965, under its original title, "Aspects of the Contradiction Between the Capitalist Relations of Production and the Socially Necessary Labor Power."

During the past twenty years the development of the forces of production in the advanced capitalist economies has led to an accelerating qualitative change in the nature of the labor power which is required by the social process of production.

I shall attempt to outline rapidly, and somewhat schematically, certain of the potentially disruptive contradictions with which this change confronts European capitalism, and the manner in which capitalism seeks to disguise or defuse or prevent them. Not claiming to exhaust the subject, I shall confine myself to pointing out contradictions on the following levels:

1. The contradiction between the growing cost of the socially necessary labor power (notably the length and cost of the training required) and the tendency of society to avoid, as far as possible, taking the financial burden upon itself;

2. The contradiction between the nature and level of training called for by the development of the forces of production and the nature and level of training which, in managerial eyes, is needed to perpetuate the hierarchic relations within industry and, more generally, the existing social relations of production;

3. The contradiction between the growing autonomy, actual or potential, of productive work and its directly social character for an increasing proportion of workers, and their status in industry and in capitalist society. Or, if you prefer, the contradiction at a particular level between

the human forces of production and the capitalist relations
of production.

The shortage of skilled labor is recognized in every European capitalist country as being one of the main obstacles
along the present course of monopolist expansion. In
France, the Fifth Plan specifically invoked the lack of
skilled workers, technicians and engineers as a reason for
postponing even the smallest reduction in working hours
until 1970. Despite the increase of unemployment in certain industries and regions, the French Government in
May 1965 argued that skilled labor was in such short
supply that an indiscriminate reduction in working hours
would bring about a general slowdown and, as a result,
even higher unemployment.

This was an implicit admission of the fact that to secure
full employment and reduction of working hours the
"skilled-worker bottleneck" would have to be eliminated,
and that the workers' demands relating to hours and working conditions could only be met by a large-scale educational program. But such a program, according to the
French Government's own pronouncements, is incompatible with the present policy of monopolistic accumulation.
It was predicted that by 1970 the number of skilled workers coming out of the state training centers would be 50
per cent greater than the number in 1964; this figure nevertheless represents *less* than a third of the number of skilled
workers required annually by industry.[1]

As in other capitalist countries (although somewhat less

[1] The situation is no better in the German Federal Republic.
Here 70 per cent of the apprentices are trained in artisan or
semi-artisan workshops where they receive no instruction in
modern techniques and are taught a skill which, in one case out
of three, they will have no opportunity to use. Efforts to give
them a minimum of theoretical instruction have been frustrated by the lack of facilities and instructors on the one hand,
and by opposition on the part of craft employers on the other.
Leo Bauer, *Der Stern*, Nos. 50 & 51, 1964.

than in Italy) the shortage of skilled labor in France means that an excessively long work week goes hand in hand with underemployment and a degree of total unemployment that is by no means negligible, particularly among the young.

The wretched state of training cannot be directly attributed to a considered policy on the part of the managing class. On the contrary, the big owners are generally aware of the urgent need for extended training programs, both larger and better, if the growth and competitiveness of the nation's industry are to be maintained. If insufficient funds are available for the purpose (only 40 per cent of the Fourth French Plan's target for training was realized), this is essentially because the development of education is a part of the growing collective needs engendered by monopolist expansion, and respect for the spontaneous process of private accumulation (subject, if necessary, to "corrective programming") prevents the government from levying sufficient taxes to make a public investment consistent with collective (that is, public) needs.[2]

In a nutshell, monopolist expansion, dissociating its direct costs from its social costs, lays upon the community the increasingly onerous burden of creating conditions favorable to monopolist growth, while at the same time denying the community the means necessary for the task.

In the field of education the following collective needs are generated by the present stage of technological evolu-

[2] This is flagrant in the case of French planning. In the field of collective amenities and social services its targets, although already falling short of ascertained requirements, have been constantly sacrificed to short-term considerations. In other whole. On the contrary, it has disregarded those needs when in and the structure of consumption to the needs of society as a whole. On the contrary, it has disregarded those needs when in practice—that is to say, in terms of monetary equilibrium—they have been found to conflict with the commercial and investment policy of private corporations.

tion: raising of the age for leaving school; increase in the number of persons holding post-secondary and university degrees, which calls for a corresponding increase in the number of educational establishments and teaching staff at all levels. Meeting these needs implies a very rapid increase in the number of students and the possibility of attracting them into teaching by offering them salaries comparable to those paid by industry: in other words, a transfer of resources from the private to the public sector.

But on most of these points the short-term interests of the capitalist sector are in conflict with its long-term interests. The problem of financing education, for a start, is strictly insoluble except by a program infringing upon the "spontaneous" tendencies of private capital accumulation. By promoting collective needs of which the cost cannot be covered by the funds remaining at the disposal of the state, this creates drastic bottlenecks which in the long run threaten the whole system's growth potential.

The inability of the bourgeois educational system to produce a sufficient number, first, of teachers, and then of skilled workers and qualified scientific personnel, is attributable to not only the economic but also the social structure.[3] Apart from the lack of facilities, it is due to the fact that candidates for secondary and higher education are selected on social grounds. What happens is that, except for some purely marginal adjustments, the cost of socially necessary education is borne by the family, which amounts to leaving professional or vocational training to the private initiative of individuals. Beyond the minimum of education required by law, the pursuit of learning is regarded as the privilege of a minority whose parents are financially able

[3] In the German Federal Republic all persons with higher academic qualifications would have to be channeled into state education in order to furnish the minimum number of teachers required by 1970. *Die Deutsche Bildungskatastrophe* (Freiburg, 1964).

to delay their entry into active life. The period of training and learning is accordingly considered "unproductive."

This system breaks down when the development of the forces of production calls for a "wider reproduction of the labor power"[4]—that is to say, the acquisition by each successive generation of adolescents of more advanced and costly professional skills than their parents possessed. European capitalist economies can provide themselves with the quantity and quality of socially necessary labor only by socializing at least a part of the cost of its creation, since there is no longer a sufficient number of families capable of financing it out of their own resources.

What is happening, although in a haphazard way, is a general tendency to include the cost of extended education in the cost of labor power itself. By implication, and in a more or less disguised form (grants, family allowances, various kinds of subsidies), the work of learning, of extending and transforming professional skills, is implicitly recognized as socially productive and necessary work whereby the individual *produces himself* in accordance with the needs of society, and establishes certain claims on society by doing so.

These claims, which have been put forward mainly by student movements, are substantially as follows: (1) payment for the socially necessary work of learning or studying; (2) provision of the necessary collective equipment and facilities; (3) a sufficiently thorough theoretical education to enable the young worker to keep abreast of scientific and technical developments, instead of being dominated and downgraded by them.

These three claims, which are common to the French, Italian and German student movements, reflect the crisis in the bourgeois educational system, particularly at university level, and relate it directly to the crisis in capitalism. The first, demanding paid study *for all*, deserves closer examination.

[4] A. Gorz, *Strategy for Labor*, Chapter 4.

It is often argued, on the left as well as on the right, that the demand that all students should be paid for their work of self-education is premature in a society where the overwhelming majority of students come from the middle or lower middle class; and that instead of subsidizing the privileged classes who send their children to the universities by socializing the entire cost of education, it would be more logical to increase the number of scholarships available to working-class students and thus "democratize" higher education.

To this the student vanguard (UNEF in France and SDS in Federal Germany)[5] reply as follows:

1. Advantage must be taken of the need for a broadening of the social basis of university education to pursue the anti-capitalist implications of this necessity to the limit. It is important to fight at once for the most advanced democratic policy, by asserting the principle that society must itself bear the cost of socially necessary training and confer—by paying a *social salary* to all students—the status of *young worker* on all pupils at universities and technical or vocational colleges who are engaged in a course of socially useful education.

There is no inherent reason why the middle- or lower-middle-class student should have a middle-class view of his future professional work. On the contrary, by conferring upon him the status of "young worker," the universal availability of higher studies—and the fight to secure this—will offset the influence of his family background and any tendency he may have to regard his studies as a private undertaking opening the way to a lucrative career.[6]

If the principle of the social and socially productive nature of studying is not established as of now, and if the students' movement—and the workers' movement—allow capitalism to make partial concessions whereby students

[5] Union Nationale des Etudiants français and Sozialistischer Deutscher Studentenbund.

[6] See "Manifesto for the Democratic Reform of Education" (UNEF, 1964).

from poor homes, but not others, are treated as "young workers," thus creating class discrimination between students, the social nature of studying and the right of every student to a social salary will have been negated from the start and will be extremely difficult to impose later on.

2. Instead of ensuring the autonomy of university work (and of the universities), the selective grant (public, but also private) based on social considerations, tends to accentuate the dependence of students either on their parents, in the case of those receiving no grant, or on the state or private bodies in the case of those receiving a grant. In effect, the two forms of subsidy, by the parents or by the state, result in the student's work being subject to a dual system of external compulsion (or veto).

a. Students receiving assistance from the state (or from private industry) are required to show exceptional ability, industry and discipline, and an unassailable conformism; whereas those not in receipt of assistance often enjoy a far greater degree of freedom in the choice and duration of their studies.

b. Selective grants based on social considerations enable the state to channel poorer students into strictly utilitarian fields of study, whereas the non-grant students may be helped by their parents to pursue studies having a greater social prestige and to enter places of learning whose avowed object is to create a bourgeois elite. The latter only accept grant students subject to conditions,[7] whereas non-grant students enter very much more easily. An increase in the number of grants will therefore not dispel class and social discrimination in the universities.

c. Whereas students receiving grants are governed in their studies by the requirements of the state (which assumes rights over them in exchange for its assistance,

[7] Conditions relating to family background, that is to say, the bourgeois idea of culture, which for the working-class student are extremely difficult to fulfill. Pierre Bourdieu and André Passeron, *Les Héritiers*, 1965.

whereas freely available further education would have the opposite effect), non-grant students depend solely on the goodwill of their parents and, in the great majority of cases, continue to be kept by them even after they have legally come of age.[8]

The demand that all students should be paid, according to *university* and not *social* criteria, which since 1964 has been put forward by UNEF, is thus a considered response

[8] See SDS, "Hochschule in der Demokratie," *Neuekritik*, Mai 1965, Chapter 5, pp. 133–41.

The inquiry carried out by MNEF (Mutuelle nationale des Etudiants de France) into the living conditions and financial resources of French students reveals that middle-class students (managerial class and liberal professions) are as a rule *less well off* than those from other levels of society, with the sole exception of the children of clerical workers.

Students totally destitute (less than 300 francs a month) are to be found at every social level. Their division into classes is as follows: 5.6 per cent working class; 7.3 per cent clerical workers; 20 per cent technical and administrative personnel; 6.6 per cent liberal professions and upper class; 14 per cent of students as a whole. That is to say, social differences are reflected only slightly or not at all in student incomes.

In total, the French state provides for only 13.3 per cent of student needs, family assistance for 51.3 per cent. Students themselves provide for 24 per cent of their requirements by part-time work (a proportion which rises to 37 per cent in the case of the children of clerical and agricultural workers, and 43 per cent in the case of children of workers in Paris).

This necessity to supplement their means by part-time work, which interferes with full-time study and accounts for the fact that three quarters of all students do not complete their studies, is to be found among students of all classes; 18 per cent of the sons of workers, farmers and retired people, 16–17 per cent of the sons of clerical workers and proprietors, 12 per cent of the sons of technical and administrative personnel, do more than ten hours part-time work a week.

The notion that "unfavored" students come essentially from a single class is flatly contradicted by the results of the inquiry. "Student budgets," from *Recherches universitaires*, No. 5, 1964.

to the crisis in bourgeois education and the partial reforms proposed by the capitalist state. In voicing the demand the student movement makes the following points:

1. That only the socialization of the cost of study can set the students free from bourgeois educational, cultural, careerist and "elitist" standards, from capitalist standards of utility and profitability, and from the pressures exerted upon them by parents, the state, industry and their own lack of time and resources.

2. That only under this system can the autonomy of intellectual, cultural and professional training be ensured, and thus the independence of the universities.

3. That it alone can create, by removing discriminations of entrance, the end of the divorce between theory and practice, science and technology, and elitist and utilitarian culture.

4. Finally, that it will from the outset accord the student his rightful place in society as a "young worker" and induce him to understand that his demand for autonomy both intellectual and vocational, and for a culture that reflects historical reality and is therefore exempt from ideological and commercial degradation, is in sharp opposition to the demands of monopoly capitalism and can only be achieved in alliance with the working-class movement.

To put it another way, the struggle of the student unions for emancipation and valorization of the student labor power is the equivalent, in the educational and cultural field, of the workers' struggle in the field of industry. But all the evidence suggests that this struggle can become and remain truly socialist, and avoid the pitfalls of reformism, only if it is extended and sustained by a strong working-class revolutionary movement. Left to itself student trade unionism, however socialist its thinking and objectives, cannot transcend the limits of corporatism, but must inevitably relapse into it if its aims are not taken up by the working-class organization and inserted from the outset into an overall social struggle, safeguarding the student world against its own idiosyncrasies and myths.[9]

I have concentrated on showing so far that the increasing cost and time required to produce the socially necessary labor power has led to a crisis in the bourgeois educational system, based as it is on social bias and private payment. The development of the forces of production provides an objective basis for the claim that higher education should be open to all, that public allowances should be paid to those engaged in study and that the universities should be radically overhauled. But this reform cannot be restricted to matters of university entrance and payment of students. The objective necessity of enlisting a far greater proportion of working-class recruits implies an absolute condemnation of the methods and content of traditional higher education, which has hitherto been regarded as a school for the elite of bourgeois society.

In place of the encyclopedic, academic and ornamental "culture" designed to create "rare spirits" above (or outside) daily reality, whose purpose is to provide an ideological justification for existing social practices, industry has now set the universities the task of producing a large number of trained professionals capable of immediate use in production, research and management. At the same time the monopolies are perfectly aware of the threat to the established order inherent in a general raising of educa-

[9] "The struggle against the technocratization of the universities cannot in any event form the strategic basis of an autonomous student movement. It makes sense only if it is part of a comprehensive strategy of the working-class movement aimed at changing the structure of the capitalist regime. That the problems of educational qualification and autonomy should have a central place within this strategy is essential but . . . [all endeavors in this sense will be meaningless unless] a vanguard political organization in student circles is capable of interpreting the significance of the industrialization of the universities in class terms." Antoine Griset and Marc Kravetz in *Les Temps Modernes*, May 1965.

tional standards. Indeed, once a given standard has been reached the demand for intellectual, professional and existential autonomy becomes as insistent among these highly qualified workers as the gnawing material needs of manual workers in the old-time industries.

That is why the monopolies, while calling for education on more "realistic" lines, at the same time seek to restrict both the quality of higher education and the number of students having access to it. "It is a bad thing," the president of Kodak-Pathé has written, "to live in a country where there is an excess of highly qualified personnel, because in times of crisis young people who have completed long periods of study without being rewarded with a suitable job represent not merely a net loss in terms of capital investment but also a threat to the established order."[10]

What is remarkable about this piece of ownership reasoning is not merely the anxiety to match the number of "highly qualified personnel" to the number of suitable jobs available *in times of crisis,* but also the strictly utilitarian view of education (which is considered a "net loss" unless it leads to a "suitable job"), and the fear that too much of it may endanger the Establishment—which may be taken to mean the capitalist relations of production and the hierarchic relations in industry.

Big Business, in short, is seeking to reconcile two opposites: on the one hand, the need created by the modern process of production for a higher development of human capabilities, and on the other hand, the political need to prevent this development from leading to an increased autonomy of the individual which would threaten the existing division of social functions and the distribution of power.

[10] Quoted from *Humanisme et Entreprise,* the propaganda organ circulated by Big Business among students at the Sorbonne under the aegis of the "Centre d'Etudes littéraires supérieures appliquées" (Center of Higher Applied Literary Studies). It is noteworthy that in three years only twenty-five students of literature completed the course laid down by the center.

The solution of the problem sought by Big Business, as
the Fouchet reforms in France clearly show, is by way of
specialization: alongside traditional elite education there is
to be a stunted utilitarian education laying all the emphasis
on technical proficiency. In order to avoid producing people whose "overrich" talents may cause them to rebel
against the discipline required of them, they are to be
hamstrung from the start. They are to be competent but
limited, zestful but docile, intelligent in their own narrow
field but stupid in all other respects. In short they are to
be specialists, incapable of relating their particular knowledge to the general movement of science, or their particular activities to the overall process of social praxis. The
aim of the Fouchet reforms is to divide education into
two separate parts. The great majority of university and
high school students are to receive purely technical instruction from which all advanced theory, as well as the
arts and philosophy, is excluded. The teaching of the hu-
manities is to be divorced from mathematics and science
so that it remains a purely intellectual pastime—as though
it were necessary to prevent people having a philosophical
background from entering jobs where their critical turn
of mind might endanger the Establishment. In other words,
technological qualification is to be kept separate from the
authentic culture which is concerned with the methods
and proceedings of creative activity in the sciences and
technology, and "culture" will be divorced from social
praxis and productive work.[11]

[11] H. Tanaka, "Education in Japan," *Recherches interna-
tionales,* No. 28, 1961. "The stress laid by the National Min-
istry of Education on the need for a wider knowledge of the
natural sciences corresponds to the requirements of the monopolies in the present stage of technological development. But a
higher level of professional qualification cannot be achieved
without raising the general educational level of workers, with
the inevitable consequence that their state of awareness, and
their ability to fight capitalism, are also raised . . . The ruling
class cannot ignore this dangerous prospect. That is why they

What is remarkable is that this policy is in no sense a requisite of technological progress: on the contrary, it is opposed to it. For it is not true that modern technology demands specialists. What it needs is polyvalent basic education concerned not with fragmented, predigested and specialized knowledge, but with initiation (or more exactly, ability at self-initiation) into methods of research and technological invention. It does not need the pupil to be stuffed with ready-made, immediately useful information: it needs him above all to be taught *to learn,* to inquire, to expand his knowledge by himself and to dominate conceptually and synthetically an entire field of activity in its connection with other related fields. Only education on these lines can enable the worker to maintain his professional skill: that is to say, to keep abreast in a world of constant technological change, and master innovations which, as may happen more than once in his working life, render his

are pursuing an educational policy designed essentially to instill knowledge useful to the development of the forces of production, while education in other fields is so ordered that it will contribute to the maintenance of the capitalist relations of production."

Also A. Minucci, "Sul rapporto classe operaia-società," *Critica Marxista,* No. 1, 1965. "The monopolies are not only artificially prolonging the phase of the fragmentation of work in the factories, but they also oppose the introduction in the schools of new educational procedures such as are called for by present-day industrial developments. All capitalist countries, in varying degrees, possess fragmented and essentially inadequate educational systems . . . The very structure of the educational system is designed to perpetuate the division of culture and education into two widely separated halves, the humanist and the logical-empirical. Thus, to the quantitative insufficiency of education is added a qualitative insufficiency which creates a gulf between technology and science, and between science and production, of which the effect is a failure to comprehend the process as a whole. It is not merely the relations of production but the schools themselves which deprive the worker of the means to master and understand the relations of production."

existing knowledge obsolete and oblige him to re-educate and familiarize himself with new methods if he is to avoid the depreciation of his skills and the loss of his job.

In objective terms, then, what technological progress calls for is not only a solid polyvalent education encompassing methodology and theory, but also training in self-education, which presupposes a drastic recasting of present teaching methods and curricula. And if Big Business is against this it is not simply on account of the social cost (specialists being cheaper to produce, and the cost of their eventual loss of skill being borne by themselves), but also because the specialist, robbed at the outset of any real hope of professional independence, is more docile and more resigned to the present order of things.

The United States precedent is not without relevance to any assessment of the chance this monopoly-capitalist educational policy has of succeeding. The remedies which European capitalism is now seeking for the crisis in bourgeois education are in many respects similar to those adopted in the United States during the thirties, of which the catastrophic balance sheet (from the bourgeois-humanist point of view, it is true) was drawn up by William H. Whyte in *The Organization Man* (1956). Whyte describes the decline of the theoretical disciplines and the discredit into which they have fallen, particularly in the fields of exact and natural science, while at the same time there has been a rapid growth, encouraged by the monopolies, of specialist schools (management, public relations, marketing, advertising, etc.) with purely utilitarian curricula adapted to the immediate requirements of industry. These have drained off the relative majority of students, dispensing "know-how" rather than any coherent sum of knowledge.

The process seemed at first to have striking advantages for private ownership. Higher education provided them with personnel who were not only immediately utilizable but already indoctrinated and integrated in the system, inasmuch as their education stimulated careerism and discouraged all critical spirit. To the extent that the traditional universities in Europe remain steeped in the old academic notions of culture they, too, leave the door wide open to private enterprise in education: that is to say, private specialist training schools, which are becoming more and more numerous, and which dispense neither comprehensive technology nor scientific theory, but simply supply recipes for a career.

By the time Whyte's book was published, however, the system he condemned had already been virtually superseded. A report by Allen Dulles, the head of CIA, comparing the number of scientists and research workers in the U.S.S.R. with those in the United States, made the Americans realize that they were falling seriously behind and prompted the U.S. Government to institute a program of theoretical instruction in all fields by means of massive injections of credit and a large increase in the number of grants.

The result of this rapid expansion, which has created overcrowded universities dispensing quasi-industrial instruction to an unprecedented mass of students having no contact with their overworked professors, has become apparent during the past few years. It has taken the form of a student revolt, often supported by members of the teaching staff, against the lack of teachers and the powerlessness of students to influence the content or nature of courses, the arrangement of curricula, the methods and conditions of work; also against the authoritarian methods of university administration; and, more or less explicitly, against the policies of American imperialism and the United States pattern of civilization.

What is emerging from this revolt, which externally resembles the revolts of the Italian students (in the Faculty of Architecture, for example) and the French students at the Sorbonne, is that after a given level of general education has been reached it becomes impossible to restrain the urge for autonomy. One cannot teach knowledge and ignorance at the same time without the victims becoming aware of the way in which they are being cheated. Specialization, however early it is practiced, cannot impose fixed limits on the inherent autonomy of cognitive praxis stimulated by wider education without the subject eventually seeking to break down those limits. In a word, autonomy cannot be made selective or relative. The capitalist dream of a specialized technician who will combine a passion for his work with total indifference to the ends it serves, professional initiative with social acquiescence, a sense of responsibility in technical matters with irresponsibility in the social and economic field, is one that cannot be realized. It is for the workers' movement to display it for the illusion it is, to demonstrate its contradictions, and to confront the repressive ideology of organizational capitalism in a struggle conducted on every level, with overall alternatives implying the reconquest of man.

During the era of manufactories and, later on, of Taylorism, capitalist relations of production found their natural extension and confirmation in work relations. Where the great majority of workers were concerned labor power consisted of a pure quantity of physical energy composed of undifferentiated and interchangeable human units having no value in themselves. They were of value only insofar as they could be used in organized external combination with other units of human energy—that is to say, insofar as they were under the orders of an owner and his subordinates, and alienated from the product and a process of production whose purposes remained estranged. The workman was required to work, not to think. It was the business of other men to relate his individual labor to that of his fellows. In short, the alienation and dehumanization of work had their natural basis in the division of labor and the process of production.

This basis of the enslavement and dehumanization of the worker by capital—and of its only possible negation, the violent suppression of manual labor, since its humanization is out of the question—is tending to disappear for a growing proportion of workers. That is not to say that technological developments, and in particular automation, are creating a new working class and a general growth of the worker's individual autonomy in his work. The process is more complicated. The old individual skills have become superfluous and—whether we are talking about bank clerks or precision lathe operators—the old skilled workers are being replaced by a new type of unskilled worker who, because of his technical responsibilities, is often required to have greater skills, and above all a higher level of general education, than his immediate job calls for. Although the job may require less individual skill and initiative, it is likely at the same time to call for broader general knowledge and an understanding of a wider sector of the process of production.[12] For example, the initiative required from an operator of multiple semi-automatic lathes may be less than that of a precision lathe operator, but the part he plays in the process of production as a whole, and his knowledge of it, may be greater. The same is true of the

[12] "The fact is that the qualities required of an automation operator, although they vary from one installation to another, cannot be fitted into the normal system of codification. His task alternates, in varying proportions, between the duties of a supervisor, sometimes carrying heavy responsibility, and collective work, both entailing in a greater or lesser degree, according to the particular case, an understanding of logical and technical structures. But it is clearly very difficult to supervise a supervisor: the chain-of-command system is at once thrown out of gear, as is the scale of skill ratings. In fact, the responsibility vested in the individual no longer corresponds to the length of his apprenticeship to a particular trade, but far more to his general level of education. Clearly the implications of this phenomenon are very different under the present system from what they would be under a system in which education, like productive work, was treated as time given by the individual to society, and remunerated as such." Pierre Rolle, "Automation: a social problem," in the *International Socialist Journal*, March/April 1965.

technician in an oil refinery or an electricity generating
station or nuclear power plant. Individual work and skill
are displaced by functions and skills that are more immediately social. The individual no longer proves his skill by
transforming inorganic matter but through social co-
operation with his fellows, that is to say, through social interchange, team work and so on. In short, the labor power
is from the start *socially* skilled; the relationship is not a
solitary relationship with matter to be worked by means of
a tool, but a relationship with the industrial process resulting from the *conscious* combining of human activities.[13]
Productivity no longer demands the combination *from outside,* by a third party, of the labor power represented by
the quantum of physical energy of a given number of
workers; it increasingly demands a *reciprocal* co-ordination
of activities by those who accomplish them—that is to say,
co-operation among teams within which the traditional bar-

[13] "As big industry develops, the creation of wealth . . . depends increasingly on the level attained by science and the
progress of technology, or on the application of science to production . . . Instead of the work being entirely included in the
process of production it is now more often the man who acts as
a supervisor and regulator of the process itself. (What is true of
mechanical equipment is equally true of the combination of
human activities and the development of human relationships.)
The worker no longer interposes between himself and the thing
the intermediary link of a modified natural object: rather he
interposes the natural process, transformed into an industrial
process, between himself and the inorganic matter of which he
is making himself master. He assists the process of production
instead of being its principal agent. Thus the central pillar of
production and wealth is neither the work directly accomplished
by the man, nor his working time, but the *appropriation of his
force of production* in general, his understanding of nature, and
his domination over it inasmuch as he acts as a member of society—in a word, it is *the development of the social individual.*"
Marx, *Grundrisse der Kritik der politischen Oekonomie* (Ber-
lin: Dietz, 1953), pp. 593–94.

riers between workmen, technicians and engineers fade
away.

The result is that the natural basis of industrial hierarchy and owner authority is tending to disappear and that
the traditional system of rating and remuneration, founded
on individual work, productivity and skill, is thrown into
crisis. The technical or scientific worker in the automated
industries is restricted to the permanent underemployment
of his abilities in his individual task, and in consequence is
prompted—to the extent that his level of consciousness allows—to transfer his interest from his individual work to
its social implications, and from his individual part in the
process of production to the significance, the operation and
the social purposes of the latter.

On the other hand, in scientific industries such as electronics, heavy equipment, research centers, etc., where the
work itself is actually or potentially of a creative nature, a
conflict is developing between the teams of technical and
scientific workers, conscious of their abilities and eager to
valorize their labor power, and the capitalist management
whose policy subordinates, and often sacrifices, this valorization to considerations of short- or medium-term profitability. In this connection we may recall the Neyrpic dispute and in particular the pioneering role played in the
Bull dispute by the technical and engineering staff of Bull-
Gambetta, who a year in advance warned the management
of its errors and of the imminence of the 1964 crisis. The
problem was transferred unsolved from the industrial to the
political level, and the condemnation of private managerial
methods became a demand for nationalization and the socialization of research throughout that branch of industry:
the development of its full capacity, and valorization of
the "human capital" involved, having shown themselves to
be impossible under capitalist management.

In a group of key industries, scientifically and economically a driving force in the system, the nature of the work
—because of its either directly social or creative and au-

tonomous character—thus increasingly tends to enter into
contradiction with capitalist management criteria and
decision-making powers. It is more or less openly felt that
tasks should be reorganized and enlarged, that the command system should be recast and workers' control over
the process of production introduced. All this appears just
within the bounds of possibility. And this very possibility
discloses the despotism of capital. It shows that the alienation and mutilation of the worker is not, and never has
been, a natural consequence of the technology employed;
that capital does not need fragmented men in order to *produce,* but (since it clings to the old centralized hierarchic
order, the arbitrary limitation of responsibilities and duties
even where this has become unnecessary and a positive
hindrance to productivity) in order to perpetuate its domination over men not only as workers but also as consumers
and citizens. The natural basis of enslavement and dehumanization is replaced by deliberate techniques gleaming
with scientific chrome and dubbed "management psychology," "human engineering," "human relations," etc.

But it would be unrealistic to imagine that this objective
contradiction between the capitalist relations of production
and the character of the labor power—its cost of production and reproduction, its mode of training and employment—will necessarily become conscious and explode. In
advanced capitalist societies this contradiction is generally
smothered by the vast apparatus of repression, indoctrination and diversion: it will only explode in special moments
of crisis. Hence the necessity of political *and cultural* work
on the part of the working-class movement to make the
contradiction clearly understood and to weld together the
scientific and technical neo-proletariat, students and teachers, and the traditional proletariat, by demonstrating the
character and prospects of solutions to their own specific
problems while taking full account of these problems' spec-
ificity and relative independence.

This by no means implies a nurturing of corporative or sectional interests. On the contrary:

A socialist party can successfully pose its candidature for the direction of society only when it is the bearer of *universal values,* which are recognized and experienced as such by a majority of all those whose humanity is denied and dislocated by the social order. These social forces must find their truth in a socialist party in order for it to be capable of victory over capitalism. The task of the party is to unite them in *a new historical bloc.*

The concept of a bloc is radically different from that of a coalition, which remains the normal type of political combination on the Left today. In such heterogeneous coalitions, with their atmosphere of promiscuous populism . . . a process of dilution occurs, in which the political program of the party—catering as it does to every group in the coalition—reduces the aspirations and demands of each *downwards* to the lowest common denominator on which they can all agree, in a kind of *descending integration.* This is what makes these parties, despite appearances, inert and conservative organizations, incapable of changing their societies in any significant way.

The structure of an historical bloc, as Gramsci conceived it, is diametrically opposed to this system of alliances. The unity of the bloc rests on an *ascending integration,* which fuses together different hopes and demands on a higher level. Partial and sectional demands are inserted into a coherent and articulated vision of the world, which confers on them a common meaning and goal. The bloc is thus a synthesis of the aspirations and identities of different groups in a global project which exceeds them all. Its critique of capitalism is the truth of each particular claim . . . The vocation of the hegemonic party is thus manifestly universal: it is the dynamic unity of all the forces and ideals in the society which are premonitions of a new human order.[14]

[14] Perry Anderson, "Problems of Socialist Strategy," in *Towards Socialism,* Fontana Library, London, 1965, p. 242.

Chapter 4

Reform and Revolution*

* Digest of a series of lectures delivered in Sweden, April 1966.

A SOCIALIST STRATEGY OF REFORMS

The working class will not unite politically or man the barricades for the sake of a 10 per cent wage increase or an extra 50,000 dwellings. It is unlikely that in the foreseeable future there will be a crisis in capitalism so acute that, in order to protect their vital interests, workers will resort to a revolutionary general strike or armed insurrection.

On the other hand, the bourgeoisie will never relinquish power without a struggle and without being compelled to do so by revolutionary action on the part of the masses.

The main problem confronting socialist strategy is consequently that of *creating the conditions,* both objective and subjective, in which mass revolutionary action becomes possible and in which the bourgeoisie may be engaged and defeated in a trial of strength.

You may not approve of the terms in which I have stated the problem, and you may hold that socialism is not necessary to the liberation and fulfillment of mankind. But if, like most of those who work with their hands or their heads, you consider, or confusedly feel, that capitalism is no more acceptable today than it was yesterday as a form of economic and social development; as a way of life and as a way by which men relate to each other, to their work, to their environment and to peoples in other parts of the world; and also in the use it makes, or fails to make, of the resources of technology and science and of the actual or potential creative ability of the individual—if, feeling or be-

lieving this, you support socialism, then the problem of
bringing it about can be stated only in those terms.

Socialism will not be achieved by a gradual reordering
of the capitalist system, designed to rationalize its functioning and institutionalize class antagonisms. It will not emerge
of its own accord out of the crises and imbalances of which
capitalism can eliminate neither the causes nor the effects,
but which it now knows how to prevent from becoming
explosive, nor will it be born of a spontaneous uprising of
the dissatisfied masses or through the anathematizing of
social traitors and revisionists. It can be brought about only
by deliberate, long-term action of which the *beginning* may
be a scaled series of reforms, but which, as it unfolds, must
grow into a series of trials of strength, more or less violent, some won and others lost, but of which the outcome
will be to mold and organize the socialist resolve and consciousness of the working classes. This is how the struggle
will develop provided each battle serves to strengthen,
within the capitalist system, the strongpoints, the weapons
and the *reasons* which enable the workers to withstand the
forces of capitalism and prevent the system from repairing
the breaches opened in its own power structure.

There is no, there can be no gradual and imperceptible
transition from capitalism to socialism. The economic and
political power of the bourgeoisie cannot be slowly nibbled
away; nor can it be destroyed by a series of partial reforms, each seemingly harmless and acceptable to capitalism, of which the final effect will be that of the stratagem
of the Trojan horse, with the secret army of socialists
finally installed in the seats of power.

It cannot be like that. The only thing that can and must
be gradual in socialist strategy is the preparatory phase
leading to the brink of crisis and the final trial of strength.[1]

[1] This view, which is that of the majority of European Marxists, is particularly well stated by Lelio Basso. "The transition
from the preliminary phases of socialism to socialism itself . . .
becomes possible only at a certain stage in the development of
the social forces and relations, when a consciousness of funda-

And this approach, which is incorrectly described as "the non-violent way to socialism," is not a matter of any *a priori* decision in favor of gradualism or *a priori* rejection of violent revolution and armed insurrection. It arises out of the necessity to create favorable conditions, both objective and subjective, and to build social and political positions of strength on the basis of which the conquest of political power by the working class will become possible.

You may object that there can be no genuinely socialist reforms so long as effective power remains in the hands of the bourgeoisie and the capitalist state remains intact. That is true. A socialist strategy of progressive reform does not mean that islands of socialism will emerge in the sea of capitalism. But it does mean the building up of working-class and popular power; it means the creation of centers of social management and of direct democracy, particularly in the major industries and co-operatives of production; it means the conquering of positions of strength in representative bodies; it means free products and services fulfilling collective needs; and this must inevitably result in intensified and deepened antagonism between the social production required by the needs and aspirations of the people, on the one hand, and the requirements of capital accumulation and power on the other.

Moreover it is essential that this antagonism should never become institutionalized, as normally happens under neo-capitalist and social democratic regimes, by the integration and subordination of working-class organizations within the state, by concertation and by compulsory arbitration. On the contrary, this antagonism must be able to express

---

mental antagonism has penetrated the masses and when their strength enables the existing order to be overthrown. Preparation for this moment is the immediate task of the workers' movement . . . This strategy may be defined as the non-violent way to socialism, with the reservation that it does not pre-judge the final form of the crisis, which may be peaceful or violent according to circumstances that are at present quite unpredictable." *Tendenze del Capitalismo europeo* (Rome, 1966).

itself through the autonomous action of unions and political organizations; it must undermine the capitalist power structure and break down the social and economic equilibrium which tends to be re-established at a higher level after every act of partial reform. We shall come back to this.

Thus a socialist policy of gradual reform cannot be conceived simply in terms of the winning of an electoral majority or the promulgation of a string of reforms by makeshift coalitions of social democrats and socialists.[2] The electoral struggle, even if it is won, has never led to the forging of the collective will and the genuine political power of the working classes. As Marx and Engels said,[3] suffrage confers the right to govern but not the power to do so. It results in the averaging out of a multiplicity of individual wishes registered in the secrecy of the ballot by men and women who, whatever the convergence of their aspirations, do not have the opportunity to organize and unite in order to fight together.

This is one of the mystifications practiced by bourgeois democracy. Its institutions are so devised as to perpetuate the dispersal and isolation of individuals and deny them all *collective power* over the organization of society; so-called popular power allows them only to delegate power permanently every four or five years to representatives having no direct contact with the masses, and to political parties which are regarded as "acceptable partners" only if they defend the superior interests of the capitalist state against the masses, instead of doing the opposite.

In short, electoral victory does not confer power. Electoral victory based on even a modest program of reform does not confer the power to put the reforms into practice. This is one of the deep-seated reasons for the persistence

[2] By socialists I mean all forces actually seeking to achieve socialism, that is to say, the abolition of the capitalist system of production and state, not merely the so-called "socialist parties," which are often nothing of the kind.

[3] In the 1872 Preface to the *Communist Manifesto*.

of conservative majorities, except in times of particularly acute crisis, and for the regular reelection of existing governments, whatever their policy may have been. For this policy always reflects, in its general tendency if not in detail, the balance of power at any given time.

A radically different policy, however eloquently it may be advocated by the opposition, will only convince and appear feasible *if the power to implement it has already been practically demonstrated*—that is to say, if the pattern of social forces has been modified by direct mass action, organized and directed by the working-class parties, leading to a crisis in the policy of the government in office.[4] In other words, the power to implement a policy of genuine reform is not to be achieved through parliament but only by the ability, demonstrated in advance, to mobilize the working classes against the prevailing policy; and this ability can be lasting and fruitful only if the forces of the opposition are capable not only of provoking a crisis in the prevailing policy but of resolving that crisis. They must not merely attack the policy but must be ready with an alternative corresponding to the new pattern of forces, or rather—since no pattern of forces is static—to the new dynamics of struggle made possible by the changed pattern.

In the absence of any change in the pattern of class

[4] It is in appearance only that this statement seems to be contradicted by electoral victories such as that of the British Labour Party in 1964 and the possible forthcoming victory of the German social democrats in 1968. Harold Wilson's victory was really due to an internal crisis in the Conservative Party, the outcome of a long process of wear and tear, and to its inability to repair the weakened position of British capitalism in the world without the support of the trade unions. Wilson's victory was not the triumph of a new policy but that of the same policy, pursued by scarcely different means but with trade-union support (extremely reluctant in its second phase), and which, broadly speaking, produced the same result. The same thing would happen in the event of a social democrat victory in Federal Germany.

forces, and of any breakdown in the economic and social
equilibrium of the system due to a mass movement of protest, electoral logic will tend inevitably to work in favor of
those political leaders for whom the role of the "left" consists essentially in promoting the same policy as the right,
but doing it better. For leaders of this kind competition
between parties is merely, in the words of Basso,[5] "competition between potential governing teams, each putting
forward its claim to run the state more efficiently." But if,
on the other hand, mass struggle succeeds in upsetting the
equilibrium of the system and plunging it into a state of
crisis without (as has happened in recent years in most of
the countries of Western Europe) this struggle leading to
the definition of a genuinely new economic policy capable
of resolving the crisis to the political and material advantage of the workers, then the situation will rapidly degenerate and the working class, despite its tactical victory, will
find itself driven back to its original positions. We have
seen many examples of this: in France, in 1937, 1947 and
1957; in Belgium in 1961; in Italy in 1962–64; and elsewhere.

The same process, the squandering of an opportunity
favorable to the working class, is liable to recur at the present time whenever the government voted into office on a
reform program is in fact no more than a makeshift alliance of neo-capitalist reformers and socialists. We are
now touching upon the genuinely political aspects of a socialist strategy of reform.

Any such strategy, I must repeat, cannot in the circumstances of present-day Europe be aimed at the immediate
establishment of socialism. Nor can it look for the immediate achievement of reforms which are directly incompatible
with the survival of the capitalist system—for example, the
nationalization of all major industries, or of all the enterprises of monopoly or oligopoly-type structure. Reforms of
this kind, embodied in a short-term program, cannot serve

[5] International Socialist Journal, No. 15.

as a strategy designed to engage a revolutionary process, during which class antagonism would be exacerbated until the final trial of strength: being aimed directly at the destruction of the capitalist system, they require as a precondition that the working class should be sufficiently mature in order for the immediate revolutionary conquest of political power to be feasible. If immediate socialism is not possible, neither is the achievement of reforms directly destructive of capitalism. Those who reject all lesser reforms on the grounds that they are merely reformist are in fact rejecting the whole possibility of a *transitional strategy* and of a process of transition to socialism.

But we need not conclude that because, in the absence of a revolutionary situation, we cannot launch out directly into reforms that would destroy the system, the socialist strategy of reforms must necessarily be confined to the kind of isolated or partial reforms which are termed "democratic" because they lack not only socialist substance but even prospects and revolutionary dynamism. What in practice distinguishes a genuinely socialist policy of reforms from reformism of the neo-capitalist or "social democratic" type is less each of the reforms and goals than, first, the presence or absence of organic links between the various reforms, second, the tempo and method of their implementation and, third, the resolve, or absence of resolve, to take advantage of the imbalance created by the initial reforms to promote further disruptive action.[6]

[6] See the attack by Kautsky, at that time supported by Lenin, on Bernstein in *Social Reform and Revolution*. "Those who on principle reject political revolution as a means of social transformation, and who seek to restrict that transformation to the measures that can be obtained from the ruling class, are *social reformers,* however opposed their ideals may be to those of the existing order . . . What distinguishes the social reformer from the revolutionary is not that he advocates reforms but that he deliberately refrains from going further."

Also Lelio Basso, op. cit.: "What characterizes reformism is not the advocacy of reforms which any Marxist must have in

The fact that social democratic leaders and socialist forces are in agreement on the necessity of *certain* reforms should not, therefore, mislead us as to the fundamental difference between their viewpoints and objectives. For a socialist strategy of reforms to become possible, this difference must not be concealed or relegated to second place by tactical agreement at the summit: on the contrary, it must be kept in the forefront of the political debate. Otherwise, by awarding a totally unmerited certificate of socialism to the social democratic leaders, the socialist movement will be paving the way for the defeat, in a welter of ideological and political confusion, of the entire workers' movement and especially its avant-garde.

These remarks apply particularly to the present European situation, in which the precarious economic balance no longer permits, as has happened at other times, the financing of new social benefits and state intervention by means of inflation. The effect of this is that any program of a "social" nature—wage increases at the lower level, housing, development of backward areas, improvements in education and the social services, etc.—must either directly assail the logic and strongholds of capitalist accumulation with a coherent set of reforms, or else it must beat a hasty retreat in face of the shattering response of the forces of capitalism to the threat of injury to their interests.

The fate of a popular front coalition government, coming into power on an agreed *minimum program* of minor reforms, but excluding everything that goes beyond the terms of the agreement, is thus virtually sealed from the start. The essence of any agreed minimum program is that, unlike a transitional program or genuine strategy of reforms, it prevents the socialist elements, if they are not to break the agreement, from taking advantage of the impetus

---

view but . . . the separation of the reformist moment from the revolutionary moment. The effect of this separation is that the reforms . . . lose all anti-capitalist potential and even become instruments of the process of integration [of the working class within the system]."

created by the initial measures, and even from staging a counter-offensive to the capitalist offensive.

The nature of that offensive is familiar to us all, since it invariably follows the pattern of events in France in 1936. The reaction of the bourgeoisie to the threat to its power and prerogatives takes the form of the flight of capital abroad, the cutting down of investments and massive lay-offs of workers, aimed in the first place at militant trade unionists—in short, of an economic crisis in which the working class is the hardest hit. This crisis (which incidentally is not due solely to the deliberate and concerted action of the bourgeoisie, but also to the impossibility of making capitalism work when its essential mechanisms are impaired) enables the bourgeoisie, negotiating from a position of strength, to bring about the revision of the government program and the spreading of its objectives over a longer period of time (in a word, postponing them till the Greek kalends). The bourgeois terms become increasingly harsh as internal rifts appear within the coalition, between the hard-liners and the moderates; and as time passes, and the economic and financial crisis becomes more acute, it is invariably the former who yield ground to the latter. For by now the situation has already been transformed. The original minimum program is already no longer practicable. Its implementation would call for draconian measures not originally contemplated (for example, exchange controls, price freezing, restriction of imports, nationalization of industrial and financial monopolies) and which can only be adopted by a government striking while the iron is hot, with the assurance of massive public support behind it.

The weeks of sterile negotiation, economic crisis and dissension in the ranks of the coalition will inevitably have weakened the militant ardor of the workers. The hard-liners are driven onto the defensive. Confusion spreads; and the forces of capitalism, knowing that time is on their side, harden their own position. The history of the coalition becomes one of steady retreat in which it multiplies concessions in order to win back the confidence of capital.

And when eventually it is succeeded by a moderate government, better able to placate the bourgeoisie and "restore the health" of the economy, the popular front coalition has nothing to its credit except the measures of partial reform introduced during its first weeks of power, which will now be emasculated, deprived of all real scope and even turned to profit by the capitalist system.

A repetition of this process, which occurred in France after 1936 and 1945, in Britain after 1950 and 1964 and in Italy after 1947 and 1963, can be prevented only if the coalition is sufficiently homogeneous and conscious of the impending struggle to be able to reply to capitalist reaction with a devastating counter-offensive in the country, among the mass of workers, and by the introduction of governmental measures prepared well in advance of its taking office.[7]

But the reaction of the workers' movement will be effective only if reforms are conceived not as a centralized, governmental course of action, proceeding from the top, for which the coalition will ask the voters for a permanent and disciplined delegation of authority, but as the implementation of an economic policy that from the start goes hand in hand with democratic reforms stimulating the development of structures of popular power and initiatives adapted to the local conditions in the factories, in the co-operatives, at regional and local levels.

[7] "An economic program genuinely intended to change the course of development can no longer be anything but global in character, with long-term objectives based on rigorous options. It cannot operate without a political and social power and an institutional framework sufficiently strong to enable it to control the formidable chain reactions it has set out to provoke. In such circumstances what good does it do to aim at unity based on a minimum short-term program; on a mass movement more concerned to defend injured interests than to organize and select them; and on a governmental formula lacking cohesion, force and the ideas necessary for a comprehensive program intended to transform society?" Lucio Magri in *Les Temps Modernes*, January 1966.

At the same time preventive measures against capitalist reaction demand that the coalition should be under no illusions as to the possibility of placating the bourgeoisie and persuading it to co-operate in good faith with the new regime.[8] This has always been the dream of social democratic leaders, even when they are supporting a popular front. They believe that at first an honest attempt should be made to work a policy based on indirect controls and freely accepted managerial disciplines. This line of approach is possible *only* if its advocates realize from the start that it cannot be a *lasting policy* but must inevitably end in a bitter struggle for which they *have to be prepared* in advance. In other words, a policy of indirect governmental control over the machinery of capitalist accumulation and distribution need not necessarily be rejected, provided it is regarded as *transitional*, paving the way for the direct control which is the unavoidable, logical outcome if the system is not to be bogged down by the retaliatory measures of the economic forces.

To suppose that the state can permanently encompass, direct and regulate the economic process without touching

---

[8] The bourgeoisie will accept the idea of co-operation, and shrink from a trial of strength only if the left-wing victory is a crushing one, preceded and sustained by overwhelming popular support, and if the governmental parties, solidly united, give every sign of continuing in office *for a very long time*. This was the case in Sweden in the early thirties, and in China in 1950, although the social context there was very different.

In the case of China the bourgeoisie co-operated with the revolution because any attempt at resistance would have been hopeless.

In the case of Sweden, then at the beginning of industrialization, it was a newly formed bourgeoisie which came to terms with social democracy, in so far as the latter not only spared, but positively reckoned on the interests and the logic of the capitalist class. So much so that after thirty years of social democracy there is still no socialist outlook in governmental policies, and the democratic life of political parties and unions is stifled by bureaucratic centralization.

the principle of private property is to ignore the political
and psychological foundations of capitalism. No doubt it
is true that *technically* a policy of selective taxation, price
controls and credit may impose a qualitative, geographical
and social pattern on the economy by controlling the
growth of its different branches, services and regions in
accordance with social criteria and global economic considerations. But what is technically possible is not possible
politically for any length of time.[9]

Reduction of the cost of growth by eliminating waste
(in the form of artificially swollen commercial and administrative costs, representation, advertising, etc.), by preventing the use of company resources for private ends, by
preventing investment in new plants and new models which
contribute nothing to technological progress or to the improvement of the products but are intended mainly to
evade taxation—all this may in theory be achieved by the
tightening of controls and the strict regulation of private
industry: for example, by reduction of the tax allowance
for publicity, by pegging prices and profits in the different
branches of industry and even (in the case of the monopolies) by laying down rules for the use to be made of
profits, and the nature and purpose of investment, under
the threat of heavy fiscal penalties.

But the enforcement of a policy of this kind would rapidly come into conflict with the logic of the capitalist system and would destroy its vitality.[10] It would in fact

[9] I pass over the extreme difficulty, for the state, of ascertain-
ing the exact use made of the real profits of private companies
except by enforcing a very oppressive system of checks and
controls.

[10] Contrary to a widely held belief, the Swedish Government
does not impose administrative regulations on the trusts and has
no knowledge of their real profits or of the real nature of their
investment programs, which come under the heading of commercial secrecy. This is due to its awareness of the fact that
capitalism without the profit motive ceases to be dynamic. The
Swedish state, which has no medium-term global economic pro-

amount to the destruction of managerial decision-making power, to the *de facto* socialization of entrepreneurial activity and to the indirect public management of private concerns. It would entail as a sanction the confiscation of excess profits, or at least their very high taxation. Thus it would rob private enterprise of all incentive to develop improved methods and innovations tending to raise profits above the level laid down by the state, and by doing so it would destroy one of the main sources of technological progress. In short, by reducing the employers to the level of civil servants, loading them down with a ponderous bureaucracy and attacking the profit motive, the state would be assailing the very heart of the capitalist system, and would cripple or sclerose it.

To attack the machinery and motivations of capitalism is senseless unless one intends *to abolish it, not to preserve it*. To assail the consequences of the system's logic is of necessity to assail this very logic itself and to plunge the system into crisis. If this crisis is not to rebound against the forces that produced it, it must be resolved by the transfer of all centers of accumulation to public management. Failing more advanced measures of socialization in the wake of the initial reforms, designed to overcome the difficulties created by their reform program itself, the coalition of reformers will fall victim to a war of attrition and the process of decay which we have described.

---

gram, confines itself to the strict control of *individual* incomes. The budgetary resources which it derives from taxation are no greater (taking into account the fact that Social Security is financed out of the budget) than the proportion of the GNP which these resources represent in other advanced capitalist countries, and they are insufficient to enable it to meet expanding collective needs. The housing shortage, regional imbalance, wage differentials in the public and private sectors, and the acute shortage of collective amenities (only 10 per cent of the requirement of nursery schools) are comparable to those in the rest of capitalist Europe, as are the cultural inequalities and the resistance of the "ruling elite" to newcomers.

So in terms of socialist strategy, although we should not reject intermediary reforms (those that do not immediately carry their anti-capitalist logic to its conclusion), it is with the strict proviso that they are to be regarded as a means and not an end, as dynamic phases in a progressive struggle, not as stopping places. Their purpose is to educate and unite the actual or potential anti-capitalist forces through the campaign for unimpeachable social and economic objectives—above all, the reorientation of economic and social development—by using, in the first place, the methods of peaceful democratic reform. But this approach should be adopted *not because it is viable or intrinsically preferable, but on the contrary because the resistance it will encounter, and the limitations and impossibilities it will bring to light, are alone capable of demonstrating the necessity of a complete changeover to socialism to those segments of the masses which are not yet prepared for such a course.*[11]

SOCIALISTS AND REFORMISTS—THE PROGRAM

Clearly a strategy of this kind can never be carried out by an alliance at the top with neo-capitalist groups—that is

[11] "The first measures designed to transform the social structure must, if their neutralization is to be avoided, be rapidly followed by further reforms and changes in the democratic organization of power . . . Democratic planning of the development and transformation of the economy presupposes a very much broader social and political front than that at present achieved by the working-class and socialist parties; and although its initial goal cannot be *socialism,* the fact remains that democratic planning will be difficult to achieve completely, and above all *lastingly,* in the context of capitalism, if, in order to preserve its existence, we do not go beyond the initial program by reforms and changes which in the end constitute a policy of socialist transformation of society. The leading forces of the movement, at least, must be fully conscious of this." Bruno Trentin, op. cit.

to say, social democratic and center parties whose intention from the outset is to restrict reforms to measures acceptable to the bourgeoisie and who require of their associates a strict acceptance of this limitation. What it calls for, on the part of the political leaders, is full awareness of the nature of the process of transition to socialism, the mechanisms involved, the real aspirations of the masses on which it can be based, and a grasp of the *relatively short span of time* during which the success or failure of the operation will be decided.

In short, a socialist strategy of reforms must aim at disrupting the system and taking advantage of its disruption to embark on the revolutionary process of transition to socialism, which, as we have seen, can only be carried out by striking while the iron is hot. This kind of strategy can be effective only in periods of flux and open conflict and far-reaching social and political upheaval. It cannot be conceived in terms of a long-drawn-out war of attrition, because any temporary stabilization means that the decisive breakthrough, which any socialist strategy must aim at, will have failed. The new balance of forces may well be more favorable to the working class than the old, the contradictions and factors opposed to capitalist logic may be more clearly marked; but these contradictions, once the struggle for reforms begins leveling off, can have only a limited bearing: both sides will attempt to use them in order to weaken the position of the other. Such essentially *tactical* skirmishes are no substitute for a comprehensive *strategy* since, however precarious the balance may be, it rests on the acceptance by both sides of the impossibility of achieving complete victory.

It is therefore unrealistic to regard those tactical engagements, which may be spread over a long period, as part of a "revolutionary process" maturing over one or two decades.[12] However precarious the balance achieved when

12 A common assumption among left-wing social democrats, including Lelio Basso.

the struggle for reform begins leveling off, it is nevertheless a balance and therefore opens a period of uneasy truce.
The contradictions which the reforms have introduced into
the system do not gnaw away its fabric and weaken it like
a long-term illness. They cannot retain their power of disruption, but, on the contrary, must lose it. There are no
anti-capitalist institutions or gains which, in the long term,
are not nibbled away, distorted, reabsorbed into the system, completely or partially emptied of their substance, if
the imbalance which they originally created is not promptly
exploited by further advances. Being compelled to coexist
with institutions which at the outset conflict with its own
logic and restrict its sphere of sovereignty, capitalism learns
to master them by indirect means. Provided it retains control of the key points of accumulation and development,
and particularly of those activities which lead to technological progress and growth, it can eventually regain all the
ground it has lost.[13]

We cannot therefore think of the transition period, or
the period of preparation for transition, as being a long
one, something like a decade. If the transition is not
promptly set in motion following the rupture caused by the
struggle for reforms, it will not happen. The reforms will
be dismembered, scattered and absorbed by the system,
and the balance will be restored at a higher level. A new
period of preparatory struggle, embodying new contradic-

[13] For example, Social Security, which should entail the socialization of all medical and pharmaceutical consumption, in
fact becomes an added source of profit to the privately owned
chemical and pharmaceutical industries. The nationalization of
basic industries, even where these are not in the red and therefore unable to raise development capital on the open market,
eventually leads to the release of private capital for investment
in other fields offering more rapid growth and higher profit.
Although at a given moment the public sector may appear to be
in a dominating position it can only remain so if it extends
its activities to the new industries created by economic development.

tions, will then be necessary to create the conditions for a new offensive. The discontinuity of socialist strategy is that of history itself.

But we need not assume for this reason that all past democratic reforms have been valueless, which would amount to writing off a century of working-class struggle. Their past gains, even partly or wholly robbed of substance, provide the workers and socialists with a springboard for further advances. This was what Lenin had in mind when he described state monopoly capitalism as the "antechamber of socialism", meaning the farthest stage hitherto reached in the socialization of the capitalist productive process, affording certain levers capable of being employed by the socialist state.

Nevertheless it must be stressed that although past gains may have rendered capitalist predominance less secure and the equilibrium of the system more fragile, *for this very reason* further piecemeal reforms and shock to the equilibrium *will become politically more difficult*. It is precisely when new anti-capitalist measures threaten to jeopardize the system as a whole that bourgeois resistance becomes most ferocious. *The nearer the system is to collapse, or the nearer it has been to collapse in the past, the more difficult it becomes to resume the attack and break down the last defenses.* The bourgeoisie has been alerted. The workers have learned the political and economic penalties of failure. What is now called for is a higher degree of preparation, resolution and awareness, if the struggle is to be continued.

The idea of "creeping socialism" which will gain ground by a gradual series of reforms until it is ready for the final "qualitative leap" corresponds to no kind of reality except perhaps the very real vigilance on the part of the bourgeoisie which the notion reflects. There can be no *cumulative effect* of a series of gradual reforms if they are introduced over a long period and without a very sharp trial of strength based on a considered strategy. It is particularly in countries where the machinery of capitalist accumulation is already virtually subject to state control, and where (even though the state makes no use of the means at its disposal against the monopolies, and indeed does the opposite) institutional reforms presenting no intrinsic difficulty would suffice to break the power of the bourgeoisie, that capitalism brings to bear its full resources in every field (ideological, political, social) to prevent the awakening of a political will capable of carrying through such reforms.

In a number of Western European countries, notably France, the Scandinavian countries and Italy, the point has now been reached where, because of the vulnerability of the system, the bourgeoisie is defending its power positions to the death and furiously resisting all the workers' claims as well as their agitation for partial reforms. Hence the necessity of raising the struggle to the level of comprehensive strategy, based on an overall vision of society, and of attacking not merely the directly intolerable effects of capitalism but the very nature of the relations of production and the civilization they create.[14]

[14] Bruno Trentin, in the work already cited, reaches similar conclusions in an analysis of the situation which is more empirical than political.

"The events of recent years have destroyed all illusions as to the possibility of a slow and painless nibbling away of the system; they demonstrate more and more clearly the insufficiency of sectional disruptions inflicted on it by the workers, if these are not part of an overall strategy. In stressing this inadequacy we are thinking not only of the capacity of the capitalist system to absorb and emasculate partial reforms, but also, and especially, of the savage reaction of injured or threatened economic forces, and of the backlash provoked by even partial reforms when they disturb an equilibrium as precarious as that in the 1960s without the workers' movement having been able to consolidate its initial gains by the prompt achievement of further *organically linked* reforms and by the *simultaneous transformation of the existing power structure* . . .

"That is why the struggle of the workers . . . must always be conceived, at least in its broad outlines, as a comprehensive

This comprehensiveness of the struggle is necessary simply because the survival of the system is now imperiled by the achievement of even partial reforms, and the bourgeoisie is aware of the fact. The bourgeoisie meets partial attacks with overall resistance. The workers' movement cannot therefore hope to be victorious in the eventual trial of strength if it is not fully aware from the start of the nature of the stakes it is playing for, and if to this overall resistance it does not oppose an overall political resolve. One cannot win a battle in which the enemy has *everything* to lose if the immediate advantage for which one is fighting does not pave the way for a victory warranting *total* engagement.

There is therefore an element of truth and an element of error in the maximalist tendencies at present developing in face of the degeneration of European social democracy and the increasing difficulty of securing better wages, working conditions and partial reforms. The error consists in postulating that every engagement must now be entered upon with the clearly stated socialist intention that its ultimate aim is the overthrow of the system. This amounts to

strategy within which the *main links* between the various stages and aspects of the battle for reforms are agreed on in advance by the working-class parties. That is why the reform program, although it may be gradually implemented, must also be in a position, *from the earliest stage of its implementation,* to impose, by means of the economic policy which sustains it, not only a general control but also a qualitative modification of the machinery of accumulation, and must have at its disposal the necessary instruments of effective power such as parliament, local and regional representative bodies, the various forms of workers' control which prove practicable and necessary, agricultural co-operatives, peasant associations, unions.

"Failing this co-ordinated strategy, and lacking an economic plan which reflects its ultimate purpose, the indispensable limited struggles of the working class will, very much more than in the past, be neutralized and diverted from their real aims by the increasingly rigid logic of the system in which they are pursued."

affirming that the revolutionary intention must *precede* the struggle and supply its impetus. That is a non-dialectical position which evades the problem by treating it as though it were already solved. For the fact is that the socialist resolve of the masses never springs out of nothing, nor is it created by political propaganda or scientific demonstration. Socialist resolve is *built* in and by the struggle for feasible objectives corresponding to the experience, needs and aspirations of the workers.

But it is still necessary for these objectives to be interrelated in terms of a strategic whole, so that, as the struggle develops and encounters the structural limits of the system, it will gain not only in breadth but in depth. It is in the vanguard of the workers' movement and among its leaders, not among the masses, that the dialectical development of the struggle presupposes an already existing socialist intention. The intention will not be asserted by speeches and revolutionary propaganda but by ability to grade the objectives, to raise the struggle to a constantly higher plane and to set "intermediary" targets, paving the way for worker power, which must necessarily be surpassed as soon as they have been achieved.

The element of truth in the present maximalist position lies, however, in the fact that the workers' movement will not progress toward socialism if socialism is not the objective meaning of its day-to-day claims and destined eventually to become its conscious (or subjective) intention. No protest or claim put forward in general and therefore abstract terms (for example, overall increase in wages and pensions, development of social services, etc.) can possess this objective meaning, if only because its fulfillment is not within the power of those making the claim and will not be the direct result of their action, even if it is successful. Moreover that kind of claim does not of itself possess an internal anti-capitalist logic requiring the immediate target to be surpassed as soon as it has been reached. It involves a graduated implementation which may be met by government action based on technical (or technocratic) reform.

The aim of these reforms does not reach beyond their limited and specific goal.

Under present conditions the working class will acquire the maturity and political strength necessary to overcome the increased resistance of the system only if its claims, by their content but also by the *manner* in which they are pressed, represent a living criticism of capitalist civilization, its social structure, productive system and entire *rationale*.

This criticism, deepening the nature of the struggle, is particularly important in the context of neo-capitalism, where the socialist movement comes up against the minor reformism of social democrat and center parties. These very often propose the *same* kind of objectives advocated by the radical left (housing, education, collective amenities, "social justice," etc.), but always with the proviso that they are to be gained without causing a breakdown in the capitalist machine—that is to say, without upsetting the economic equilibrium or weakening the position of the bourgeoisie.

The favorite theme of the social democrats is the contention that all problems can be solved or rendered tolerable, all material needs satisfied, within the framework of the existing system, given sufficient time and discipline. No need to "break up the joint" or engage in any trial of strength: we have simply to be patient and realistic, to act responsibly and trust our leaders. Let every man keep his proper place and the neo-capitalist state will serve the best interests of all.

For socialists it is no doubt useful to point out that the reformists deny themselves the means of carrying out their own program; that the program will either never be realized or will be subject to such long delays that its remedies will have been rendered out-of-date by changed conditions; and that in any case it is possible to ask for more and do better by going further in transforming the structure. But however pertinent they may be, arguments of this kind are not enough. They amount simply to countering prom-

ises of relative improvement with promises of more rapid
or drastic relative improvement. What they do not say, and
what the reformists loudly proclaim, is that the more rapid
or drastic improvements must entail a major crisis in the
system. "You want to smash the machine," the moderates
argue. "We want to make it work better."

So long as it adopts a platform of *relative,* general improvement, the socialist movement is ill equipped to meet
this position. If it encourages the idea that the difference
between its policy and that of the reformists is merely one
of *degree,* and that it is basically pursuing the same objectives but with greater energy and intransigence, prepared
if need be to bring things to the point of a trial of strength
with capitalism, it has very little prospect of winning the
support of social democratic voters and constituting itself
the dominant force of the working-class movement. A
mere difference of degree is not enough to woo the masses
away from the slow but "safe" path of minor reforms on to
the perilous and arduous road of direct clash with the
forces of capital.

People will not be prepared to accept the risks of a serious political and monetary crisis and a head-on battle with
the bourgeoisie simply for the sake of 250,000 new houses
a year instead of 200,000, a 10 per cent wage increase
instead of 5 per cent and a slightly shorter work week. The
game would not be worth the candle, if only because the
more ambitious policy of the socialists would start by provoking a savage backlash on the part of the system, a
major disturbance of the economy and, in all likelihood,
a deterioration in the material circumstances of the workers, for a short time at least.

Moderate social democratic propaganda achieves its
greatest effectiveness by asking: "Why be in such a hurry?
Why try to force things when, with a little patience and
discipline, you can get what you want *within a reasonable
time and in a calm and orderly fashion?* Is it worthwhile
to risk a major crisis for the sake of doing in five years

what can be done in seven or eight without any drastic changes?"

This is the question stated by the European social democrats, and the socialist movement can answer it only by stressing the existence of a *fundamental* difference between its policy and the policy of the reformists.[15] The difference is not merely one of degree, timing and method in achieving the same aims as the social democrats, but better and faster: it is a *total* difference justifying the acceptance of a total risk. Only insofar as it can convincingly demonstrate that its actions and purposes are not those of the reformists, that it is not concerned with relative and partial improvements but with *absolute and global betterment,* can the socialist movement hope to advance and assert itself as the dominant force in the workers' movement.

Absolute and global betterment does not, of course, mean promising an immediate earthly paradise, by the instant creation of a socialist order. It means that every par-

[15] Attempts to attract social democracy to the left by glossing over divergencies, stressing common objectives and offering help in their achievement, make sense only if the movement for unity is strong enough among the masses to induce social democracy to join an anti-capitalist alliance, a thing that has happened only in times of acute crisis or internal and external danger. But the "left-wing front" thus constituted has always been defensive and tactical, instead of offensive and strategic. Once the reactionary threat has been averted strategic divergencies have led to the breakup of the alliance. It then becomes clear that the latter was not really directed against the bourgeois state but against pre-capitalist, pre-bourgeois elements and structures arising out of the unfinished state of the bourgeois revolution.

Lucio Magri notes this in *Les Temps Modernes,* January 1966, and he adds: "The cement binding the Front together therefore crumbles away. This cement was in fact the common struggle against a power system incapable of ensuring any social progress whatever and compelled to resort to political violence and war to disguise its social weakness and inability to serve the interests of a real majority."

tial improvement, every reform that is campaigned for, shall be related in the context of a comprehensive plan designed to produce an overall change. The import of this change must transcend all the minor gains which in one way or another contribute to it. The absolute betterment it seeks is the emancipation of all those who are exploited by the capitalist system, oppressed, degraded and sterilized in what constitutes their social value and their self-respect as individuals—their work as members of society.

Certainly reformists and socialists want a number of the same things, but they do not want them for the same reasons or in the same way. Reform, to the moderates, means simply "things"—wages, pensions, collective amenities—to be loftily bestowed by the state on the mass of underlings, who are to be kept dispersed and impotent within the system. But what matters to the socialists, as much or more than "things," is the sovereign *power* of the workers to determine for themselves the conditions of their social co-operation and to subject to their collective will the content, goal and division of their labor.

Therein lies the profound difference between reformism and socialism. It is the difference between conceded reforms which perpetuate the subordinate position of the working class in the factories and in society, and reforms dictated, effected and controlled by the masses themselves, based on their capacity for self-management and their own initiative. Finally it is the difference between merely technical, governmental reforms and those which are genuinely democratic, this being understood to mean that they are *of necessity* anti-capitalist. As Lelio Basso has written: "To fight for true democracy, for real participation at all levels in the management of collective interests, for all forms of collective control and in particular the control by the workers of all aspects of the production process . . . this is in effect to fight against the capitalists' power of decision . . . An essential element in the conflict is the struggle of the working class for its own right to self-manage the utilization of its labor power, with all the consequences this entails affecting the organization of work in the factories, the rating of skills, the administration of deferred wages (national insurance), etc."

Thus the difference in intention between neo-capitalist and anti-capitalist reform must necessarily be paralleled by a difference of method. The liberating value of the reforms can be apparent only if this was already present in the mass action designed to bring them into effect. Where the method is concerned, the difference between technical and democratic reform is the difference between institutional reform coldly applied and reform enforced in hot blood by collective action. In the formal sense any reform, including workers' control, may be robbed of its revolutionary significance and absorbed by capitalism if it is introduced by act of government and operated under bureaucratic control—that is to say, reduced to the status of a "thing."

Certain maximalists conclude from this that all reforms are meaningless while the capitalist state continues to exist. They are right when it is a matter of reforms from above, volunteered and institutionalized in cold blood, but wrong in the case of reforms brought about in hot blood by active struggle from below. It is impossible to separate any reform from the action of which it is the product, and impossible to achieve democratic and anti-capitalist reform by action which is neither one nor the other. The emancipation of the working class can become a total objective for the workers, warranting total risk, only if in the course of the struggle they have learned something about self-management, initiative and collective decision—in a word, if they have had a foretaste of what emancipation means.

THE TOTAL ALTERNATIVE—THE PROBLEM OF ALLIANCES

Whenever the socialist movement has found itself confronted by a strongly entrenched social democracy, dynamic neo-capitalism, it has been obliged to shift its emphasis from a short-term program of partial, immediate demands toward a *policy of total qualitative change*. That is what is implied by the constant references to "the total alternative," and the "pattern" of development, of civilization and social organization, the formulation of which is now seen by the more advanced wings of the European Marxist movement to be the most urgent and important task confronting it.

The fact is simply that rag-tag programs concerned with adding up all immediate demands and grievances are no longer plausible. They lack the wider vision and coherence which are essential—not only in terms of economic logic, but still more in political, ideological terms—to a "total alternative" designed to weld the objectively anti-capitalist social forces into a whole which can only be the *synthesis* at a higher level of their immediate demands, needs, interests and aspirations, and not merely the sum of these. The case of Sweden affords a particularly clear example extending beyond that country, which is often taken as a model by European social democrats: a prefiguration of the kind of society toward which most European neo-capitalist countries are evolving.

Swedish social democracy postulated that it was possible, within the framework of capitalism and accepting its mechanisms, to pursue a policy of social welfare, collective amenities and high wages linked to high productivity. The policy is based on direct taxation but goes hand in hand with a social system based on individual consumption. This has resulted in an acute, twofold contradiction.

On the one hand, the growth of social services and amenities, being financed by direct taxation, has been achieved by the actual socialization of private savings, causing a serious crisis in the mechanism of capitalist accumulation, stagnation on the stock market and a diminution of funds for the financing of private enterprise. On the other hand, there has been no countervailing increase of prosperity in the social sector. On the contrary, there is an acute housing and urban development problem, an acute shortage of medical and teaching personnel, an accelerated rural depopulation, and so on.

Thus the expansion of social services and state intervention, being subordinated to the expansion of industrial capitalism, has been insufficient to cover the social needs created by the latter but enough to make difficulties for it by drying up some of its sources of financing.

Social democracy is thus faced with a dilemma. The rapid expansion of collective social services and the growth of monopoly expansion cannot be achieved simultaneously. There has to be a choice. Either public spending must be restricted (with a consequent aggravation of the shortages already mentioned) so as to increase private saving and consumption for the benefit of capitalism; or alternatively the social services and public intervention must be expanded more rapidly than in the past. The latter course entails a far more drastic process of socialization, including further nationalization, collectivization of savings and investment, and comprehensive economic planning giving priority to collective consumption and services over all forms of affluent consumption.

The choice is not simply a technical one. It cannot fail to have a profound impact on the pattern of social development, consumption, civilization and the way of life.

The first term of the alternative is one which the majority of workers instinctively reject. But that is not to say that the second, although it is the logical response to popular needs and aspirations, can automatically count on the support of the majority.

The difficulty of converting logical analysis into practical politics arises (apart from the fact that logical thinking is never practiced by all the interested parties) from the wide disparity between different strata of workers. The immediate interests of the large category of better-paid manual workers (notably in the building trades, heavy engineering and shipbuilding industries) do not automatically coincide with those of lower-paid workers (particularly women workers) in the public services and underdeveloped or "remote" areas, or with those of technical and scientific workers.

Where their immediate interests are concerned, the more highly paid workers do not spontaneously favor a policy of advanced socialization. Trade-union and social democratic ideology has taught them to place wage claims and "consumer values" at the top of their list of priorities: work is to be regarded as a daily purgatory; capitalist standards of productivity and organization, though oppressive and intolerable, must be accepted as a matter of practical necessity; all that really counts is the pay envelope. Work, in short, is presented as the purgatory through which we have to pass on our way to the heaven of individual consumption when the day's work is done. By this view, the first term of the alternative—proposing some relief from the heavy burden of direct taxation, and increased individual affluence rather than social consumption—is more immediately attractive to a section of the working class than a policy of advanced socialization.

Demands for higher wages, though essential to workers in the low salary categories and in the underdeveloped areas, cannot therefore serve as a unifying theme for the workers' movement as a whole. The political unity of the working class, which is the indispensable condition of the second term of the alternative, can only be based on themes transcending immediate interests. Work in the ideological and political fields, criticism of the "consumer society," the devising and propounding of a new social pattern—these are the essentials.

It is necessary to show that the oppression and alienation endured during working hours for the sake of liberation in non-work can only lead to the alienation of consumption and leisure; that in order to procure the consumption and leisure benefits which "liberate" him from oppression in his work, the worker is compelled by an infernal logic to work faster and longer, to accept overtime and output bonuses, until he forfeits the possibility,

material as well as psychological, of any kind of liberation; that the man at work is the same as the man not
working, and that the one cannot be liberated without the
other. It is also necessary to show that the basic class interest of all workers is to put an end to their subordinate
position in work and as consumers, and to gain control
of the organization and purposes of social production; that
although wage increases are the first consideration of a
large mass of workers, the granting of these does not in
itself end capitalist exploitation; and that in any case the
wage level is subject to objective limitations, and that there
are limits, both objective and subjective, to the satisfactions that can be derived from individual earnings in the
absence of a sufficient development of public services and
amenities.

So long as production policy is dictated by private capital, and consumption, culture and the way of life are dominated by bourgeois values, there is no road to better living
except through higher earnings. But if the capitalist relations of production are to be abolished, it is because better
living implies less, and less intensive, work, the adaptation
of work to the biological and psychological equilibrium of
the worker, better public services and amenities, and
greater opportunities for direct communication and culture, both in and out of work, for the worker himself and
for his children.

On the other hand, the distortions and limitations imposed on scientific, technological and cultural development
by capitalist criteria of profitability; the waste of economic
resources and human energies resulting from financial and
geographical concentration; the underemployment of human potentialities by the authoritarian organization of
work; the contradiction between the law of maximum productivity on the one hand, and on the other the waste
caused by constant innovations of no practical value and
costly sales campaigns—all these contradictions, inherent

in advanced capitalism, are as important, when we come
to question the whole system, as the more obvious and
immediate causes of discontent. They imply a criticism
of the way of life and the values and rationale of capitalism.

We cannot of course proceed from these and similar
considerations to the abstract formulation of blueprinted
solutions, or of any purely speculative "alternative model."
The superiority of a revolutionary mass party over political
machines concerned with gaining power and governing
under existing conditions, lies in the fact that it can (and
must) give rise to aspirations and challenges which imply
a radical change. But a revolutionary mass party must
exercise its functions as leader and educator without
claiming to know in advance the answers to the questions
it asks: not solely because the answers cannot be found
within the framework of the existing system, but also
because the process of working them out, through con-
frontations and continuous debate at the lower level, is in-
comparably the best way of inducing participation, promoting awareness and self-education in the workers, giving
them an active bearing on the party and the new society
to be created, and causing them to understand, through
the democratic workings of the party, the profoundly authoritarian and anti-democratic nature of the society in
which they are living.

The promotion and stimulation of collective thought and
democratic debate is also the party's best means of evolving
the methods and goals of the struggle, testing its theories
in the light of practical experience and determining the
forms of action best suited to local conditions and to the
sensibilities and capacity for the masses' initiative.

This continuous process of research and collective
thinking, associating the party rank and file with the shaping of its policy and calling upon it to choose between
different courses of action, must inevitably extend beyond
the party itself, which cannot live as a recluse. Its capacity

for hegemony depends on how far its inner life, its activities and its political views attract the mass of workers
who are either unorganized or under the influence of different ideologies. In an economically advanced society,
where the working class is highly differentiated both in
its origins (urban-industrial, agricultural, petty bourgeois)
and in the nature of its work (manual, technical, intellectual), the party must at all times take the diversity of
needs and aspirations into account, and it can exercise its
leadership only by seeking to transcend this diversity toward a higher unity which will respect the relative autonomy of its diverse elements.

The policy of transition to socialism, the "pattern" of the
transitional society and indeed of socialist society itself,
must of necessity recognize this diversity. In the advanced
capitalist countries the revolutionary party cannot hope to
win power, or exercise it, by itself. It needs to form alliances with all the social, political and intellectual forces
that reject the logic of capitalism and can be won over to
a coherent policy of transition which is clear as to its socialist aims. At the same time the work of formulating
this transitional policy, especially as regards the political
and institutional reforms which need to be accomplished,
cannot be successfully carried out solely by the leadership
of the party, even if (or particularly if) it is by far the
strongest party of the working class.

The attraction which the rank-and-file activity of the
party has for the unorganized mass, and for the rank and
file of other organizations, is itself dependent, both in its
intensity and in its capacity for development, on the attraction of its long-term, and very long-term, policies for
actual or potential allies of the revolutionary party. Hence
the necessity for the latter to accept other socialist movements as *permanent* partners in the *common* task of research and formulation designed to establish the program
and methods of the transition to socialism, and to accept
a variety of movements and parties during the transitional

period and even during the period of building socialism itself.

The present or past electoral value of these permanent partners is not the determining factor in their choice. More important than their numerical strength is the representative nature of their militant basis, their authentically socialist tendency and their genuine independence. For the revolutionary mass party to ally itself lastingly with other bodies, even weak ones, and to conduct research jointly with them, is to demonstrate in practice, and not simply in words, that its respect for political pluralism and the independence of allies is something more than a tactical concession. It is also, both by the method of work and the coherence of the jointly formulated transitional policy (or "comprehensive alternative"), a source of powerful attraction to the rank and file and the left wing of the social democratic and Christian socialist movements.

The revolutionary party, therefore, should on no account rebuff by its doctrinal attitudes the masses influenced by social democracy or the traditional reformist movements. On the other hand, it must not be trapped into the kind of summit negotiations which are promptly brought to a standstill by ideological or doctrinal differences, or led into a morass of bargaining over a "minimal common program." Nor should it attempt a surface unity of the working-class movement (or of some of its components) by the federation of existing organizations, that is to say, by the juxtaposition of their machinery. This will rapidly dissolve in a process of haggling between the various leaders; it will resemble a parliament or a "shadow cabinet" which will soon cut itself off from the masses and discourage the militants, who will find themselves unable to influence decisions and priorities handed down from the summit and dictated far more by internal, organizational considerations than by any collective impulse coming from below. What is needed is the unification of the genuinely socialist elements by the working out of a coherent common program embracing long-term and even

very long-term policies,[16] as well as immediate problems
and a medium-term program. The coherence of this program, the open nature of the discussions and their impact
on the militant rank and file, which will be called upon to
play its part in the process of unification—all this will be
very much more effective and attract far more support
than approaches to the traditional reformist parties, which
are always open to the suspicion of tactical opportunism.
The minor reformism of social democracy can be defeated only by a direct appeal to the masses under its influence, not by dickering with its organization. And the
best way of winning over the masses is to offer them an
"alternative": a coherent socialist policy with clearly
stated options, and democratic methods of procedure which
social democracy, by its nature, is incapable of adopting.

THE IDEOLOGICAL FRONT—NEW TASKS FOR THE
REVOLUTIONARY PARTY

The continuing work of research and formulation cannot be confined to the strictly political and programmatic
field. The starting point, in making the masses political-
minded, is not politics or solely the process of action and
struggle. Their involvement and political choice are in fact
the outcome of a growth of awareness which does not start
with politics—the organization and structure of society—
but with the fragmentary and direct recognition that
change is *necessary because it is possible*.

The demand for change, in other words, does not arise
out of the *impossibility* of tolerating the existing state of

16 One of the weaknesses of the "Grenoble colloquy" in May
1966 was that it confined itself to a short and medium-term
"possibilist" program, and thereby excluded all consideration of
the problems of the transition to socialism and even the means
of preparing for it. The really basic questions affecting socialist
awareness and action *cannot even be raised* in a short-term context—that is to say, within the framework of capitalism.

affairs, but out of the *possibility* of no longer having to tolerate it. It is the demonstration of this possibility (whether immediate or not, and whether capable or not of being expressed in action), in every field of social and individual life, which is one of the basic elements in the ideological work of a revolutionary movement.[17]

[17] Ideological work is nothing but the unification at a particular level—that of consciousness—of diverse aspirations and interests. An ideology will or will not be a mystification according to whether it is syncretic or synthetic.

The neo-capitalist ideologies aim to unify various particular interests of the bourgeoisie and to merge these with the interests and immediate aspirations of the higher-paid workers, whom they assimilate into the bourgeoisie under the ideological label of "middle class." This syncretic unification is made to look real by propounding numerous crude and incomplete analyses and interpretations of the social relations of production under modern capitalism.

The synthetic unification of the interests and aspirations of the working classes rests on unembellished scientific analysis insofar as it proceeds from the subordinate position of those classes in capitalist society. But the main features of this subordination are not the same for all categories of wage and salary earners. Their unification therefore calls for more subtle analysis, taking into account the specific material, cultural and professional aspirations and interests of both manual and intellectual workers. The synthesis must therefore be conceived in terms of a wider perspective, transcending immediate interests toward the creation of a richer system of human and social relations—that is to say, conceived in terms of common requirements or values which can be made universal. The synthesis will of necessity remain incomplete so long as class divisions, and even the social division of labor, have not been superseded.

Since there is a strong element of mystification and propaganda in the prevailing neo-capitalist ideology, a part of the workers' struggle against it must consist of counter-propaganda and oversimplification. It is this practical necessity which has been restrictively labeled "ideological work." But although it is essential to translate ideological work into propaganda—slogans, catch phrases, polemics—it is no less essential not to con-

The domination of one class over another is not exercised solely by means of political and economic power, but also through its evaluation of the possible and the impossible, the future and the past, the useful and the useless, the rational and the irrational, the good and the bad. This evaluation is inherent in the entire social fabric and determines its resilience to change. It pervades our daily language (main instrument or obstacle to awareness), shapes the media and the way in which science and technology are assessed; it permeates *life* itself (that is, the fundamental needs, called "instincts," and immediate relations of individuals with one another—for example, sexual relationships). This means that possibilities, aspirations and needs which are incompatible with existing social relations are repressed and censored (in the Freudian, not the police sense) at the level where they might become aware of themselves, by the standards of the dominant ideology and way of life.

This way of life prides itself not only on its "values," but on a "value-free" realism peculiar to all conservative ideologies. It is "unrealistic" to suppose that a healthy economy can dispense with commercial competition, private profit, the repressive discipline of work and the threat of unemployment. Intensified exploitation of the worker, his nervous exhaustion and mental stupefaction, are the "inevitable" consequences of technological progress. There is no such thing as a "comprehensive alternative" to capitalism; the worker will always remain a worker, this being a technical necessity. The individual will always be "selfish"; his "instincts" will always be anti-social and must therefore be repressed. And so on.

The overcoming of this deep-seated indoctrination, which is rooted in the material relations, is one of the es-

---

fuse the two things. The propaganda will be ineffective if it is not based on strict analysis and careful research, and it will lose its effect if the research is distorted or censored or lost sight of simply for the sake of scoring immediate political points.

sential tasks of the revolutionary movement. It can be done only if the possibility—not necessarily immediate—of partial or total liberation can be demonstrated, and if it can be shown that the repressed needs, the desire for change and liberation, need not assume the form of scattered and acrimonious grievances convinced in advance of the fruitlessness of revolt, but can gain confidence in their legitimacy and reality. Even the most intolerable consequences of a new work organization, for example, are grudgingly accepted, after a first outburst of anger, if management can show, as it generally can, that they were technically essential and commercially profitable. The instinctive opposition of the workers can go beyond that first ineffectual outburst, gain confidence in the legitimacy and reality of its own case, and be translated into resolute struggle, only if the union is able to put forward an alternative pattern wholly opposed to that of management, based on a different concept of work and the worker, and on a notion of "rationality" which encompasses the individual's physical and mental needs, his relation to the tools he uses and to his fellows.

This form of approach, demonstrating the necessity of change by arguing its possibility, and thereby bringing to life the latent needs which society has repressed, is valid for every aspect of the relation of the individual to his work, to social production, to society as a complex environment of natural and cultural relationships. The work of ideological research and formulation, apart from its political aspects, is thus a *cultural* undertaking designed to subvert the values currently accepted by society and to make the people aware of its alienations.

The revolutionary movement's hegemony and effectiveness will be fortified by its ability to promote independent research in fields such as city planning, architecture, social medicine, pedagogics, psychology and sexual education. Contradictions may be discovered in all these fields between available possibilities and society's inability to realize these in a liberating sense. The same fields also show contra-

dictions between meaningful work as a city planner, architect, doctor, educator, psychologist, etc., and the restrictions imposed on them by the capitalist system.

The revolutionary party's capacity for hegemony is
therefore directly bound up with the extent to which it has
gained a foothold in the intellectual professions and intellectual circles. It will be capable of countering bourgeois
ideology only insofar as it is inspiring to these sections'
thinking and wins their co-operation in the quest for an
"alternative model," while leaving them free to conduct
their research. Although intellectuals, as bearers of universal and universally accessible knowledge, clearly must
be willing to renounce their privileged status, sectional interests and technocratic power so as to "serve the people,"
they nevertheless are needed as intellectuals to furnish the
dominated classes with a language and means of expression which will make them conscious of the reality of their
subordination and exploitation. If it cannot express itself,
a need is incapable of recognizing its own reality. When
the workers' experience of working-class conditions is not
given expression but denied or silenced by all those who,
through the media, constitute the "public conscience," each
worker will remain doubtful as to whether other workers
feel as he does.[18] The repressive class nature of culture is
not reflected solely or even mainly in the social background
of students. It is reflected in a much more fundamental

[18] Hence, also, the importance of free communication and
interchange. But direct communication, self-expression and the
awareness to which this gives rise, are hindered not only by a
repressive factory discipline and a housing policy which dis-
perses the workers at the end of the day's work, but also by
thought conditioning, language, the behavior patterns instilled
in the schools and by the mass media. The latter end by becoming a screen between experience and the consciousness of
that experience. The retrogression of proletarian culture and
cultural centers is very largely due to the shrinking possibility
of direct communication and the growth of the mass culture
(a form of de-culturizing) disseminated by the mass media.

sense in the nonexistence or extreme poverty of a specific
working-class culture (literature, drama and cinema), that
could enable the workers themselves to convey what they
feel and experience.

To bring popularized bourgeois culture to the masses is
not the way to fight the class bias of culture and abolish
bourgeois cultural privilege. On the contrary, what is
needed is not that the working class should be impregnated with bourgeois culture, but that culture should be
impregnated with the experience, the values, the tasks and
problems which the workers encounter daily in their work,
after work and in their struggles. The class nature of bourgeois culture is demonstrated by the fact that the working
class is not central to works of art and that the latter do
not view society as it truly is in the eyes of the workers.
We have an ample literature—technological, sociological,
moralistic and political—depicting the workers as they appear *to* capitalist society, but very little about that society,
at all levels, as it appears to the workers. What little has
been conveyed about the experience of industrial labor
and the *professional culture* inherent in even the less-
skilled tasks stems mainly from a few Soviet novels and
arid sociological studies intended for the non-working-class
public. A terrible silence has descended upon working-class
reality, and it is this which allows it to be daily affirmed
that the condition of the workers has become acceptable,
even comfortable, and that class distinctions are vanishing.

This silence can be broken only with the help of intellectuals. Attempts, notably in the German Democratic Republic, to create a working-class culture by encouraging
writers and artists in the factories has largely failed. Cultural creation in any form implies *skills* requiring apprenticeship and the mastery of specific techniques, notably the
development of a language and forms of expression capable
of reflecting working-class experience with its wealth of
individual and collective problems past and present. Such
a language will be available to all as their "common
wealth" only when it has been evolved by a few, and this,

to a large extent, still remains to be done. Although it is finally a collective undertaking, it cannot be immediately collective: for although its purpose is to prove the existence of working-class culture—which is today a variety of local, trade and oral subcultures—it must first provide the means, at present lacking, which will enable the working class to recognize its own culture and to express it. This is where the mediation of intellectuals is needed, not merely in the form, for example, of Brecht's plays, or of novels or reporting "in depth," but also in the sense of giving the working class a voice it will recognize as its own because it expresses what the workers generally experience in silence and solitude.

First efforts in this direction have been attempted in various countries[19] with the help of students and university staff—taped interviews with workers on the factory floor or at the gates; questionnaires calling not only for facts but for opinions; film documentaries; biographies of workers and militants showing how their lives are conditioned by the history of the company and the owning dynasty, and by developments in the fields of economy, science, technology and the international labor movement. These have then been processed and fed back to the workers' collectives which participated in their making, so that the collective work might be collectively discussed and the workers, seeing themselves as the collective subject of the work and of the values, the needs and the language arising out of it, might become aware of themselves as the potential creators of a new culture and not merely the underprivileged consumers of a culture that is alien to them.

The destruction of the bourgeois cultural monopoly cannot be achieved by the mass dissemination of previous cultural matter. Mass dissemination of "culture" is simply the

[19] Sporadic attempts at "worker investigations" in Italy, Norway and Germany have acquired a certain notoriety because of the strikes and great unrest they provoked, although this was not their original intention.

distribution of another line of consumer goods. In its various forms—television, movies, paperbacks, newspapers —it depends on the centralized communication system, which is what we mean when we talk about the "mass media." That is to say, the "media of mass communication" do not allow the mass of individuals to communicate *with each other.* They simply permit news and cultural products to be communicated *to the masses,* which, by the one-sided nature of the process, are reduced to isolated silence as the passive recipients of the communication.

It is not mass consumption of culture that will break the bourgeois cultural monopoly, but only the creation by the dominated classes of their own culture.[20] The task of animating, inspiring and guiding the creation of this culture, and stimulating free self-expression and the collective exchange and discussion of ideas and experiences among the masses, is one of the essential functions of the revolutionary party, and one in which it can succeed only if it has a mass base, particularly in places of production and education. It can, moreover, succeed only by encouraging the widest possible spread of democracy and initiative among the masses where people work and live collectively; by encouraging free debate on every level, so that the needs that society represses may be expressed and become consciously manifest in all their depth and diversity; and by attracting intellectual elements which will give the working class its voice and language, and perceive, reveal and formulate its deepest needs, unifying these on the higher level of a new perspective and an anti-capitalist "alternative."

[20] In the same way, it is not the broadening of the type of education dispensed in high schools and universities that will "democratize" education, but a radical reform of methods and content which will break down barriers between intellectual and manual, theoretical and practical, and individual and collective work—barriers which are entirely arbitrary from the point of view of the acquisition and development of knowledge.

In nearly all these respects the task of the revolutionary party, and the form of organization it calls for, are appreciably different, in advanced capitalist societies, from the task and structure of the Bolshevik Party. This is not to say that revolution in the West can expect to achieve its aims solely by peaceful means. Nothing could be less certain. The destruction of the bourgeois apparatus of repression is one of the tasks that a revolutionary party must be equal to. But it is no longer the first priority, as it was fifty years ago. The fact that it may have to be undertaken is not sufficient reason, under present conditions, for creating a Leninist party (or an armed vanguard on Guevara lines) in the West. Unlike the Tsarist autocracy (or the Latin American military dictatorships) the function of the modern capitalist state is not only one of repression. Its power is based, in the first instance, not on the police and the army, but on its political-ideological capacity to present itself as a *legitimate* mediator between antagonistic classes. It is on this political and ideological ground that it has first to be fought, if the neutralization of its repressive apparatus is to become possible (which does not, of course, rule out direct action tending to show that its power is based on legalized violence).

But there is more than this. Whatever its leaders intended, the Bolshevik concept of the party as an organized vanguard, distinct from the masses, contained the germs of most of the subsequent degeneration of "soviet" power. The elitist concept of an organized vanguard was not an essential requirement of the struggle and of the revolutionary party. It was the historic circumstance of clandestine revolutionary struggle in a country where the peasant population was largely illiterate that enforced the separation of the vanguard from the masses, the centralization of political planning and decision making, and the concentration of all the powers of leadership in the hands of a small body of professional revolutionaries, depositories of a truth which had to be "carried to the masses."

For revolutionary struggle in contemporary Western Eu-

rope the conditions are fundamentally different. The basic
task of the revolutionary party is not to direct and control
from above, but to stimulate and *deliver* the capacity for
initiative, improvisation and self-organization of the masses
themselves. The party's task is not to put forward its *own*
pre-formed doctrines as a basis of struggle, or to affix
political-strategic aims (such as could only have been conceived by a detached, centralized leadership) to acts of
struggle which are bound to appear "primitive." The party
must no longer be a vanguard separate from the masses
or an organization detached from the struggle, but an active element within the masses which, like a ferment,
stimulates action wherever this is possible, helping the
masses to create their own organs of struggle and collective
leadership, and to achieve the political vision implied by
the carrying of their own experience to its logical conclusion.

Insofar as the party is a central organization it is to be
regarded as a necessary evil: necessary because there has
to be a center where local experience can be compared and
co-ordinated, where it can achieve a unified outlook and
be transformed into a political strategy to confront the
bourgeois state. But nevertheless an evil because, facing a
centralized power, it reflects the necessity to centralize a
revolutionary undertaking of which the final aim is to do
away with *all* state centralization. As a central organization,
the party must be understood to be a temporary structure
necessary for getting rid of the bourgeois state but *which
must thereafter get rid of itself*.

The essential characteristic of any truly revolutionary
movement is that the organization developed during and
in the outcome of the struggle is not the same as that which
existed at the beginning. Having at the start made use of
existing organizations, it liquidates these on the way and
substitutes those organs of self-government and self-
administration which the sovereign base has evolved for
the perpetuation of its sovereignty. A truly revolutionary
movement is distinguished by the fact that, having un-

leashed or stimulated a mass movement, it is prompt to dissolve into it, to favor the birth of sovereign assemblies and to accept the liquidation of all hierarchic structures and all separation between leaders and led. The slogan of revolution is not "all power to the party," but "all power to the soviets"—that is to say, to the sovereign assemblies of the producers.

That the party is a provisional structure, destined to be constantly questioned and re-created by the revolution itself, should be clearly apparent from its internal functioning and the style of its leadership. The destruction of the bourgeois state by the political victory of the party is not the completion of a revolution. It may indeed be the funeral of the revolution, if all the power is concentrated within the party apparatus. Or it may be the beginning of a process of continuous revolution—that is to say, of the repeated liquidation of the hierarchic structure, and bureaucratic rigidities which tend to re-emerge.

Chapter 5

Arduous Socialism*

* Amplified text of a lecture delivered in February 1966 at the Mexican National School of Political and Social Sciences.

. . . Others believe that oppression is due exclusively to the private ownership of the means of production, and that with the expropriation of capital the liberty of the workers will be automatically assured. This, too, does not seem to us correct. Socialist power may expropriate the capitalist and thus create the premises for the workers' freedom: but if the organization of production in the factory and the country as a whole continues to be bureaucratized under a rigidly centralized decision-making system, the workers will be subjected to social production as an alien process and in certain respects will find themselves in a state of subordination similar to that in capitalist countries.

Vittorio Foa, Secretary of the CGIL

ALIENATION WITHOUT EXPLOITATION

In his *Critique of the Gotha Program,* and in scattered notes in Parts II and III of *Das Kapital,* Marx refers to three conditions essential for the creation of a communist society:

1. Victory over scarcity, whereby it will become possible to satisfy the needs of all and of everyone, as shaped by history.

2. "Polytechnism" or the polyvalent education of all, allowing a continuous rotation or simultaneous exercise of manual, administrative, technical and free creative work. This interchangeability of functions is necessary in order to abolish specializations, mutilations, social stratifications and the state, and to achieve the voluntary division of

labor within society and the self-management by associated individuals of all the aspects of their social activity.

3. The abolition of work as "an obligation enforced by poverty and external goals"; this being also a condition for the voluntary division of labor, and requiring that scarcity in every form has been overcome, including scarcity of time.

The three conditions are based on a common stipulation, namely, "the full development of the forces of production." This means not only the development of capacities of production, but also the devising of *techniques* of production enabling the individual to accomplish his share of socially necessary work in a relatively short time, without overexertion and in a *manner* favoring the expansion of his human faculties.

In short, communism, as Marx saw it, was to be a collective activity controlling its own development as well as its collective product, freely achieved by the voluntary association of individuals. It must abolish everything external to the individual, all alienated social roles that do not rest on personal choice and conscious aims. It must adapt the process of production to human needs as regards what is produced but also the manner of producing it.

To recall these preconditions of a communist society is to realize that, far from being overtaken by present developments, they have drawn further ahead of them, so that today they appear to us even more remote than they did to Marx some one hundred and ten years ago, when in the first outline of *Das Kapital* he predicted the automation of the productive process. In other words, the meaning history had for Marx (its only possible meaning: the reconquest by individuals of the inhuman forces which their own activities have generated amidst the prevailing scarcity) has not only not been overtaken, but seems to have receded as a possible goal.

One of the reasons for this apparent recession is that the socialist revolution has not occurred at the highest level of the development of the forces of production, but at its lowest level.

The fact that the first successful socialist revolution took place in Russia has had far-reaching consequences for the workers' and socialist movements in the advanced capitalist countries. Russia, in 1917, was in only the early stage of industrialization. Even today about 40 per cent of its working population is in the agricultural sector, as opposed to 20 per cent in France, 10 per cent in the Netherlands and 6.7 per cent in the United States. Any attempt at comparison between the industrial civilization of Russia and that of the United States is therefore invalidated by the disparity between their respective stages of development, just as is the attitude which consists in basing oneself on the American model to evaluate capitalism, or on the Soviet model to evaluate socialism.

A great many writers appear to believe that the degree of economic development achieved by American capitalism is attributable to capitalism *as such* and prefigures the future of all capitalist societies. This is to overlook the fact that American capitalism developed in unique circumstances which cannot be duplicated in any other capitalist country, notably, and precisely, *because of the very existence of the United States and the kind of domination it exercises*. To say that capitalism is capable of producing everywhere else what it has produced in the United States is simply propaganda; and to maintain, as a French writer recently did, that European workers would reject socialism if they were offered the alternative of wages on the American scale is to ignore the fact that French capitalism, for example, is incapable of paying wages on that scale. That it may acquire this capacity in twenty years' time is neither here nor there: the Vietnamese and Algerians revolted against France to gain rights and possibilities which the French had possessed since 1789.

If it is therefore unacceptable to base a judgment of capitalism on the internal achievements of the most advanced capitalist country without taking into account its relations with the rest of the world, it is no less unacceptable, on the other hand, to judge socialism by the comparable achievements of the U.S.S.R. without taking Russian history into account. At the present time there are only two industrially developed socialist countries, East Germany and Czechoslovakia. For historical reasons they are only now beginning to look for an original pattern of development suited to their stage of evolution.

Until now socialism has presented itself as the shortest road, indeed the only possible road, to development, bearing in mind the absence of an *independent* national bourgeoisie; and, moreover, taking into account the obstacles placed in the way of balanced economic development by imperialism. In no country has socialist revolution taken the form of the collective appropriation of an already developed productive potential, and therefore of the subordination of economic necessities to the demands of collective and individual human liberation, such as the creation of a genuine democracy founded on the power of the producers to regulate production and exchange according to their needs.

Socialism has until now been regarded as a method of accumulation whose efficiency and superiority reside in management of the economy as a whole. That is why the construction of the foundations of socialism has necessarily been accompanied by a weakening of direct democracy, of popular power as it existed during the period of the revolutionary conquest of power. During this early phase the intolerable conditions to which everyone was subjected made it possible to unite the laboring classes in a common struggle. Only by concerted action of all can conditions be changed; therefore, each individual requires of his fellows the form of union characteristic of an active group, and within the combat group each individual finds himself in a reciprocal relationship with the whole.

During the period of revolutionary union for the conquest of power, individual liberty coincides with collective liberty, and the sovereignty of the individual exists *for* the group and *through* the group for the purpose of achieving a *common goal* identical to his own aims. But this coincidence cannot survive the winning power, at least not until scarcity has been overcome. It cannot survive because the first task of the victorious revolution is to diversify the communities of producers in view of the diversity of tasks to be accomplished.

The nature of these tasks, at the existing level of development of the forces of production, prevents their interchangeability: specialized subgroups, corresponding to the horizontal and vertical division of tasks, have to be set up. In the initial stage each subgroup may derive its power from direct democracy, on the pattern of factory soviets or self-managing communes. But the problem of co-ordinating the activities of these local groups arises very quickly. This co-ordination *might* be achieved by democratic mediations *if* the groups were free to make the optimization of *local* conditions their main concern. But that is precisely what they cannot be allowed to do in conditions of underdevelopment and scarcity. The first task of local producers must necessarily be the creation of a *surplus* for investment, and the investment policy must be related to a long-term development *strategy* of which the necessity may not always be apparent to local groups, and which may be in contradiction to their immediate needs.

The democracy of soviets or self-managing communes must therefore be subordinated to a group specializing in the planning and co-ordinating of the economy as a whole, that is to say, a sovereign, central group, the state, which robs the low-level groups of at least part of their sovereignty, being the embodiment of a Truth and Unity of their activity which becomes external to them.

This process, which Sartre has examined at length in his *Critique de la raison dialectique,* is common to all socialist revolutions in underdeveloped countries, including the Yugoslav revolution even *after* 1950. In my view we must not deceive ourselves as to the possibility of preserving the sovereignty and democracy of producer groups during the phase of the construction of the *bases* of socialism. We must on the contrary accept the dialectical necessity of some state centralization, and it is only by doing so that we can, from the outset, build in institutional safeguards which will limit and control the process of centralization and arm the revolution against bureaucratism, terror and despotism.

The socialism of scarcity and accumulation, although it abolishes exploitation, cannot, therefore, claim to put an end to alienation. It *cannot do so* because, during this phase, the relations of production cannot be wholly transparent to the producers, and also because the whole process of production is still governed by the laws of political economy, the science of rational allocation of scarce resources. This economic logic is, of course, opposed to the ultimate aims of communism; but it is a material impossibility, under present conditions in Yugoslavia, U.S.S.R., Cuba or China, to subordinate production to the needs as they are felt, or to those which would become manifest if they were encouraged to determine themselves freely. From the time of Lenin, on the contrary, socialist man has been defined as embodying—and encouraged to—*subordination of his individual needs to the requirements of production.* The satisfaction of needs has been assimilated to the simple reproduction of the labor power, which has been required to reproduce itself as cheaply as possible.

Thus the society of socialist accumulation has perpetuated the divorce between the concrete individual and the social individual, between individual interest and the general interest. But it has sought to interiorize the divorce by asking the individual to repress his individual needs *himself* in the interest of the community as a whole.

In capitalist society, on the contrary, individual needs and the necessities of accumulation are *separated* and may take the form of class antagonism. The functions of accumulation and production, indeed, are generally separated, the one being the province of the capitalist, individual or collective, the other that of the class of workers and employees, and of the peasantry. The contradiction between the logic of accumulation demands (which is to produce in order to produce more, and to work in order to obtain maximum profit) and the logic of human needs (which is to work in order to create a human world and life) *may* have a degree of free play under capitalism. This can happen *if* and *when* the working class has gained trade-union and political rights, which is far from being the case everywhere. When it has acquired these rights it is *possible* for it to contest the inert demands of capital in the name of the living demands of the people subjected to capitalism. And it is possible, on the basis of this contestation, for the working class to define the project of a radically different society in which production will be subordinated to needs— needs whose nature and priorities will grow in scope and depth as the level of consciousness and awareness rises. It is only through this work of contestation, reflection and struggle that the project, the pattern of socialist democracy and socialist man, can be born.

But clearly in the U.S.S.R. contestation and reflection of this kind were necessarily repressed. Under the conditions that existed in 1917, of extreme scarcity, constant external danger, and the insufficient or total lack of skill of a labor force torn away from agriculture, there could be no question of subordinating the *manner of producing* to the need for broadening human faculties through work, or of adapting the *nature of the product* to individual needs. In other words, the moment of positive contestation which, under capitalism, finds its expression in the trade union and the workers' party, could be allowed no expression under the socialism of scarcity and accumulation.

On the contrary, the logic and the task of accumulation had to be carried by the working-class leaders themselves, and so one found these leaders, at every level, reinventing an ethic of productivity which in certain respects resembled the ethic of the puritan bourgeoisie in the heroic age of capitalism: namely, an ethic of self-denial, frugality, austerity, unremitting labor and self-discipline, and also of moral vigor, prudery, cleanliness and sexual repression. Man, according to this ethic, was not brought into this world to enjoy himself and cultivate his senses, but to surpass himself in his passion for work; he would reap his reward in the future society for the sake of which he was sacrificing the here and now.

It is the historical circumstances of socialist accumulation and the ethics of productivity they determined which account for many of the shortcomings of present-day socialist society, shortcomings which appear all the more paradoxical since they run counter to the aims of communism. An example is the backward state of socialist architecture and city planning, which have thus far been little concerned to create an urban environment in which people can live and move in comfort. Research in these fields has only just begun. The same is true of research in the fields of the arts, education and psychology, and of many fields of theoretical science. It is also true of research—essential to the communist outlook—concerning the adaptation to man of the conditions, the environment and the techniques of production, and concerning the optimum pattern of the division of labor and consumption.

In short, rather like the puritan bourgeoisie of the last century, the socialism of accumulation has deliberately relegated to the background (and censored, in the Freudian use of the word) all those needs which were not directly productive—that is to say, whose satisfaction was not necessary to the reproduction or increase of labor power. In the U.S.S.R., at least, the arts of living, cultural creativity and artistic taste and standards, have remained more or less stagnant at the pre-revolutionary level. Except in the Balkan republics, accumulative socialism has created an industrial landscape of which the main characteristic is its utilitarian drabness.

This deliberate choice of general austerity, accompanied by a general rise in the standard of living and education, constitutes a perfectly rational and efficient policy—but only up to a point. The point where it ceases to be efficient has now been reached in most European socialist countries, and its drawbacks are becoming clearly and retroactively apparent in a number of fields.

THE NEED FOR DEMOCRATIZATION

I shall start with the field of consumption, or, more exactly, the pattern of consumption. The socialist ethic has for so long been based on the principle that man consumes in order to work that socialism has been taken aback when the development of the forces of production has permitted the production and consumption of the "superfluous." Much has been written to the effect that the crisis in the system of central planning has been due, among other causes, to the impossibility of *distributing* the superfluous. It is undoubtedly the case that whereas, in conditions of general scarcity, the distribution of *necessary but scarce* products is simple, the distribution of *abundant or superfluous* products is more difficult: when one has emerged from the state of vital necessity, consumer demands and therefore decisions to buy become unpredictable. Central planning has been confronted by the problem of overproduction and under-sale of products such as washing machines, radios and clothes which corresponded to neither the needs nor the tastes of the people.

But what thus far has been far less discussed is the fact that this crisis in central planning is also, and mainly, a crisis of the *criteria* whereby the production of non-indispensable goods, their quantity, style and quality, is decided. In principle, under a socialist economy, these are matters that should be decided by the free choice of the associated producers. Theoretically one would expect this choice to be governed by an overall concept of the socialist civilization yet to be created; by concern for the progressive enrichment of individual needs and therefore of the

content of collective life, and for the progressive fulfillment of those needs by the growth of free social services
and consumptions—rather than individual ones—in a word,
by a coherent scale of priorities.

None of this has happened, for, in reality, production
policy has never been decided by the producers themselves.
During the period of general scarcity and intensive accumulation there could be no question of permitting free expression of the workers' needs. On the contrary, considering
the absolute material impossibility of fulfilling those needs,
the producers were asked to dismiss them from their minds
and, as good militants, repress them in others as well as in
themselves, treating them as shameful weakness, the Evil
in every man that prevented him from devoting himself
unreservedly to the general interest, to the Good, of which
the State Plan was the embodiment.

This practically unavoidable gulf between the general
interest (that of accumulation and of the Plan) and individual and collective needs inevitably prevented *positive*
reflection on the pattern of life and civilization of the future
socialist society. The Plan could not be the "democratic
expression" of concrete needs, its priorities could not be
democratically determined. It is true that in creating the
foundations of socialism the expressed intention was the
future satisfaction of social needs. But between that future
and the present lay such an immense complexity of mediations, such a *dense* period of time, that for the present
it was necessary to repress the consciousness and the expression of needs. Authoritarian planification and bureaucratic centralization of decisions were the scarcely avoid-
able outcome of this situation.[1]

[1] They were particularly difficult to avoid in Russia, where
the Bolshevik Party was an elite vanguard with hardly any roots
in the predominantly peasant mass of the people; where most of
the best elements of the party—and even of the proletariat itself
—had been wiped out by the civil war; and where the destruction caused by the civil war had led to a situation of famine and
exhaustion which China did not experience to the same extent.
Moreover, whereas the Chinese Communist Party was built

Theoretical research as to the nature and pattern of
the needs which socialism was eventually to satisfy thus
became a purely academic exercise. Such needs could not
be grasped and specified in their living reality, nor could
the validity of patterns of life and consumption be verified

---

up as a mass vanguard in the process of a protracted people's
war, and considered itself the instrument of a revolution whose
subject was to be the people itself, the Bolshevik Party was
structurally and ideologically elitist, drawing its inspiration from
Western European Marxism and believing in the intrinsic superiority of Western methods (in the fields of technology and
industrialization).

But however great the impact of those historical factors,
which led to the aggravation of the authoritarian and bureaucratic style of Bolshevik government, bureaucracy and authoritarianism must not be regarded as evils that an underdeveloped
country can avoid completely during the period of transition
to socialism. This is borne out by the Chinese Cultural Revolution. The Chinese leadership has been careful not to set so
rapid a pace of industrialization and accumulation as to force
extraneous methods of production, management and leadership
upon masses that were not prepared to receive them; it has been
careful to ensure that economic development would bring immediate benefits to the masses; and it has not allowed the methods and pace of development to be imposed from above by an
elite of technocrats and bureaucrats who would tend to become
a new class, holding material privileges and the monopoly of
power.

It is all the more noteworthy that the formation of such a
class could not be avoided in China, a fact that is confirmed
by the Cultural Revolution against bureaucratic and capitalist
methods and mentalities within the Chinese party. The latter's
top leadership itself is well aware that the tendency towards
bureaucratization and reversion to capitalist social relations is
rooted in the material conditions of the transitional period itself, insofar as the requirements of accumulation which dominate this period have a logic of their own which is always in
virtual contradiction with the needs and the level of consciousness of the masses. The intensifying of this contradiction into
new social divisions can be counteracted, but the root cannot
be eliminated. Like revolution itself, the Cultural Revolution
cannot be completed once and for all.

by democratic discussion in producers' or low-level party assemblies. Just as the Plan itself, during the period of forced accumulation, was a bureaucratic concept imposed from above, so was all thinking about the pattern of civilization an ideological emanation from above. The party might expound general notions on the pattern of proletarian life as opposed to that of bourgeois societies, and insist on the priority of collective needs and consumption over individual needs and consumption, but none of these ideas could take root in the experience of the masses. These ideas were, for one thing, strongly contaminated with productivist propaganda. They were, on the other hand, suspect for very understandable reasons. In a situation where all essential goods, from potatoes to needles and thread, were in short supply or of poor quality, the emphasis on collective priorities sounded like an ideological excuse for central planning failures and the impoverishment which was poisoning everyday life.

Two conditions had to be fulfilled before any concrete research on the long-term shaping of socialist civilization could be undertaken. First, the stresses of daily life had to be relieved by a greater supply of everyday necessities, and secondly the whole system had to be democratized, to permit free research and the free, collective discussion of priorities and the pattern of life and work. But this free debate can be fruitful only if it is guided by a vanguard. The party can fulfill the functions of a vanguard only if it ceases to identify itself with tasks of administration and management which are cut off from the masses.

The fulfillment of the first condition, the raising of the standard of living, did not in the early stage call for any reform of the system of central planning. The unsatisfied needs were so universal that the administration could hardly go wrong in operating on purely pragmatic lines, regardless of what consumption priorities it might have in mind. But in the long run it is a matter of some importance whether a socialist society gets through a period of acute scarcity by increasing everyday consumer goods in a purely pragmatic way, or whether it does so by foreshadowing, through its scale of priorities, a new pattern of society, qualitatively different from that of capitalism, and a general concept of "true wealth"—that is to say, of the human potentialities which may be developed by production of the superfluous.

Socialism, in short, had to cease to be a state of scarcity, austerity and drabness; it had to satisfy individual daily needs so that the emphasis laid on cultural and collective needs, and their collective fulfillment, might be seen to be genuine. But as it moved in this direction it also had to demonstrate that the socialist pattern of consumption was not a tardy imitation but an innovation qualitatively superior to the capitalist pattern.

Thus far this demonstration has been lacking. Everything has happened as though production and consumption policy, even in its long-term implications, was mainly an imitation of capitalism. Priority has been given to the type of individual equipment popularized by so-called affluent capitalism. This was normal in the case of such things as bicycles, motorcycles, radios and canned foods, but less so in the case of cameras, refrigerators and individual washing machines, since the housing shortage and smallness of apartments create acute problems for the town dweller, and since the installation and improvement of cheap collective services—such as public transport, shops, nursery schools, house canteens or restaurants, delivery laundries— would free women from domestic chores and hold greater advantage on all levels. Why, for example, was it thought necessary to produce washing machines, notably in the U.S.S.R. and Czechoslovakia? And why, since the dismissal of Khrushchev (who had different views on this particular matter), has the U.S.S.R. been concerned with the development of private motoring?[2]

[2] There can be no objection to this development from the point of view of quantity. The U.S.S.R. will have a population of about 250 million in 1972, and by then will be producing a million private cars a year.

Three factors of unequal importance seem to have operated.

1. Semi-durable equipment is comparatively easy to produce in existing plants and by existing technical methods. Its production enables at least a part of the unemployment or latent underemployment in the U.S.S.R., Poland, Hungary and Yugoslavia to be rapidly absorbed. It also enables factory managers and planning officials to achieve a rapid expansion in the volume of production, since it is easier to meet the *quantitative* requirements of the Plan by the production of "semi-durables" than by installing or improving collective services.

2. The "luxury" character of these products, in the local context, provides an outlet for the excess purchasing power of the higher strata of city workers. For a long time there were no goods available for people in this category, who were earning from twice to five times as much as manual workers, to spend their money on.

3. Individual equipment is what capitalist industry offers the families and what capitalism regards as the yardstick of development and of living standards.

What is open to criticism is the quality of the vehicles being produced. It seems that, at least in the early stages of the program, these are to be developments of Western models which, as regards their use value, are far from being ideal. The priorities of use for motor vehicles in a socialist society may be grouped under three headings: (1) transportation for *kolkhozians* over short and medium distances; (2) urban transportation —taxis and hired cars; (3) hired pleasure vehicles for excursionists and vacationers covering short and medium distances.

The first purpose would be best served by a vehicle combining the qualities of a jeep (or Citroën *deux-chevaux*) and a mini-bus; the second calls for a vehicle of small size and power, extremely simple mechanically and for preference electrically propelled; the third requires an appropriate version of the second, still to be developed.

The Western-type vehicle, clumsy, complicated, fast, fragile and costly, corresponds far more to the Western *consumer image* than to any of these uses.

Failing an overall idea of socialist civilization these three factors were becoming decisive. The masses of the "socialist" countries, having for so long been deprived of the superfluous and of the amenities of daily life, were inclined to compare their own state with that of workers in the capitalist countries and, since they had no other basis of comparison, to measure their standard of living in terms of the American pattern of consumption. Their leaders did the same.

But this is a trend that cannot be justified by pragmatic or technological arguments, however easy and convenient they may be. Marxism has laid sufficient stress on the ideological implications of technical decisions for this aspect of the matter not to be disregarded. The adoption, by socialist leaders, of "Western" consumer patterns as references is not an unimportant choice (any more than the adoption of American production techniques, as we shall see). That pattern has been so often, and rightly, criticized by Western Marxists, that the slogan proclaimed by Khrushchev in 1956, the "overtaking" of the United States, looks like a serious deviation.

We must look more closely at the reasons for this "consumer" policy, which now threatens to become irreversible. Clearly, individual equipment and collective equipment are often incompatible with each other. The privately owned washing machine, for example, operates against the installation of public laundries. The privately owned car upsets the whole urban structure and communications to the point that it eventually hampers the rational exploitation of public transport and militates against a great many forms of group and community leisure activity and life (notably by destroying the neighborhood as a living environment).

The tendency (particularly manifest in Hungary and Czechoslovakia) to reestablish, within limits, the free market as an indicator of consumer needs, cannot be regarded simply as a "democratization" of administrative planning. It is subject to the same criticism as the chatter about "consumer sovereignty" in capitalist countries. This criticism may be summarized as follows:

1. The consumer is never sovereign. He is only able to choose between a variety of products, but he has no power to bring about the production of other articles, more suited to his needs, in place of those offered to him. The production of the superfluous creates and shapes needs at least as much as it fulfills them. The market is not a democratic confrontation, on equal terms, between a variety of sovereign demands and a variety of offers designed to meet them. It is a place where huge production and sales oligopolies, possessing very wide powers of decision, encounter a fragmented multiplicity of buyers who, because of their dispersed state, are totally powerless to influence the production decisions of the firms. The nature of the market prevents it from being a place where collective choices can be formed or the collective will asserted. It is a place where fetishized products confront their fragmented producers, cut off from their own product, who have now become the "consumers."

2. Economic democracy, that is to say, socialism, means that production policy, and therefore all decisions relating to the nature and priorities of consumption, must be controlled by the "associated producers." No distinction between producer and consumer can be acceptable in a socialist outlook. The needs which production is required to satisfy are those of the workers themselves, and the use value of any given product has to be assessed in terms of the amount of social labor it entails. The need for the product has to be weighed against other needs which, because of it, may have to go unsatisfied (for example, the need for more spare time), and against other ways of producing it (more or less costly in terms of work). For example, should everyone have four pairs of short-lived shoes a year, or one solid pair and two short-lived ones? Should emphasis be laid on the improvement of collective services or on the supply of individual equipment, and in what proportions? Should there be a mediocre television

receiver in every apartment, or a television room in every apartment house, with equipment of the highest possible quality?

A production policy based on needs implies weighing the advantages of producing the superfluous against its cost in labor. This is possible, and has a meaning, only if the associated producers at every level—the factory, the sector, the union, the commune, the region—possess real economic power. This power of decision, of course, can be effective only if the decisions have been reached collectively after free discussion at the lowest level, in the institutions of direct democracy. Discussion and choice at this level clearly need to be enlightened and informed. *That is the role of the party.* It is within the bosom of the party that the vanguard of the proletariat can formulate the patterns of long-term production and consumption policies, testing these by democratic debate in the party's local assemblies, and then passing on their proposals (or the suggested alternatives) to the producers' assemblies.

The obvious prerequisites of all this are *autonomy of the party in relation to the administration,* autonomy of the union, and internal democracy within the party. That little if any progress has been made in the discussion and formulation of long- and short-term patterns of socialist civilization is largely due to the fact that the autonomy of the party, and its internal democracy, were suppressed during the period of forced accumulation in favor of control by the apparatus. Every apparatus tends to perpetuate its own power, and this is *one* of the reasons for the tendency to imitate the capitalist consumer society. Just as the dispersed and fragmented producer-consumers, having no collective influence over production policy, cannot conceive of any improvement of their condition except in terms of higher individual consumption, so the spontaneous tendency of the apparatus is to increase individual consumption *in order* to maintain and consolidate its own power and to maintain the producers in the state of individual consumers. By preventing the formation of a collective will, and the exercise of collective power in the field of production, the authoritarian administrators of the economy transform needs into needs of individual consumption—that is, into needs of escape and withdrawal into private life— and then for better or worse satisfy them on that level, to avoid having to make more far-reaching (political) concessions, or to prevent grievances from finding political expression.

This analysis of the situation, which is widespread among Czech communist intellectuals, has led them to the following conclusions:

1. The political monopoly of the party *apparatus* is the main factor in the depolitization of the masses, that is to say, in their lack of interest in everything outside the sphere of private life.

2. This depolitization is particularly manifest in the demand for individual consumer goods.

3. The apparatus pays for the maintenance of its political monopoly by anticipating this demand and encouraging individual consumption, thus distracting the workers from making democratic demands ("consume and shut up").

4. The building of socialism can take place only through democratization—the party must again become the party, the administration the administration, the union the union and the Plan the Plan.

WORK, LEISURE, CULTURE

However great the differences in other respects may be between capitalist and socialist societies, however great the disparity between their respective aims and priorities in the fields of education, culture, the best use of natural and human resources, health and social policy and so on, the reasons for the depolitization of the masses on the one hand and the emphasis on private consumption on the other hand are *formally* the same in both systems. The first of these reasons is that the individual, both as a producer and as a citizen, is deprived of all real power (which can only be collective) over the policies and conditions of production which shape his life both at work and outside it. Submitting to society rather than consciously creating it, and incapable of coinciding with his social reality, the individual tends to withdraw into the private sphere, regarded as the only one over which he has any control.

But there is more than this. His withdrawal into the private sphere—which in an advanced capitalist society means the sphere of so-called affluent consumption, and its illusory symbols of a sovereignty deprived of all substance —is not in the first place, or predominantly, the attitude of a *citizen* confronted by *society* but that of a *worker*, deprived of initiative, responsibility and the possibility of self-development in his work, who seeks compensation in non-work. That this attitude should be tolerated and even encouraged by the social system may at first sight look like a step towards liberation. But it is by no means a positive step *if the compensations offered in non-work become a pretext for justifying the authoritarian and oppressive organization of work (and of society) which created the search for compensation in the first place.*

It is impossible, particularly in a Marxist or communist outlook, to sustain the argument that technological progress has destroyed all creative forms of work, and that therefore production work is to be regarded as a boring necessity that the individual has to put up with so that he might find personal fulfillment by shrugging off work and absorbing himself in leisure activities. This thesis[3] can be

---

[3] Supported by some French sociologists, Marxist and otherwise, who, in fact, postpone the matter of industrial democracy until the era of automation, and use it as an argument for warping or rejecting the demand for worker control. This demand, although dispersed, is deeply rooted not only among the younger workers, possessing higher social qualifications than formerly, who suffer from the insufficient use made of their skills, but also among the new skilled workers (technicians,

sustained only if the forces of production have been so highly developed that a man's leisure occupations may be regarded as his *main social activity,* and his directly productive work as merely accessory (not only because of the short time it takes, but because of the power of automatic processes), that is to say, as *a sideline of his personal social work.* The essentials of communication, material and verbal exchanges, would in these circumstances take place outside the sphere of material production and would be based on a general affluence or social wealth. The integration of the individual within society, and the permanent reappropriation of the latter, would occur in the constant reordering of the social field (mainly cultural) by the free association and voluntary collaboration of individuals for the main *social* purpose (sanctioned by the cultural standards of society) of developing intellectual, emotional, aesthetic and political relationships and exchanges. Economic relations, those of work and production, would then cease to be the dominant and determining factor in social relations. The reign of necessity would have given way to the reign of liberty.

But that state of affairs is far from actually existing, if indeed it may exist some day. And so long as it does not exist *social relations will continue to be determined by work and production relations.* Social production will continue to be based mainly on human labor; social work will continue to be the individual's major activity, and it is mainly through his work that he will be an integrated member of society. It is *for and by* a certain type of productive work that his personality will be shaped.

If that work excludes personal initiative, responsibility, grouping, voluntary collaboration and free exchanges between individuals, the development of their faculties and

---

designers, production engineers, etc.) whose standard of education makes it difficult for them to accommodate themselves to the industrial hierarchy and the subordinate functions, lacking in responsibility, which are allotted to them in the productive system.

their autonomy, then the individual will be no more able to recognize himself in his social relations and in society than in the social work which society requires of him. The escape from the working world, and from the *social relations* which that world imposes, will be one and the same thing; he will seek to get away from both and find compensation elsewhere. And the fact that his withdrawal and compensatory activities cannot substitute a new order of *social relations* for that determined by the productive system means that his leisure activities can never become *effective social activities:* they can only be *private* and bring meager, abstract or imaginary satisfactions, such as games, fishing, shows, day-dreaming, hobbies, drink and excursions—all things whose only value is *in opposition to daily work and the prevailing social relations,* and which do nothing for the free development of the real man.

Consciously or otherwise, all patterns of the so-called "civilization of leisure" are based simply on the *quantitative* expansion of these private and gratuitous activities. They presuppose more free time for more excursions, private club games, hobbies, reading, entertainment, but these activities never lose, through their multiplication, their gratuitous nature of "vacation" from society and never acquire a creative social quality.

A society that introduces the thirty-two-hour or twenty-four-hour work week without at the same time changing the relations of production and work—where individuals after work disperse to their suburbs to watch television, dig their gardens, hold card parties, prowl the streets in "hooligan" gangs or join hobby groups—will have made no progress toward a higher form of civilization: it will simply be reproducing the American big-town subproletarian civilization on a larger scale.

Marx was thinking of something very different from the growth of leisure considered as socially meaningless time when he envisaged "the free development of human faculties" as being the full development of the social individual. That full and free development can in no circumstances be conceived as the fruit of *private* activity, even in a group.[4] The individual does not develop or liberate himself by attending night classes to acquire craftsmanship or a knowledge of foreign languages and literature; or by playing games in a closed circle, or by Sunday painting and poetry, or by traveling about the country. To the present-day industrial worker all these activities are meaningless except as compensations for the monotony of his work and the poverty of human relations in work. They prevent the atrophy of certain faculties but do not permit their full realization. They are imaginary forms of liberation, games and escapism. Rejecting (or putting in parentheses) the social world without creating any other, they have no objectivity, and no real object.

There can, then, be no proletarian culture until the barrier dividing the world of work from the world of leisure has been broken down. Leisure activity can be no more than a compensation and a way of passing the time, with no cultural (and therefore social) relevance, until it has found an extension, an outlet and a practical application, in the most important of all social activities—namely, work. So long as this, while continuing to govern social relations, excludes, represses or discourages the free expansion of individual faculties, culture will tend to remain a private luxury, an abstract adornment and the negation of the real social individual, not his fulfillment. Its social value will not really be recognized, since a society which compels men to work like robots can only with difficulty recognize the importance, or even the possibility, of their human fulfillment. Such a society will be inclined to regard culture as merely one *utilitarian* activity among others (self-improvement courses, night schools, etc.) and to neg-

---

[4] The group itself may very well be private, that is to say, designed to create an atmosphere of intimacy and freedom *opposed to and outside* the social relations and therefore more or less forced and artificial—clubs, sports and holiday associations, sects, chapels, etc.

lect all aspects of leisure-time activities which do not increase *directly* productive labor power.

It is essential for the creation of a popular culture that social work should call for the full development of human faculties and enable them to be used in the interest of all. There can be no emancipation of the social individual in his free time unless he is also emancipated in his main social activity—work.

Such emancipation was clearly impossible under the socialism of scarcity. Decisions affecting the division of labor and the *manner* of working could no more be left to "the freely associated producers" than could decisions affecting production policy. This became impossible once the Soviet leadership had given top priority to industrialization and forced accumulation, subordinating political to economic considerations and widening the gulf between the leadership and the masses. The situation was further aggravated by the decision to impose Western techniques of production, and consequently a division of labor similar to that under capitalism, upon newly urbanized peasant masses. The adoption of advanced capitalist methods inevitably rendered even more acute the shortage of competent technical and managerial personnel, thus increasing the power and privileges of the "cadres," their estrangement from the workers, and their reluctance to submit to control from below and to rely upon the creative initiative of the masses.[5] In short, the introduction of capitalist methods

[5] Czechoslovakia and East Germany are special cases. Although the possibility of worker democracy existed in both countries, it was not able to be developed because of the international conditions in which socialism was built. Both countries were brought into the socialist camp at a time when, encircled, threatened from outside and devastated by war, they were forced into autarky. Both countries did more than their share in assisting the reconstruction of the Soviet economy, and both suffered from its impoverishment. For political reasons arising out of the international situation, the Czechoslovak rev-

and production techniques produced the same oppressive working conditions and social divisions as existed in capitalist societies, the same discipline and the same paramilitary hierarchy. It is scarcely surprising that we should find the same tendency to withdrawal among workers under both systems, the same desire to escape from industrial reality.

The key to the emancipation of the workers and to industrial and socialist democracy, the first condition of the power of the workers in production centers and in society, is therefore the abolition of methods of production and organization of work that remain as dehumanizing as they were a hundred years ago. Until they are abolished, the self-determination of the worker in his work, his needs, his consumption and his social relations will encounter obstacles difficult to overcome. To say this is to say nothing

---

olution—which, regardless of the form it took, represented a majority movement—brought about an acute shortage of qualified personnel by removing "cadres" of bourgeois or petit bourgeois origin and replacing them with proletarian "cadres"—a kind of workers' primitivism which did not begin to be corrected until about 1960.

In East Germany the original forms of worker power that emerged after 1945 were progressively reduced from 1948 onward, following a program of accumulation which was rendered more intensive by the fact that the German Democratic Republic had not only to achieve its own reconstruction but also to pay extremely heavy reparations to its eastern neighbors (some industrial plants were shipped to Russia and reconstructed as many as three times). The main cause of the 1953 revolt was the re-establishment of authoritarian relations of production and work. The revolt led to notable concessions on the part of the state. Workers' production councils were never destroyed in East Germany. They have been gradually incorporated into the state apparatus, while the stifling of worker power at the lower level has been accompanied by an increase of private and social consumption which has finally put East Germany first among the socialist countries in regard to living standards, education and social services.

new. Marx understood it in the last century. Communism does not mean equality in work, consumption and culture. It means the emancipation of the worker by the abolition of wage labor itself, and this calls for a development of the forces of production that has not thus far been achieved.

TRADE UNION, PARTY AND STATE

The only way to create a society founded on the liberation of the worker, in which the social individual is in control of his consumption and social relations *because* he is in control of his productive work and work relations, is to recognize the original contradiction between his needs as a worker and as a consumer. Although exploitation is abolished in a socialist society, that contradiction still exists to the extent that scarcity still exists. To deny it by postulating a unity of producer and consumer which does not exist in practice is to require the subordination of the producer to the consumer, the sacrifice of needs and aspirations regarding men's working lives to the need for higher consumption (and therefore higher production). To deny this contradiction is to deny alienation in work, and to prevent this alienation from becoming conscious.

If the contradiction is to be overcome, and alienation in work abolished, both phenomena must be recognized. This recognition implies the free play of dialectical tension between needs in the field of work and needs in the field of consumption. This means the free expression and representation of needs *at the specific levels* where they appear —at the level of daily life on the one hand and of working conditions and relations in work on the other. And the only way of ensuring the representation and free expression of these needs at these specific levels is by preserving the *independence and representative nature* of the unions, both at work and in society.

The superiority of socialist civilization over capitalism is not simply a matter of more rational organization, greater equality, fuller satisfaction of social needs and better collective services and amenities. The fundamental and decisive superiority of socialism lies in the liberation of the worker at the level of the productive act and of relations of production. This will have been achieved only when the collective ownership of the means of production also means that the worker feels himself to be "at home" in the plant and in his work because he has the power to regulate the production process according to his needs, both in its development and in the social and technical distribution of tasks. The power of the working class is also the freedom of the workers to impose their collective will on their conditions of work.

Only an independent union, enjoying the confidence of the workers because it *unconditionally* defends, both in the factory and in society, the specific needs and aspirations born of work itself in the places of production, can really *know* those needs, formulate them and act for the purpose of optimizing the conditions of work and life. Does the pursuit of this goal conflict (in theory) with the pursuit of maximum productivity and production?[6] That is all the

[6] I say "in theory" because although management tends to postulate this conflict and consider it as the reason for the industrial hierarchy, it is notorious that, even on assembly lines, output can be increased by measures of optimization which diversify the work and restore a degree of initiative and responsibility to the worker—job rotation, job enrichment, rest breaks, self-management at shop level, on the assembly line, in the work teams, of the technical division of tasks and of the organization of work, etc.

Vance Packard quotes the striking example of Non-Linear Systems, Inc., which enriched jobs by giving small teams of workers—or individual assembly workers—complete intelligible tasks to perform calling for the exercise of responsibility and initiative. At the same time clocking-in was eliminated. The result was that the number of work hours required for the manufacture of a computer was halved, and customer complaints reduced by 90 per cent.

more reason for entrusting the two aspects of the matter
to separate bodies. There is otherwise a danger that the
pursuit of optimization—in each town or plant or region—
will be neglected and production will remain the province
of technicians and productivists. Only through the independence of the union, its freedom to contest and put forward demands in opposition to management and economic
planning, and respect for its function—which is to look for
optimum working conditions and methods within the factory and living conditions outside it—can a dialectical tension be established between the demands of worker liberation and those of economic and technical efficiency.

This need for the union (and also the party) to be independent of management, government and the Plan, was
implicitly recognized at the Eighth Congress of the League
of Yugoslav Communists in November 1964 and has been
explicitly affirmed by leading Western European Communist parties.

This independence requires two complementary aspects:
(1) freedom to put forward demands, and (2) the power of
the workers to determine the working conditions of production.

(1) The union's freedom to advance day-to-day claims
is one of the principal means by which the collective needs
arising from the industrial environment become conscious.
It is necessary for these needs to be *collectively* formulated,
through the process of debate and collective thinking, if
they are not to be repressed, only to surface again as individual desires of escape and attitudes of solitary withdrawal. For it is through freedom of criticism and the expression of *collective* demands that the proletariat can
arrive at an understanding of the kind of civilization and
the scale of priorities its emancipation implies, and that its
adhesion to the Plan may be safeguarded, as well as the
democratic nature of the latter. Union demands give the
planners indispensable warnings and indications as to the
Plan's content, which in turn will be determined *and re-*

vised in permanent collaboration with the union, without the latter being *responsible* for its execution.

This last point needs to be emphasized. The cost of putting any plan into effect can never be precisely estimated in advance, if only because the new needs to which its execution gives rise (in Marxist terms, the value of the necessary labor power) cannot be exactly predicted. Only freedom of demand enables the inadequacies of the estimations to be perceived in time and corrected: such matters, for example, as the modification or deterioration of working conditions caused by technological reorganization or the restructuring of a branch of industry, and the shortages, inacceptable in practice, which a certain order of priorities threatens to create. Moreover, only freedom of demand can enable the value of the labor power—that is to say, the qualitative and quantitative needs—to be known in any particular set of circumstances, material and historical, local and regional. Without this information, and without sufficient flexibility and adjustment of work and wage conditions according to the needs born of work in a constantly changing environment, certain forms of work will be subjectively underpaid. The workers will be inclined to abandon them and forced labor will be necessary —that is to say, the adoption of authoritarian methods and the divorce of the leaders from the masses.[7]

[7] Bruno Trentin, in his address to the Gramsci Institute Conference on "Tendencies of European Capitalism" (1965):

"A part of the social costs involved in the implementation of a plan of development are *derived* costs, which are difficult to foresee, regarding both their nature and their extent. We have to consider the social repercussions which the process of industrial restructuring and technological transformation required by a national development plan will inevitably produce in the system of skill ratings, output norms, composition of teams, levels of employment and, in general, on the organization of work in factories. They are repercussions which, because of the prejudice, or at the least because of the new problems they

(2) On the other hand, we have only to read Soviet novels such as *Engineer Bakhirev,* by Galina Nicolaieva, to understand why it is that a factory manager, whether under a socialist or a capitalist regime, cannot get the best value out of the productive potential for which he is responsible unless he is under constant pressure from the workers, and constantly informed, by their freely expressed criticisms, of bottlenecks, latent possibilities, and necessary or possible improvements in working conditions. Hence the importance of this second aspect of union independence, worker power over the production process: that is to say,

---

create for the worker, will call for corrective or compensatory measures which only the unions can advocate in effective and consistent terms. It is through union demands . . . finally, that the social costs of a development plan find expression and *become measurable.*

"A general wage policy, or any other form of *a priori* centralization of goals, tends to prevent these unforeseeable elements from ever being included in the *real* and measurable costs of the plan itself. Thus it tends to conceal these real costs, at least quantitatively, from the society as a whole. And this brings the worst possible solution to the very delicate and complex problem of the relation between the plan and the laboring classes, and of the integration of the latter in a democratic system functioning genuinely at every level of society.

"We are here touching upon a matter of great importance for the whole methodology of planning. Upon its solution depends the capacity of any development plan to express, throughout the period of its execution, a genuine adhesion of the *majority* of workers, and to correct its aims, if necessary by modifying its fundamental decisions with the conscious, and always more democratically articulated, support of the social forces concerned. And I do not hesitate to state my belief that certain of the considerations I have submitted to you apply equally . . . to socialist planning, particularly when it has to deal with an advanced economy.

"Setting aside the numerous "technical" deficiencies in the forecasts of a socialist plan, I think it unlikely, if not impossible, that it will be able, *at the stage of its formulation,* however democratic, to resolve the countless unforeseeable prob-

over the organization of work, the composition of teams, the work speeds, the consequences of technical innovation and even their nature. Clearly the aim of this worker power must be to strike a balance between maximum efficiency and optimum efficiency. In particular it must enable the workers themselves to determine the best balance between the following variables: maximum satisfaction in work; maximum production and monetary earnings; maximum free time.

The implications of this system are clear. As soon as wages become sufficient to cover basic needs, the workers will be brought to ask themselves what their priorities should be—improved working conditions, increased wages or more free time? They will be brought to discuss these matters, not individually but *collectively,* with genuine col-

lems arising out of the objective contradictions which its implementation will create between the concrete interests of well-defined groups of workers, on the one hand, and what are *presumed* to be the interests of the whole community on the other. Even in a socialist society I think it highly improbable that the plan can anticipate all the social costs of its implementation . . .

"Even in a socialist context, and particularly in the case of industrially advanced economies, nothing can replace the autonomous function of the union, which alone is capable of converting the unknown factor represented by "derived" social costs into *definable and measurable* social costs, and of bringing to light the objective contradictions inherent in the application of the plan in such a manner as to enable the collectivity genuinely to resolve them, instead of evading them.

"This function of the union calls for a form of action which cannot be the mechanical endorsement of the policy of the central planning organisms but must consist of *both participation and contestation.* The union should not claim to represent by its action the community as a whole but only a *part* of society whose interests are to be brought to the attention of the representative and executive organisms of the state at every stage of implementation of the plan by means of a dialectical relation that is both collaboration and contestation."

lective power to alter their condition. And they will be
brought to seek not merely an increase of their individual
monetary consumption in return for more intensive work,
but also—and principally, once a certain point has been
reached—a *qualitative* improvement of their *common* situation both at work and in their community. They will be
able to decide, for example, whether to give priority to
individual wage increases or to free social services (nursery schools, transport, laundries, cultural amenities, vacation centers, etc.). They will be able to influence the orientation of technological innovations and the use to be made
of the plant's surplus (or profit).

But the matter cannot be left there. What we have said
earlier about the limitations and insufficiencies of local unionism and unionism in general applies also, in some degree, to socialist societies. The role of the union is to ensure the representation and unconditional defense of the
needs which arise out of work and the conditions under
which that work is performed, and to see to it that the
decisions embodied in the Plan take those needs into account. But it is not the union's role to formulate the general, long-term economic and social policies which imply
decisions of ideological and political nature, that is, the
definition of a pattern of civilization. That is the role of the
party. But for the party to carry out this task two things
are necessary. First, it must recover its autonomy in relation to the specialized administrative and economic organisms whose operations are governed by short-term technical imperatives. Such bodies are not necessarily able to
discern the implications of measures that seem the most
practical and effective at a given moment. And secondly,
the broad policies proposed by the party must be related to
living, concrete reality as it is experienced by the people
directly engaged in production work. But this reality can
only become manifest through the independence and
through the free and open debate of the specific groups

(unions, farm co-operatives, workers' councils, youth organizations, etc.) in which the people are organized.

That is to say, the party can fulfill its function as a guide only if it ceases to identify itself with the administration, the state apparatus, and the management of plants and current affairs, so that it can concentrate upon the political-ideological implications of the seemingly technical decisions that are constantly being made at those levels. The less it is committed to day-to-day technical decisions, the more it will have the farsightedness and authority needed to direct these in the long-term, global sense. And if this orientation is to be effective, if it is to stimulate the democratic participation—the politization—of the masses, it obviously cannot be imposed from above. It requires the party to be present at all levels, not to pass peremptory judgment but to clarify the debate, to unveil the political implications of seemingly technical options and to explain their meaning and long-term effect on that level: in a word, to raise the debate by introducing criteria of a higher level than those of the technicians.

This independent presence of the party, leading but not directly ruling, becomes more necessary as decision making becomes less centralized and the problems to be solved become increasingly technical. At this stage conflicts are liable to arise between particular interests of plants or industries, between macro-economic and micro-economic considerations, and between central planners, industrial managers, unions, workers' councils, etc. Such conflicts cannot be settled from above in any satisfactory way; they cannot be solved through temporary, pragmatic compromises which entail the risk of endangering or obscuring the overall aims of the socialist policy. These aims must be present at every level through the party's mediation, as the choice of a civilization in the process of permanent, collective formulation.

It is no accident that the Yugoslavs, having had a long experience of decentralization and also of the disadvantage of "practicism,"[8] have come to enunciate clearly the problem of the separation of party and state, and of the autonomy of different groups and social organisms having specific aims. The following is an extract from a report from Belgrade by Giuseppe Boffa which appeared in *Unità,* on September 15, 1966.

In their self-critical analysis of their movement the Yugo-slav Communists affirm that their League has become too exclusively a "power party" concerned with matters of direct state management, and has been led to substitute itself for the organs of the state in dealing with economic and administrative problems, as a result of which it has neglected the political and ideological questions which should be its principal field of activity. The party, they say, is more given to "ordering" than to "guiding." This is true both at the summit and at the lower level, that is to say, in plants, where party intervention is an obstacle to self-management. One of the leaders exclaimed: "Are we a party of bureaucrats or a workers' party?"

This state of affairs had two major drawbacks. On the one hand, the party and its leaders very often made decisions, notably in economic matters, for which they did not possess the requisite competence, thus short-circuiting the competent organisms and undermining their authority. On the other hand, being preoccupied with these administrative tasks, the party has paid little attention to the great political and ideological questions agitating the country and has thus lost its influence over the masses, their way of thinking and acting. This is particularly noticeable among the young people.

These are not problems peculiar to the Yugoslavs, and they did not discover them overnight. . . . They conclude that the party must be separated from the state, which means also separating it from such other social organisms as unions,

[8] The word designates (and denounces) the identification of the party with the practical tasks of administration and management, and its degeneration into a pragmatic bureaucracy. See the report of Edvard Kardelj to the Eighth Congress of the League of Yugoslav Communists, published in *Economie et Politique,* March 1965.

self-management organisms, the Socialist Alliance, and abandoning the "conveyor belt" thesis, which, rejected in theory, has never been abolished in practice. The party should become less and less the body exercising power . . . It should on the contrary seek to become the real ideological and political "guide" of society, not through its "ideological monopoly" but through its ceaseless work of confrontation and persuasion.

. . . In short, the League should everywhere become the political party fighting for self-management and direct democracy, both at the summit of the state and in every plant where the centralizing and authoritarian tendencies of the manager or his representatives need to be checked. Ideological discussion should also be more freely developed in party organizations.

These remarks are not intended as an abstract criticism of European socialist regimes. They seek, rather, to define certain material and historical circumstances which for the workers in those countries have given rise to forms of alienation different from those created by capitalist industry but not always easier to accept. But we must not conclude from this that the two systems are the same and that they can be treated alike. For the majority of socialist countries the choice was not between a socialist and authoritarian process of accumulation and one which is capitalist and "democratic"; the alternative was, and still is, for two thirds of mankind, between a reactionary dictatorship incapable of valid social development, on the lines of Guatemala, Brazil, Turkey or South Korea, and a popular dictatorship such as we see in Cuba, China and North Vietnam.

But for the workers' movement in the advanced capitalist countries the fact remains that the socialism of accumulation as practiced in Eastern Europe is not a valid pattern or a way of solving the problems of advanced industrial civilization. In other words, the Soviet experience cannot serve as a basis for evaluating socialist policies in Western Europe or North America.

Chapter 6

Colonialism at Home and Abroad*

* Text of a lecture delivered at the Mexican National School of Political and Social Sciences, Mexico, February 1966.

Colonialism is not an *external* practice of monopoly capitalism. It is, in the first place, an internal practice. Its first victims are not the exploited, oppressed and dismembered nations but the populations living in the metropoles, in the dominant countries.

That is the thesis I propose to illustrate here. It may appear surprising, even outrageous, since it runs counter to widespread and convenient oversimplifications. The custom in these days is to divide the world crudely into two camps, that of the highly developed imperialist nations and that of the dominated and exploited nations. The current view is that the problem confronting the next few decades is that of the emancipation of nations representing 54 per cent of the world's population but sharing only 16 per cent of the world's wealth. The rich nations and the "proletarian peoples" are set in opposition to one another as if they were both monolithic blocs. This idea of *global* antagonism may be natural and useful to peoples engaged in armed resistance to the invading forces of imperialist power, but it is a concept which in the long run is likely to rebound upon its protagonists.

In the first place, there is the risk that the division of the world into imperialist and oppressed *nations* will encourage a belief in the national *unity* of peoples in the struggle against imperialism. This belief in "national democratic states" was in high repute in the U.S.S.R. during the last phase of the Algerian war. Since then it has lapsed into the background. Because although *certain* wars of liberation (in North Africa, South Asia and the Caribbean)

were *at a given moment* national wars in which the bourgeois classes participated as co-leaders, once national independence had been legally and formally achieved the liberated nations became rapidly divided within themselves
on the question of what *content* their independence was
to be given. The bourgeois classes, although they may
have been in the forefront of the struggle for liberation,
now allied themselves with their former external enemies
against their domestic class enemies, and in their own class
interests re-alienated a substantial part of the national independence. In Africa especially, all the newly liberated
countries have reverted to a state of political and economic
dependence on imperialism, except those where liberation
has been followed by the establishment of a socialist-
oriented state.

The division of the world into imperialist and oppressed
nations has the further disadvantage that it cuts the world
revolutionary movement in two. It is easy to reply that the
laboring classes in the advanced capitalist world today are
not revolutionary, and that there is little to be gained by
uniting with them. The argument, although it may be immediately and tactically valid, cannot be sustained in a
context of long-term strategy. It amounts to abandoning
all hope for socialism in the advanced capitalist countries, and to envisaging a world where the so-called rich
nations will all be on one side of the barricades and the
poor nations on the other, and in which socialism can be
achieved in the advanced countries only as a result of
world war.

That is why I think it is important to stress the fact that
the dividing line between development and underdevelopment, dominating economic powers and dominated populations, colonizers and colonized, is one that runs not only
between nations but also *within* every nation in the capitalist world. The unity of the world revolutionary movement is not a problem that should be posed simply in terms
of political-ideological solidarity with anti-imperialist movements; we have also to show that there is a concrete con-

vergence and solidarity between the interests and struggles of both underdeveloped and developed peoples. The best approach, I think, is through a critique of the pattern of monopolist development, which enables us to see that colonialism is not merely an *external* practice of modern capitalism, but also an *internal* practice going on within the imperialist country and extending without any break in continuity to countries beyond its frontiers.

This fact is beginning to be recognized in the United States by what is now called the "New Left." The New Left was born originally of moral indignation at racism and poverty within the country, and quite naturally it has come to relate the struggle against poverty and oppression at home to the struggle not only against the outward *manifestations* of American imperialism but also against the whole economic *system* on which American imperialism abroad and internal poverty rest.

The fact that monopoly capitalism is incapable of solving the problems of employment (or unemployment), education, balanced development of the national economic "space," inequality of income and opportunity, conservation of natural resources, development of collective services and social infrastructure, etc.—this is the essential fact on which criticism of the new forms of economic imperialism must be based. It shows not only that the struggle against imperialism abroad can find allies within the imperialist country, provided it fights imperialism in the name of a different pattern of development and civilization, but also that neo-colonialism can no more solve those problems in its dependent countries than it can at home. I will start, therefore, by recalling certain facts concerning the United States and other advanced capitalist countries.

In 1965, after five years of economic "boom," there were in the United States 38 million people, 20 per cent of the population, whose family incomes were below the $3,000 per annum regarded as the American minimum. To these may be added another 20 per cent whose incomes, ranging from $2,800 to $4,812, were below the $5,500–

$6,500 reckoned by the Bureau of Labor Statistics to be necessary to ensure, to an urban family of four, a "modest but decent" standard of living.

This poor or destitute population may be divided into three broad categories.

1. The urbanized inhabitants of undeveloped regions, or of regions structurally undermined by the decay and disappearance of a local industry.

2. The small farmers, representing a quarter of the American farmers but whose output is economically negligible.

3. The sub-proletariat in the big towns, composed of young people and recent immigrants from rural districts who are unable to find jobs, members of racial minorities, old people, and 17.6 million employees in services such as laundries, hotels, restaurants and hospitals which pay less than the minimum wage.

The poverty of this sub-proletarianized mass is structural not transitory. Michael Harrington, in *Dissent,* quotes the following facts. The poor represent 20 per cent of all Americans. But 25 per cent of all children come from the poorest families and are in turn condemned to poverty by their low standard of education, verging on illiteracy. The great majority of the 25 per cent of recruits rejected by the Army because of an inadequate educational background come from poor families.

In 1965, despite the economic "boom," the conscription of an additional 200,000 soldiers, and orders for military supplies arising out of the war in Vietnam, the official unemployment figure was still 5 per cent of the working population. If we include people in part-time employment, and those who have given up looking for work, the figure rises to 6–10 per cent. The working-age population is increasing at the rate of 1.5 million a year. Between 1957 and 1963 the number of industrial jobs fell by 300,000. The 600,000 new jobs created in the private sector during this period were almost entirely in the "service" sector.

The United States, that is to say, presents certain social

and regional contradictions resembling the relationship between a dominant economy and a dominated one. Its internal development has broadly proceeded from its urban centers in the East, with their industrial concentrations and financial dynasties. The power of the New England bourgeoisie over the development of the economy was for a long time undisputed. Not until oil was discovered in Texas and sources of private accumulation were created by public finance (i.e., creation of war industries in California) did other large industrial and financial centers emerge at the other end of the country.

But the existence of several poles of development, policy making and economic power has not led to a balanced expansion of the nation's human and material resources. The reverse has happened. The geographical concentration of the process of capital accumulation has been accompanied, inevitably, by the relative or even absolute impoverishment of other regions, which have been used by the power centers as reservoirs of labor, raw materials and agricultural products. As happened in the European overseas empires, these "peripheral" regions have provided the metropoles with their savings, their labor-power and their people without having the right to reinvest the capital accumulated by their efforts in their own area. No new industries, for example, have been created to take the place of the coal mines when pits have been worked out or have ceased to be profitable. Thus whole areas have become zones of unemployment and poverty, in some cases robbed of their substance to the point of no return—that is, the point at which, from lack of a sufficient youthful population, and of industrial and cultural centers, they can no longer be developed. They sometimes revert to the desert.

This process of geographical concentration, entailing the abandonment of vast, formerly prosperous areas and the overcrowding of others, cannot be ascribed solely to the United States colonial tradition. The same phenomenon is to be seen today in Latin America and Western Europe. Outside the Paris and Rhone Valley areas there is scarcely any region of France which in ten years' time will be able to find employment for a reasonable proportion of the new generation which will have reached working age, or will have given up agriculture. The economic development of France is directed almost entirely from Paris. The old industrial regions have for a century past been used as sources of minerals, raw materials and production goods without any attempt having been made to valorize or process these products locally. The bulk of the surplus created by regional activities has been invested elsewhere, mainly in the Paris region, which is by far the main consumption and processing center in the country. It is exactly as though the provinces were colonies of the Paris metropolis. The speculative operations of the Paris banks, unconcerned with safeguarding the different regions against inevitable conjunctural hazards by diversifying their activities or processing and adapting their primary products, have in some cases reduced them to mono-production—textiles in the North and the Vosges, shoes in the Choletais, steel in Lorraine, wine in the Midi, and, more recently, natural gas and sulphur in Aquitaine.

Because of this quasi-colonial type of development the structural crises in the old established industries (textiles, boilermaking, coal mining, steel making, shipbuilding, etc.) and in traditional agriculture have taken the form of dramatic regional crises which have nowhere been resolved by the redeployment of activities according to local needs and resources. Any such development can be possible only if the regions and their local communities possess powers of economic and political initiative. The latent possibilities of a region, its human and economic potential, can be determined, and local energies and resources fully mobilized, only if the region enjoys genuine autonomy, through its own elected assemblies, and above all if its economic policy making is subject to a degree of popular democratic control and orientation which is clearly incompatible with private management.

Failing this, regional problems are "solved" by the reduction or suppression, without any countervailing action, of insufficiently profitable activities, according to the short-term profit standards of industrial and financial groups. Local populations are encouraged to migrate to urban areas, there to swell the flow of sub-proletarians coming from more distant countries, especially the former colonies. The movement from the country to the cities is accepted by French "planners" as a normal process. According to their predictions a quarter of the entire French population will be concentrated in the Paris region by 1980, and a quarter of the working population will be concentrated there by 1970. The West, the Center and part of the South-west will then be in danger of reaching the point of no return, preventing their future development.

This point of no return has already been reached in some parts of central France, in Sicily and in southern Italy. The latter country and, in recent years, Spain, afford a particularly striking example of internal colonialism. Migration from the South to the North, both in Italy and in Spain, has depopulated potentially rich agricultural areas, aggravated the shortage of food products meant for domestic consumption, accentuated economic dependence on the export markets of richer countries and, in short, driven industrial production along what may be termed "the Japanese way": that is, priority production in insufficiently developed countries of "gadgets" and "affluent" consumer goods for export to wealthier countries in exchange for machines, patents and food.

The policy of poles of industrial development, adopted in most capitalist countries, is no doubt advantageous from the point of view of the large private corporations, but it is certainly not so for the economy as a whole. The pole is generally a large or medium-sized town around which the state, at public expense, creates industrial zones which private industry is then "encouraged" to occupy by fiscal allowances, subsidies, grants of land, buildings, roads, etc. The industries which do so are generally subsidiaries of native or foreign monopolies. They are not concerned with regional development, but with the establishment of export industries oriented toward already developed regions—such as assembly workshops, heavy industries in the first processing stage and subcontracting plants.

Industrial development of this kind, based on medium-term profit assessments, attracts people over a wide area. But the population attracted from the surrounding countryside is very much less drawn by the industry itself than by the parasitical and tertiary activities that spring up around it: small shopkeepers, landlords, dealers in food and drink, middlemen of all kinds interposing a series of speculative transactions between the producer and consumer of food products and ordinary consumer goods. Far from fostering the region's balanced development, diversifying and enriching local activities, human relations and regional culture, the new industrial "pole" does the reverse: it debases the life of the region and destroys local culture, and creates a sub-proletariat which acquires the frivolities and perversions of industrial civilization without the advantages, particularly in the matter of education. The proliferation of speculative activities, notably in the commercial, land and real estate fields, the cost of the urban infrastructure and services, and the loss of agricultural production, finally represent a burden upon the region many times greater than the cost of balanced, progressive development suited to its needs.

This type of internal colonialism must not be confused with the indispensable process of concentration in densely populated agrarian districts, which is one of the primary conditions of agricultural development. Agrarian concentration, by the merging of small holdings and a partial exodus of the rural population, is essential to the production of an agricultural surplus, which is the only means of providing funds for investment in agriculture itself as well as in industrialization. But it is precisely *not* with this that we are dealing here. The exodus from the land to the point of no return is due to the fact that agrarian concentration —by land reform and the creation and capital endowment of co-operatives—is not taking place. It is not happening because the agrarian economy has already been pillaged and colonized by big capital, by big agriculturalists and feudal proprietors whose financial and political interests are closely allied to those of monopoly capital. In addition to these there are the trusts in the food industry, in fertilizers, in cattle feed, and in commerce, which integrate agriculture instead of themselves being integrated by it, treating it simply as a source of raw materials, robbing it of the possibility of autonomous development and appropriating the surplus it creates for investment outside agriculture and outside the region.

The crisis in agriculture has led to some investment in the opposite sense, that is to say, to large-scale, highly mechanized capitalist farming projects in some of the depressed areas. This is of little importance, for the following reasons:

1. Capitalist agriculture still accelerates the crisis by concerning itself principally with produce and cultivation which give the easiest and quickest gain in productivity, and concentrating investment upon these, to the detriment of other agricultural activities.

2. It neither produces all the varieties of products that are needed nor gives priority to those which are most important to the economy in general. It is more like the mining industry, which works for the benefit of an anarchic and speculative world market, not to supply local or national requirements.

3. In this it resembles external colonialism, with which it shares some financial and political characteristics, being closely involved with commercial and agro-industrial capitalism. Agrarian capital dominates agricultural sales co-operatives, credit systems, agricultural unions and politics. It confiscates a very large part of the surplus of the agricultural sector, absorbs most of the state subsidies, forces the collectivity to sell at a loss or destroy the surplus produced with a profit, and thus does its share in the looting of society.

So in the relations between industrial, commercial and agrarian capital on the one hand, and the rest of the economy on the other, we may discern aspects typical of the colonial relationship. These are not confined to the economic plane. It is also politically necessary for corporate capital to prevent the peasants from uniting, from extending their co-operative activity to other fields related to agriculture, thereby reconquering their autonomy, taking control of the manufacture or purchase of equipment used in agriculture, and liberating themselves from subordination to big capital in the processing and distribution of agricultural products.

In general, monopolist development tends to accentuate regional as well as sectoral disparities. The uneven development of different sectors would do no harm if the more rapidly growing sectors lent impetus to the rest and to the economy as a whole. But this does not happen. Under the system of monopolist accumulation the key industries, those whose development in fact takes priority, are those promising the most rapid gains in productivity; they do not manufacture capital equipment but consumer goods, particularly "durable goods"—that is, things for individual consumers.

These industries are the prime movers even in semi-developed capitalist countries such as Spain, Japan and some of the Latin American countries. They specialize in non-essentials, in the manufacture of articles which are necessary neither for the satisfaction of elementary needs nor as means of production. These are the so-called "affluent" goods: private cars, home refrigerators and washing machines, televisions and transistor sets. Industries operating in this field require a high degree of technical and financial concentration. They drain away the savings of not only the parasitical strata of society but also the popular strata, to the detriment of other fields of investment and development.

Hence the familiar spectacle, in America and Europe, of slums with televisions, shantytowns with private cars, homes with refrigerators but without bathrooms or running water, illiteracy with transistor sets. And it is not only in the semi-developed economies, but also in those that are highly developed, that monopolist expansion, instead of abolishing scarcity, merely shifts it to other levels. The priority given to "affluent" goods means fewer schools and hospitals, fewer cultural, agricultural and industrial infrastructures; it means a perpetual housing and slum crisis and insufficient public resources for combating air and water pollution and providing necessarily non-profit collective services; it means that highways, parking lots and high-speed urban trafficways are given precedence over improved systems of public transport and the rebuilding of towns to make them habitable.

The objections to "affluent" consumption are not based on moral considerations, nor need we condemn the process because it creates "artificial" demands in order to satisfy them. It is certainly true that the monopolies "manipulate" the public, individually and collectively, to promote superfluous consumption, and that this manipulation diverts profound needs into superficial desires, mystifies the demand for free time and autonomy with the endless invention and rapid obsolescence of gimmicks and status articles—anything from electric toothbrushes to gold faucets, from the electric carving knife to the individual shoe-polishing machine. There would be no harm in these frivolities if basic needs had everywhere been satisfied, and if the individual were free to work harder to buy whatever nonsense he liked, or to work less and do without. But he lacks this freedom and it is because he lacks it that "affluent" goods correspond to a genuine historical-social craving, although a manipulated one: the craving to "get your money's worth," since you have to give up your time to earn money whether you like it or not.

The conditioning of the public mind is effected less by direct advertising than by the system itself, which orders the distribution of public and private investment so that the individual can satisfy his needs only by acquiring the individual goods offered by the oligopolies. The private car, for example, is a real necessity because of the anarchic state of urbanism. Slums, air pollution, extensive urbanization and the inadequacy of public transport make it an essential means of escape, recuperation and transportation. At the same time, private motoring prevents the remedying of a state of affairs for which it only offers a palliative.

What has to be condemned is not "affluent" consumption *as such,* but the priority given to it, and the fact that it sterilizes a large part of the economic surplus *before* fundamental needs have been satisfied and conditions created for the free flowering of human faculties.

It is *a fortiori* absurd, if not criminal, to permit the circulation of "affluent" goods in a country still in the first stages of industrialization. The sudden appearance in the hands of a privileged minority, native or foreign, of the technical gadgets of an advanced society must necessarily have a corrupting effect on the Andalusian, Calabrian or Mexican peasantry. They see the results and by-products of technical-scientific civilization without even knowing anything about the system and methods that produced them. To the peasant masses these things have a quality of magic. The gulf between civilizations thus abruptly contrasted is so immense that to them no means of bridging it is conceivable. For the Andalusian day laborer, for example, the only way of acquiring the blessings of technology is money: but no amount of *work* will enable him to earn enough money. So all his needs are perverted and mystified into money needs.

In the metropoles themselves, scarcely educated adolescents in the poorer quarters of the cities undergo a similar process: their reaction is violence and a taste for violence, which is not only a direct and despairing negation of the social order and its privileges but also a form of magical appropriation, by consumption-destruction, of the prevailing civilization. Direct violence is the spontaneous response to a civilization which offers itself as something to be consumed, not something to be created. Violence is the truth of a civilization which has cut off the consumer from the producer and the producer from the product, uprooting the individual from his natural and human environment, and which has quantified—that is to say, reduced to external relationships—the relationship (in work) between man, his tools and nature, the relationship (in his habitat) between man and his environment, and the relations between man and man.

As René Dumont, Frantz Fanon and Mao Tse-tung have all stressed in their different ways, it is of the first importance, in an underdeveloped country, to base development policy not on the planting of poles of growth and advanced industry in rural settings, but on a series of transitions designed to encourage the qualitative and quantitative development of human resources. One of the great lessons of the Chinese revolution is that an essential condition of long-term development is a healthy, solid agriculture, capable of its own wider reproduction.

Industrialization must never be allowed to give rise to the pillage of the rest of the economy. It must, on the one hand, grow up from the roots, that is to say, be shaped in accordance with the needs of the majority of the population, which is rural, under the control of agricultural working communities and by the creation, at their initiative, of local industries which are complementary to agriculture; and it must, on the other hand, operate from top to bottom only insofar as the creation of modern industrial complexes near the big cities serves to raise the level of agricultural productivity and the local industries complementary to agriculture. In other words, heavy industry can be a prime mover of the economy as a whole, ensuring its balanced development, only if it starts by supplying other sectors—and primarily agriculture—with production goods which raise the productivity and accumulative capacity of every sector.

Between the wooden plow drawn by men or animals, and the tractor-drawn multiple plow, there lies a series of intermediate stages which have to be taken into account, not only to maintain full employment but also because a national culture can be forged only by enhancing work culture and by the appropriation of nature, not by the brutal destruction of the traditional relationship between labor and nature.

I am far from suggesting, in these remarks, that development should be autarchic. It should be autonomous, which is quite another matter. This autonomy does not rule out the use of foreign techniques, or even the acceptance of loans or gifts, or, subject to reservations, foreign investment. Autonomous development means that the impetus of growth should come from within the society and should be based on the full use of its own material and human resources. It does not mean that a developing society must go through all the historical and technical stages which, in the past, have accompanied the transformation of essentially agrarian economies into industrialized economies, mechanized and automated. If this were necessary the gulf separating the developed world from the underdeveloped world would continue to grow wider instead of being bridged.

Nevertheless, although foreign help and even investment should be sought, it alone cannot solve the problem of development, either quantitative or qualitative. It can contribute to balanced development only on the following conditions:

1. That foreign aid or investment is fitted into the framework of an overall plan for the economy, the intentions of which it must respect.

2. That foreign technical personnel charged with carrying out a program of aid must be under the administrative and technical control of the beneficiary country, which obviously presupposes the existence in that country of technical personnel trained in several foreign schools and industries, and thus qualified to compare the advantages of different foreign techniques and combine them in the best possible way. A multi-national aid program is always preferable to aid from a single large country.

3. That the plant supplied shall be "normalized" so as

not to be dependent on the techniques or raw materials of the country supplying it.

4. That in the case of aid from private sources all materials shall be supplied on a rental-sale basis, so that after amortization and normal remuneration of the capital involved, they become the property of the beneficiary country.

5. That foreign techniques (licenses and patents) shall also become the property of the beneficiary country after amortization, and that during the amortization period they may be improved and modified without any restriction being placed on their use.

The above conditions have all been secured by Yugoslavia, to name one example. They are realistic by normal capitalist financial and commercial standards. The question is not whether capitalism will accept them but whether the developing country will have the *political* strength to insist upon them in order to safeguard its prospects of autonomous, balanced development.

I need not repeat here what has so often been said, that foreign, especially North American, investment policy has never aimed at stimulating the process of industrialization and development and that it does not have this effect. I will merely recall certain aspects of the new economic imperialism, basing what I have to say on a remarkable study by the Pakistani economist Hamza Alavi.[1]

Alavi points out, in the first place, that between 1950 and 1960, the balance of movements of American capital showed a surplus: although this was the period of the Marshall Plan and the big American military aid program, during which the United States exported $23 billion in public funds (mainly for military purposes) and $20 billion in private capital, $19 billion in foreign capital were invested in the United States during the period, while American investment abroad brought in $25 billion. Thus in the purely monetary sense American investments over a long period

[1] "Imperialism Old and New," *Socialist Register*, 1964.

represent a burden on the "beneficiaries," to which must
be added the flight of private capital from those countries
encouraged by the American system of free exchange.

Alavi goes on to distinguish between the old form of imperialism, based on the plundering of natural mineral resources, which never led to any kind of industrial development, and the new imperialism, which favors investment
in industrial sectors that *already exist*. Private foreign investment never *creates* an industry where one did not exist;
it thrusts its way into a process of industrialization that is
already taking place in order to control and restrict it, govern its policy and gain possession of the market it is creating. Monopoly capitalism, writes Alavi, "seeks to thwart
any real efforts in the underdeveloped countries to make
progress toward industrialization, which would affect the
secure exploitation of these markets. To the extent that it
cannot prevent progress toward industrialization, it seeks
to contain the drive toward it and to secure for itself participation in what cannot be prevented. But the nature of
this participation is such that in effect it undermines further progress. For the emphasis is on assembly and packag-
ing plants for foreign products, which so often go under
the label of manufacturing establishments. This effectively
circumvents measures taken to protect domestic industry."

Using neo-colonial practices in India as illustrations,
Alavi then describes how the native economy is robbed and
its development hampered. The repatriation of monopoly
super profits, which was the driving force of the old colonialism, is now of only secondary importance in the new
economic colonialism because the process is often limited,
in semi-colonies or nominally independent countries, by
their permanent balance-of-payments deficit, and the rapid
devaluation and difficult convertability of the national currency. If economic colonization were to aim primarily at
the repatriation of profits, the monopolies would be obliged
to insist upon financial stabilization, which means a defla-
tionary policy. But this would necessarily narrow the domestic market of the dominated country, limiting or pre-

venting its growth. Relatively stable expansion is possible only in modern, structured states. Where such states do not exist imperialism has no interest in letting them be created, for this would imply an upheaval in social relations and oblige imperialism to negotiate instead of dominating.

That is why the North American monopolies in particular tend to appropriate their profits in a secretive way, preferably before the goods they manufacture in foreign countries are marketed. Instead of incurring the risks of direct investment, they prefer to participate financially in "national" firms to which, under exclusive contracts, they sell raw materials, manufactured parts or, most often, the right to use patents under license. The charges for using patents and the super profits on the raw materials furnished to the "national firm" amount to a sum *higher than the total profits realized by that firm.* But as they can be entered in the "national" company's books as "imports of goods and services" their payment in foreign currency does not encounter the same political and psychological obstacles as the repatriation of profits.

These methods camouflage the looting of the dominated country without diminishing it. The repatriation of direct or indirect profits by foreign monopolies means that they are not available for investment or reinvestment within the dominated economy. Moreover, the technical progress of the latter comes within the sphere of influence of the foreign trust, which is enabled to dictate the pace of development and technical progress in a whole group of dominated countries. The training of skilled workers, with which the foreign companies are often credited, either does not happen at all or only on a small scale. Technical and administrative personnel are more often than not furnished by the trust, which also enforces rigid pre-established specifications for goods or parts manufactured locally, forbids any modifications and, in cases where the local branch is authorized to undertake any form of technical research, secures rights in the result and reserves its eventual exploitation for itself.

Even the international relations between a group of

countries come to be governed by the strategy of foreign monopolies. These decide, according to their own requirements, the international division of labor between Western European countries, for example, or Latin American countries. Certain American monopolies select a particular country—for example, West Germany or Mexico—as a base for the commercial conquest of a whole region of the world. By this means American imperialism creates countries which are *imperialist by proxy*, that is to say, countries that dominate others *in the interests of a third country by which they themselves are dominated*. American imperialism thus imposes national or provincial specializations at a low stage of industrialization, determines the development and the degree of progress in all the countries within the area, regulates international exchanges over an entire subcontinent, and in doing so places further obstacles in the way of the independence of each individual country and of the group of countries as a whole.

The dominated countries' opportunities for self-determination are not weakened in the economic field alone. Political intervention by the dominant country is continental. Only in extreme cases does this take the form of direct intervention, overthrowing regimes or governments, fomenting putsches, financing mercenary armies or sending in troops under false pretenses. Indirect intervention is less obtrusive and often more effective, and it consists of more than bribing national leaders, financing political parties, trade unions and regimes, and threatening retaliation if any injury should be done to the private interests of the metropolis. The mere knowledge that the metropolis *might* disapprove of the political victory of a particular party may be enough for the fear of retaliation to cause a swing in favor of the pro-American party, without any threat having been uttered.

Nationalism, which is the spontaneous reaction to this state of dependency, is not a sufficient answer, nor is it the right one. Democracy and internal autonomy can be gained in any country only through the conquest of its real sovereignty, and this can no longer be achieved on a national basis in the face of monopolies whose strategy is international. Moreover the urge to national sovereignty may contain political and economic elements as reactionary as the servile acceptance of external domination. In particular— as in Gaullist France, Franco's Spain or Pakistan—anti-Americanism may simply reflect the clash of two forms of imperialism, unequally powerful but equally evil, between which there is nothing to choose; the question is only to escape them both, by playing one against the other.

This brings me back to my starting point. Although nationalism may be a positive, progressive impulse, legitimate in the cultural sense, it is quite insufficient for combatting imperialism in the economic and political field. On the contrary, it enables imperialism to play one dominated country against another, to profit by the traditional rivalry of the weak and oppressed, and to create oppressors who will dominate their neighbors in the interests of imperialism, compensating themselves for their own humiliation by preying upon the weak.

The real field in which political autonomy and self-determined development can be regained is the political-economic field. But here the struggle can be effectively pursued only by the co-ordinated efforts of a number of nations, in the same continent or even in different continents. And it will achieve complete liberation only if its goals and principles speak to the hearts and minds of those forces within the capitalist world which are already fighting against the model of monopoly development, against the myths of the "affluent society" and against internal colonialism. Imperialism cannot be beaten at its periphery unless it is also attacked at its center, the metropolis itself.

That is why I believe that the situation and the problems confronting workers and socialist movements in the advanced capitalist countries are of vital importance for the peoples of the entire world, and why the present backward state of these movements, due to historical reasons, is a matter of serious concern, and not only for themselves.

The reverses which the workers' movement in the West has suffered during recent decades, its often low level of international consciousness, and the fact that capitalism has not been overthrown in any advanced country and is not likely to be in the near future—all this largely explains the divisions within the world revolutionary movement, and the impatience and skepticism with which certain anti-imperialist forces view the European workers' parties. All these things operate against a centralized anti-imperialist strategy on a worldwide scale.

In these days, as the recent Tricontinental Conference in Havana has shown, there can only be several separate, largely autonomous strategies. But the necessity for autonomous regional strategies does not mean that the division of anti-imperialist forces must be accepted. The very diversity of strategies makes it more necessary that they should be *co-ordinated*.

Chapter 7

Sartre and Marx

A Marxist can approach the *Critique de la raison dialectique,* the most recent of Sartre's philosophical works, in a number of ways. It would be possible to write a historicocritical essay on the complex dialectical relationship between Sartre and Marxism as a movement. It would be equally possible to write an essay on the history of philosophy, discussing Sartre's place in contemporary thought, showing the internal logic that led a philosopher whose starting point was the "cogito" of Husserl to move toward dialectical materialism, and studying the validity of this development and its compatibility with Marx's method itself. Finally, and best of all, it would be possible to do both at the same time—using the regressive-progressive method which Sartre himself recommends. In this case, one would start from Sartre's work as the singular enterprise of an individual, and then proceed to situate it in the historical context that conditioned it, showing how Sartre grappled with the problems of his time in general and Marxism in particular. This would provide a critical reconstruction of his own particular way of surpassing his problems and of being surpassed by them.

So far, none of these three possible approaches has been attempted by Marxist scholars. Whether in France, in Italy or elsewhere, most of them have postulated from the outset that Sartre must be an idealist since he has not repudiated his early work and its phenomenological method. And some have tried to prove this postulate by taking issue with the Sartrian vocabulary. Let us, therefore, define the aim and method of Sartre's work, before examining how it is related to and what it adds to contemporary Marxist thought.

The aim of the *Critique* is to found dialectical materialism as a method and to define the sector of being to which it is applicable. It is not as such an attempt to apply it practically in a specific field of inquiry. Put another way, the structures, notions and categories brought into play in the *Critique* are not yet operational, but pertain to the critique of a method which has been applied empirically by Marxists with success, without becoming conscious of itself and of its own possibility.

The attempt to found dialectical materialism is undoubtedly related in all sorts of ways to the work of the later Husserl. Husserl said of science in his time: "It has become unable to account for itself." This judgment is valid *a fortiori* for the human sciences and for dialectical materialism. Scientific praxis, by failing to question its own status, and by claiming to put lived experience in parentheses, has become opaque to its own practitioners. Man absents himself from the science he produces and it sheds no light on him. The sciences that study man take him for their object, ignoring the fact that the object is itself the subject (as a man of science) inquiring into it. They thereby prevent themselves from ever accounting for their own method and possibility. Finally, just as the man of science cannot understand his own practice from the point of view of the sciences which he produces, so Marxism has been unable to account for Marxists. In other words, Marxists become unable to account for themselves.

Husserl, in *The Crisis of European Sciences,* remarked:

> We lack the real insight by which the cognitive subject could account not only for his effective operations and innovations, but also for all the implied meanings that remain obscure and sedimented, all the underlying presuppositions of his instruments, notions, propositions and theories.
>
> Do not science and the scientific method today resemble a precision machine—a machine which is obviously rendering useful service, and which anyone can learn to manipulate

correctly, without having the least idea of the possibility and internal necessity of this kind of operation?

Thus scientific method, having developed into the progressive accomplishment of a job, is a *technë* [technique] which can be transmitted, but which does not thereby necessarily transmit its true meaning. Therefore theoretical tasks and achievements that can only dominate the infinity of their themes by the infinities of method, and the latter only by technical thought and activity, devoid of meaning, will be able to remain genuinely and pristinely meaningful only *if* the man of science has developed the capacity to return to the *original meaning* of all his notions and methods.[1]

In order to provide a foundation for the possibility of true knowledge, Husserl sought to rid scientific thought of objectivism—and the psychologism, epiphenomenism, dogmatism and skepticism which resulted from it—by restoring the original experience of the world as we live it. Sartre's efforts to provide a foundation for dialectical reason are close to those of Husserl, at least at first sight: the dialectic has no foundation unless it first experiences itself "as a double movement in knowledge and in being."[2]

DIALECTIC AND SCIENCE

Unless the existence of a sector of dialectical intelligibility is irrefutably confirmed in the unity of experience as deriving from the individuals, as "the logic of action," we can only speculate or make dogmatic assertions about it. The kind of dogmatism that asserts the *a priori* existence of a Dialectic of Nature and wishes to make human history into no more than a specific variant of natural history inevitably ends in skepticism: indeed, if human history is only one section of a much vaster and enveloping totalization and is ruled by the supposed finality of developments

[1] *Die Krisis der europäischen Wissenschaften.*
[2] *Critique de la raison dialectique* (Paris: Gallimard, 1960), p. 10.

in nature, then its truth lies outside itself and there can be no true knowledge.

As Kojève remarked, "If Nature is creative in the same way as man, then truth or genuine science are only possible at the end of time." The upholders of the Dialectic of Nature imagine that they can get out of this difficulty by allowing to man the privileged faculty of understanding the total meaning of developments in nature, while remaining immanent within them. But this metaphysical postulate—also to be found in religious systems, where man is supposed capable of knowing God and his Purposes—makes true knowledge dependent on a postulate and on the faith one has in it. This is why transcendental materialism can avoid skepticism only by refusing to question its own method, out of sheer dogmatism.

By making the meaning of human history depend on that of natural history, human history is subjected to a dialectic outside itself, in a way which Marx seems to reject when he writes, in the 1844 Manuscripts, that "man is his own origin."[3]

"If we do not want to make the dialectic into a divine

---

[3] "This external materialism imposes the dialectic as exteriority. Man's nature is found outside him in an *a priori* principle of extra-human Nature, in a history that starts with the nebulae. In this dialectic partial totalizations do not even have a provisional value. They do not exist. Everything is always reduced to the totality of natural history . . . Thus any real thought as it is actually formed in the concrete movement of History is taken for a deformation of its object. . . . But just when this skeptical objectivism is complete we suddenly find that it has been dogmatically imposed on us, in other words that it is the Truth of Being as it appears in the universal consciousness. The spirit sees the dialectic as the law of the world. The result is that we fall back into a completely dogmatic idealism . . . However we look at it, transcendental materialism leads to the irrational: either by suppressing empirical man's thought, or by creating a noumenal consciousness which imposes its law at will, or by finding in 'nature alone' the laws of dialectical reasoning as contingent facts." *Critique*, pp. 124–25, 128.

law, a metaphysical destiny, then it must spring from individuals and not from some kind of supra-individual ensemble."[4]

In other words, the dialectic can have no foundation unless the individual—not, of course, conceived as a monad, but grasped in the totality of his conditions and relations as a totalization in process of retotalization[5]—can experience it in his own praxis.[6]

But why this "privileged" position of the individual? The answer is quite simple and leads us back to Marx. It is that there is no certainty, no meaning, no comprehension except for somebody. For example, to establish if History has a dialectical intelligibility (or more simply if it is intelligible at all) there is no other way than to seek to understand it. But as to understand means for everyone "I understand," this means to see if History can be reconstructed from a

[4] Ibid., p. 131.

[5] Totality and totalization: "To act means to modify the figure of the given in such a way that a field is structured which, to the actor, constitutes a meaningful totality. This totality is the presupposition for any particular meaningful action within it. In other words, the totality is broken up into finite provinces of meaning, each of which is the scene of particular types of action. While man, as an acting being, is constantly engaged in structuring the world as a meaningful totality (since otherwise he could not meaningfully act within it), this process is never completed. Totality, then, is never a fait accompli, but is always in process of being constructed. Therefore the term totalization can be applied to this meaning-building process." Berger and Pullberg, "Reification and the Social Critique of Consciousness," *New Left Review*, January–February 1966.

[6] Praxis and process: "When what is going on in a group can be traced to the authorship of its members it will be termed praxis, and it will be thus far comprehensible. Behavior, however, may have become too far alienated from anyone's responsibility to be directly comprehensible in terms of the deeds of any identifiable agents. But it will still be intelligible if one can retrace the steps from 'what is going on' (process) to 'who is doing what' (praxis)." R. D. Laing, *New Left Review*, p. 8.

multiplicity of individual praxes, which as partial and conscious totalizations are capable of understanding themselves. History is intelligible to dialectical knowledge if it can be understood as a totalization of totalizations. But the criterion of intelligibility cannot be that God, or Nature, or my father, or the leader claim to have understood: it is that *I understand* (and therefore that everyone can understand). The criterion of intelligibility is self-evidence.

Is this a privilege granted to the subject? Certainly, as the demand to understand—and particularly the demand to understand History, which is made "by individuals pursuing their own ends" and which *makes* individuals and turns back on them as necessity insofar as others make it—is a demand of the "subject" and not of the "object." If I pose in advance that there is an intelligibility or a dialectic or a History, but that we cannot understand it, I find myself in the same kind of relation to it as the believer is with God. More seriously, I deny in advance the possibility of communism—what Marx called in *The German Ideology* the possibility for "united individuals" to "submit to their power" and to "make impossible all that exists independently of them," the possibility of their becoming the "subjects of History" and of recognizing themselves in it as in the product of their own voluntary and conscious collaboration.

The fact is that any discourse on Being that tries to abstract from the speaker and to grasp Being beyond the cognitive situation (i.e., the practical relations) of the speaker, is implicitly a metaphysical discourse: it claims to pronounce on Being in the absence of men. Any certainty that lacks the criterion of being certain for me (of being self-evidence) on the basis of lived experience, is an act of faith that sooner or later leads to dogmatism. Conversely, the only way to eliminate metaphysics is always to refer the affirmation or the investigation to the praxis—historically situated, methodologically defined, oriented towards determinate goals—of the investigator. In other words, any research or affirmation must have its critical counterpart:

must take responsibility for itself as a project in progress, producing its own goals, its own tools and its own principles. Any other course is to grant a metaphysical privilege to the inhuman.

The Dialectic

To return to the dialectic: if it is to appear with complete transparency, if it is not to be a fact of nature or an empirical and unintelligible law such as the law of falling bodies, it must itself be intelligible. It must be one with the knowledge it has of itself; in other words, totalizing knowledge must be homogeneous with the totalization it takes knowledge of, and the known totalization must include a knowledge of itself (or the permanent possibility of that knowledge) as its own structure.[7] The dialectic, then, for the individual who understands it, is the living logic of his own praxis insofar as this operates the totalization of diversity and is totalized by the praxis of others. In brief, until the contrary is proved, dialectical reason is of transparent and certain value only in that sector of being which is the practical totalization by men of inorganic matter and the totalization of praxis by worked matter: human history. It is of value for this sector on condition that it is possible to reconstruct from the individual praxis collective realities and practical ensembles[8] which are fully intelligible.

THE INTELLIGIBILITY OF MATERIAL DIALECTIC

For Marxists, the theoretical and practical issues at stake in this attempt at reconstruction are obviously immense. It is not, as many of them believe, a question of starting from the solitary individual. In the section entitled "Critique de l'Experience Critique," on the contrary, Sartre points out

[7] *Critique,* p. 137–39.
[8] Practical ensembles: general term for human multiplicities.

that "only a man living inside a sector of totalization can grasp the ties of interiority that unite him with the totalizing movement." He goes on:

> The epistemological point of departure must always be *consciousness* as apodictic certainty of itself, and as consciousness *of* some object or other. But we are not concerned here with interrogating consciousness about itself: the object it must set itself is precisely *life*, i.e., the objective being of the investigator in a world of Others, insofar as this being has totalized itself from birth, and will totalize itself until death. It follows that the individual disappears as an historical category: alienation, the practico-inert, series, groups, classes, the components of History, work, individual and common praxis —each man has lived, and lives, all these as interiority. If the movement of dialectical Reason exists, this movement produces this life, this membership of such and such a class, such an environment, such groups; it is the totalization itself which provokes his successes and failures through the vicissitudes of his community, his particular joy and pain; here are the dialectical ties that appear in his love or family relations, his friendships and the "relations of production" that have stamped his life. Starting from this, his own life, *his understanding of his own life must lead to the denial of its singular determination in favor of a search for its dialectical intelligibility in the whole human adventure.*[9]

The endeavor to reconstruct from individual praxes the dialectical intelligibility of the material mediations whereby, at various levels, praxis inverts into the passive anti-dialectical unity of materially structured economic and social processes, possessing their own laws of motion, does not of course prevent these processes from being the object of a specific scientific study regulated by analytic reason. This type of reason can be applied, for example, to monetary circulation or capital accumulation precisely insofar as these are praxes made passive in the exteriority of the inert, turning against agents, and governing them from the outside according to inflexible, insurmountable laws. How-

[9] *Critique*, p. 142. My emphasis.

ever, analytic reason is by its nature incapable of re-establishing at the foundation of these processes, considered in themselves, the multiplicity of the praxes that sustain them and that make them insurmountable for each agent. In other words, although it is legitimate to a certain level of investigation, analytic reason is incapable of rendering intelligible laws which it presents as quasi-natural.

The scope of Sartre's enterprise is to establish the dialectical intelligibility of historical processes solely (which is not the same as studying these processes themselves), and by the same stroke to provide a reciprocity of perspective that permits an understanding of the individual as the alienated agent of history. The following observations will serve to stress the importance of this undertaking.

1. If, as certain sociologists—both Marxist and non-Marxist—maintain, the individual is to be explained by materially structured social wholes without these being intelligible as results of multiple individual praxes, then society cannot be known except as an external object and from an external (non-dialectical) point of view. The individuals, similarly, can only be known from outside as a purely passive product. Moreover, specialists are needed to know the individuals' "true reality." What about the status of these specialists? Aren't they individuals too? Of course they are; but they claim for themselves, as neutral bearers of a transcendent science, the privilege of explaining what the individuals really are, while denying that they themselves and their explanations must or can be explained likewise. Thus, the subjectivity that was to be eliminated returns through the back door: it is now the sociologist who claims dogmatically for his sole self the possibility of an absolute knowledge of all others; he poses as the sole subject, the absolute subjectivity, the solipsistic witness from the beyond, in his claim to know individuals as pure objects through a society that he alone grasps as their truth. Thus everyone is explicable to the sociologist, except he himself who does the explaining.

2. If the individual is explicable through the society, but the society is not intelligible through individuals—that is, if the "forces" that act in history are impermeable and radically heterogeneous to organic praxis—then socialism as the socialization of man can never coincide with socialism as the humanization of the social. It cannot come *from* individuals as their reappropriation by collective praxis of the resultant of their individual praxes. It can only come *to* individuals by the evolution of their society according to its inner logic. The positivist (or transcendental materialist) hypothesis is that the historical process is impermeable to dialectical intelligibility. If so, then socialism, born of an external logic, will also remain external to individuals and will not be a submission of Society and History to individuals and their demands, but a submission of individuals to Society and its demands on them; not the "full development" but the negation of individuals, not the transparency of the social for individual praxis, but the opacity of the individual for himself, insofar as his being and his truth have become completely external to him. Thus the social individual is not the individual recognizing himself and achieving himself in the community, but the individual radically denying himself—his needs, his interests, his certainties—for the sake of a society he experiences as the absolute Other, to the point of feeling guilty not to feel at one with it.[10] We know that this conception of socialism prevailed for a long period, that it still has its adherents, that it profoundly affected Marxist philosophy,

[10] A very good description of this conception, in its subjective aspect, can be found in Kazimierz Brandys' *Defense of Granada*. It is neatly reflected in Czech popular humor in the following joke: The director of the State Plan confided in a militant well known for his intelligence, that the national economy was in a lamentable state, and asked his advice. The militant advised the rigorous application of the official line, expounding this with eloquence. "I know all that," said the director. "It's your personal opinion I'm after. Have you got one?" "Oh yes," replied the militant, "but I'm wrong."

and that it must therefore be liquidated on this terrain as well.

Sartre clearly indicates that this was one of his aims and that, on the other hand, his work was inserted within Marxism and had the strictly limited object of testing out the possibility of a dialectical intellection.

Scope and Aims

Sartre's attempted reconstruction could not, in fact, yet bear on history itself. His aim was to establish beforehand the dialectical intelligibility of the elementary and formal structures of which history is the "totalization without a totalizer." He was concerned to forge from regressive experience the instruments for a dialectical understanding of history to "discover the intelligibility of practical structures and the dialectical relations which link the different forms of active multiplicity."[11]

I must now show by some rather long quotations how the circularity of certain Sartrian arguments is the object of an express warning from Sartre himself. He very precisely delimits the scope and aims of his work:

The experience of the dialectic is itself dialectical: which means that it proceeds and organizes itself at all levels. It is both the experience of living, as living is acting and suffering, and the rationality of praxis; it must be regressive since it sets out from the lived to rediscover gradually all the structures of praxis. However, I must warn that the experiment attempted here, although by itself historical like any other project, is not intended to be a study of the movement of history, the evolution of labor, of the relations of production, of the class struggle. Its goal is simply to discover and to establish dialectical rationality, that is to say, the complex play of praxis and totalization.

When we have reached the most general conditions of these, that is materiality, it will be time to reconstruct from the starting point of our experience a schema of the intelli-

11 *Critique*, pp. 754–55.

gibility proper to totalization . . . So our task cannot *in any way* be the reconstruction of real history in its development, any more than it can consist of a concrete study of the forms of production or of the groups that the sociologist or the anthropologist studies. Our problem is to provide a critique. No doubt this problem is itself raised by History. But our task is precisely to try out, to criticize, and to found—*in history,* and at this moment in the development of human societies—the instruments of thought by means of which History thinks itself, inasmuch as they are at the same time the practical instruments by means of which it makes itself. . . . Our real aim is a theoretical one. It can be formulated as follows: under what conditions is the knowledge of *a history* possible? Within what limits can the connections be revealed as *necessary?*[12]

From the fact that Sartre shows how the group can arise from the series and how the series can be reborn from the group, it should not be concluded that Sartre poses—consciously or otherwise—any *a priori* impossibility of disalienation, and withdraws desperately into solipsism. Sartre himself writes:

It will in no case be sufficient to demonstrate the generation of ensembles by individuals, or inversely to show how individuals are produced by the ensembles which they compose. In each case, it will be necessary to show the dialectical intelligibility of these transformations. This will of course be a *formal* intelligibility. By this we mean that it is necessary to understand the bonds of praxis—as self-aware—with all the complex multiplicities which are organized through praxis and in which the latter loses itself as praxis in order to become *praxis-process*. But we in no way aspire—and we will have the opportunity to repeat this yet more clearly—to determine the concrete history of these metamorphoses of praxis. In particular, we shall see later that the concrete individual becomes a member of very diverse ensembles, for example, of what I shall call *series* and *groups*. It is no part of our project to determine if series have preceded groups or vice versa, either originally or at any given moment of History.

12 Ibid., pp. 134–35.

On the contrary: we shall see that groups are born out of series and that they often end by serializing themselves in their turn. Thus our *sole* concern will be to show the passage of series to groups and of groups to series as constant fluctuations of our practical multiplicity, and to verify the intelligibility of these reversible processes. . . . However, although each moment of regression may appear more complex and more general than the isolated and superficial moment of our individual praxis, it remains from another point of view purely abstract, that is to say that it is yet only a *possibility*. In fact, we shall by this formal procedure achieve a dialectical *circularity*: either considering formally the relations of the group and the series in so far as each of these two ensembles may produce the other, or grasping in experience the individual as the practical foundation for such an ensemble and the ensemble in question as producing the individual in his reality as an historical agent. This circularity exists; it is even (as much for Engels as for Hegel) a characteristic of the dialectical order and of its intelligibility. It nonetheless remains true that circular reversibility is in contradiction with the irreversibility of History as it presents itself to experience. If it is true abstractly that groups and series may produce each other indifferently, it is also true that it is historically such and such a group which, by its serialization, has produced such and such a series (or the other way around), and that if the series has given rise to a new group, this latter, whatever it may be, is irreducible to the first.[13]

ALIENATION

Before proceeding further and posing the question of the relevance of the *Critique* for Marxist inquiry, I should like to suggest certain reflections on the relationship of the *Critique* with *Being and Nothingness,* on the vicissitudes of the Sartrian *cogito* and on the problem of alienation.

One of the aims of *Being and Nothingness* was to give a foundation to psychology and, more especially, to psycho-

[13] Ibid., pp. 153–55.

analysis—by ridding them of mechanist explanations and by giving a theoretical foundation to a method which, in practice, implied the possibility for the individual to rework himself and to make himself master of his existential choice. Sartre begins by expelling from consciousness the objects which psychologists have placed there in their attempt to "explain psychic life": images, sensations, feelings, emotions. Psychologists portray these as flowing through consciousness, conceived of as a passive milieu. Sartre expels the motives, drives, motivations, instincts which are held to govern conscious behavior from behind the scenes and explain it, without themselves being intelligible. He wanted to restore consciousness to itself as freedom, translucidity, activity through and through, total and undifferentiated comprehension of its own behavior, and its own foundation. It is only if this restitution is possible that morality has a meaning. If it is not possible, if the individual is governed from outside or from behind by external and unconscious determinisms, he does not belong to himself and there is no sense in asking him to account for his actions, to answer for the world to the degree to which he makes it, or to humanize it.

The purifying reflection which was the *cogito* of *Being and Nothingness* remains, however, purely abstract. Making freedom once again the ground of all action—including flight from and refusal of freedom, that is to say, bad faith —Sartre demonstrated the possibility in principle of a reconquest over alienation in its subjective dimension, while founding the *formal* possibility of this alienation. He did not, on the other hand, make *real* existence intelligible: the reasons why bad faith is infinitely more widespread than authenticity were a matter, in *Being and Nothingness,* of pure contingency. That work only indicated the ontological reasons why human reality may—or is given to—be misled about itself. If you prefer, *Being and Nothingness* allows one to understand how it is possible that a being who is free praxis may take himself for a statue, a machine or a thing, how it is possible that he may not gain an explicit and thematic awareness of his being praxis. In the *Critique*

Sartre is concerned, on the contrary, to analyze the reality
of alienation as necessity—*practical* necessity in *this* world,
which cannot be transcended by a simple subjective con-
version, and which becomes intelligible only if one goes beyond the framework of the reflexive *cogito,* not in order to
abandon it forever, but rather to return to it constantly.

The *cogito,* in the *Critique,* no longer concerns in fact
the formal (ontological) structures of interiority of the relation of the for-itself to the in-itself and to the Other. It is
constantly transcended by the attempt to grasp the material
mediations by which this relation, in its practical, objective
reality, is deviated, degraded, alienated in a world of inorganic inertia, sealed—that is to say, rendered practically
impossible to transcend—by other praxes. The *cogito* of the
Critique thus no longer refers to the for-itself in its relation
to the in-itself, but to the for-itself in so far as—being a
reworking of the material field towards an end, that is to
say, being praxis and being work—it extends outside itself,
into the materiality and the time of things, in which its
totalizing action (that is to say, the action of reorganizing
the diversity of the given toward an end) *is acted* by the
quasi-totalization in exteriority, in the world of the inert,
of its praxis as one praxis among others exercised at the
same time.

This being-acted, this collapse of praxis into the sealed
inertia of matter which gives back to me my action as that
of another, remote-controlled toward other ends (which
may be those of nobody), and turning against my own
ends, this is one of the forms of alienation, and presents itself immediately to experience. The necessity of alienation,
however, no longer has this character of immediate evidence. The necessity of alienation is not the same, for
Sartre, as the necessity of objectification, but as that of objectification in a world of scarcity and of sociality as series
and as passive being.[14] Sartre writes most notably:

> From the moment when impotence becomes the truth of prac-
> tical power and counter-finality the profound meaning of the

14 Ibid., pp. 358–77.

end pursued, when praxis discovers *its* freedom as the means chosen elsewhere to reduce it to slavery, the individual suddenly rediscovers himself in a world in which free action is the fundamental mystification. He no longer knows freedom except . . . as propaganda of the rulers against the ruled. But one must understand that this experience is no longer that of the act, that of the result become concrete; it is no longer the positive moment in which one *does,* but the negative moment in which one is produced in passivity by what the practico-inert field has done with what one has just done.[15]

[Necessity] is the moment in which, by the very freedom which produces it, the Thing, transformed by other freedoms at work, presents *through its own characteristics* the objectification of the agent as a rigorously foreseeable and yet totally unforeseen alteration[16] of the ends he pursues. . . . Necessity does not manifest itself in the action of the isolated organism or in the succession of physical-chemical facts; the reign of necessity is this domain—real, but still abstract, of History—in which inorganic materiality encloses human multiplicity and transforms producers into its product. Necessity, as a limit to freedom . . . is the revolving field of stricken materiality in so far as it is affirmed and snatched away at the same time, for all and in all free actions, by all free actions as Others; this is what forges our chains.[17]

While, in *Being and Nothingness,* there were the formal couples for-itself–in-itself, freedom–contingency, transcendence–facticity, in the *Critique* one finds: praxis–practico-inert, dialectic–anti-dialectic (that is to say, passive totalization of a multiplicity of praxes by the inert), constituent dialectic–constituted dialectic. Sartre explicitly excludes from the notion of alienation the objectification of solitary praxis in a passive matter which this praxis has produced or transformed in accordance with its original

---

[15] Ibid., p. 373.

[16] *Alteration* has the sense of deterioration as well as modification. Sartre employs it and alterity because they imply theft of my praxis by the Other.

[17] *Critique,* pp. 375–76.

ends, and even if it fails to achieve these ends. He shows
on the contrary that failure[18] can in no way be assimilated
to an alienation (or to an experience of necessity as alienation): the failure of a solitary act exercised in a field in
which it is acting alone, where the failure is due to the
opacity of matter, is foreseen-unforeseeable: unforeseeable
because matter is opaque, but foreseen because its opacity
gives us the certainty that the unforeseen may happen.
You split wood with an ax, the handle gives and the blade
flies off and strikes you on the head, or the ax slips and you
split your shin: this type of accident was foreseen. Far
from presenting itself as a counter-finality or a necessity, it
appears to you as the consequence, prepared by yourself,
of your foolishness, of your clumsiness ("I could have expected it, I was a fool"), in short, as your own act. The
experience of alienation, on the other hand, is, among
other things, the experience of a curse of matter which
turns my actions or their result against me, to the advantage
of the ends of another, or which makes it impossible for
me not to give reality freely to the prefabricated being
which comes toward me like a sentence pronounced over
me and engraved in things. Now, things do not dominate
man and are not insurmountable for him except in so far
as they have absorbed and are sustained by other activities elsewhere—in so far as they are not purely passive, but
are like a passive activity, a materialized practice, the
practico-inert.

THE SUPPRESSIBILITY OF ALIENATION

By taking great care to show that man can be alienated
only in as much as he is praxis, and that his alienation can
originate only in the praxis of others (in *Being and Nothingness* Sartre wrote: "only freedom can limit freedom"),
Sartre rejects all religious and metaphysical definitions of

18 Ibid., pp. 282–83 and 749–50.

alienation as pertaining to the subject in his relation to
Being or to Nature. Alienation is neither a natural fatality
nor an inherent characteristic of human nature; it is the
negative destiny which praxis suffers through the praxis of
others as mediated by worked matter, on the basis of determinate material circumstances (some of which, most
notably scarcity, have a natural origin). The necessity of
alienation, in other words, is something historical and not
something ontological or metaphysical. In principle, it must
therefore be possible to liquidate it. The negative destiny
which comes to men by man is a human destiny which
men must, in principle, be capable of reconquering and
submitting to their control. But this liquidation of a destiny
which comes to each of us by all (in so far as they themselves are alienated) can be achieved only when those material circumstances on the basis of which the praxis of all
is for each man a hostile force, are themselves abolished
by the practical unification of all.

This, however—which is the profound meaning of history—is not something that can be achieved at any time
and at will. Although the inert processes that betray, negate
and alienate human praxis are a resultant of the latter,
they are not its creation. The practico-inert processes are
themselves produced on the basis of natural circumstances.
And these in fact constitute an obstacle to the durable
positive unification of human praxis as long as scarcity
persists. Scarcity, as defined by Sartre, is an original factual
negation of organic life. Life can perpetuate itself only
through a practical negation of this factual negation: all
living beings have to struggle against a hostile world in
which their existence is threatened, in which "there is not
enough for everyone" and in which, therefore, every individual potentially endangers the life of others by drawing
on scarce resources. The relation between individuals thus
bears originally the imprint of the negative circumstances
—that is, of scarcity—on the basis of which they are established. Every individual is a potential supernumerary in so
far as he may be "the one too many" to whom survival—

or satisfaction of needs—may be denied by the others' struggle to get enough. And conversely every individual is a potential "counter-man"—"a wolf to man"—in so far as he may deny survival or satisfaction of their needs to the others.

The necessity of conflict, of violence, of man's otherness for man has its ultimate factual foundation in scarcity. Scarcity is a negation imposed on man externally by nature and has to be internalized as negation of Nature by man and of man by man. It makes for the fact that history cannot be natural history, and that human beings cannot live in harmony with Nature: they have to transform the natural environment through work in order to survive, they have to be praxis and anti-physis; they have to produce their subsistence and the conditions for their subsistence. From this point of view, scarcity "founds the possibility of history"; it is "its passive motor." History begins when the factual impossibility of man is perceived as "the impossibility of this impossibility," that is, when men, revolting against destiny, set out to render the impossible possible.

The way Sartre deals with this theme is an implicit reminder of Marx's philosophy: communism will be the end of prehistory and the beginning of *human* history; and the factual precondition of communism is that scarcity should give way to abundance, that nature should be mastered in such a way as to cease being hostile to human life.

The importance given by Sartre to the category of scarcity is by no means relevant only to underdeveloped countries. Both the theory and the reality of relative immiseration in capitalist societies can be understood only if the fact of scarcity is taken into account. A Marxist starting from the analyses of the *Critique* could show that industrial development reproduces scarcity at other levels—scarcity of time, of men, of primary resources, of energy, etc. —and that all new scarcities, including those which have become apparent in socialist countries, stem precisely from basic scarcity.

For a Marxist today must refuse to isolate developed countries from others; he must, on the contrary, situate them in a global context in which every local and partial victory over scarcity brings with it a displacement of scarcity into other areas. This alone enables one to understand the aggravation of imperialist wars, inter-imperialist struggles and even, of late, rifts within the socialist camp. This obviously does not mean that struggle against scarcity should be considered hopeless. It simply means that in a world where three quarters of mankind are still undernourished, and two thirds are actually starving, in a world where the foreseeable (and even, locally, the present) population growth is greatly outstripping production of food, human life remains precarious. The industrial regions are enclaves in a world which lacks the minimum necessary for survival. Famine and the struggle against famine remain the defining truth of this century and probably of the century to come. Victory over scarcity—abundance—remains *for us* inconceivable.

Sartre thus ranges himself against those Marxists—there are fewer and fewer of them, it is true—who consider scarcity a circumstance and product of the capitalist phase of development. Furthermore, since Sartre considers violence as internalized scarcity—that is, the negation of man in exteriority becomes the negation of the Other by each Other acting in a situation of scarcity—it is understandable that for Sartre socialism cannot yet suppress violence in human relations, nor alienation as the sealed inorganic negation of human praxis. Socialism cannot yet abolish "the reign of necessity."

Yet the suppressibility of the reign of necessity is clearly shown by Sartre when he describes the particular and short-lived situations in which individuals, when confronted with a threat against "all of us," cease struggling each for himself and unite so as to face together an obstacle or an enemy that could not be mastered by a multiplicity of dispersed individual actions. The active unity of human praxis

which then emerges—the "fused group"[19]—is the paradigm
of all egalitarian concepts of what a liberated fraternal
community should be. The fused group is the one and only
type of dialectical totalization in which the overall resultant
of a multiplicity of individual praxes is, as a result of voluntary co-operation, homogeneous to each of them. In the
fused group, alienation is—at least temporarily—abolished.
To understand the significance of this experience and the
reason why the fused group cannot, in the present world,
overcome for long the necessity of alienation, we have to
deal shortly with the two main types of practical ensembles—or modes of totalization—that make up the fabric of
history.

In the world of scarcity, ignorance and necessity, the
most common practical ensemble is what Sartre calls the
"series":[20] a multiplicity of dispersed individual praxes,
each struggling toward its own ends. The cohesion of these
praxes is purely external. For example, hundreds of thou-
sands of peasants, each attempting to enlarge his piece of
land, cut the trees on the hill slopes. The multiplicity of
their dispersed praxes is unified externally according to the
laws of inert materiality and reverts itself against "all" families as an external negation of their ends: erosion, flood-
ings, natural catastrophes are the anti-human totalization
of discrete practical totalizations. Processes of this type—in
particular social processes like fluctuations of the market,
business cycles, traffic jams, etc.—are what Sartre calls the
"practico-inert."[21] They are "a reversed praxis," a "passive power," an "inert synthesis" of praxes, "a bond of
materiality which surpasses and alterates the simple human
relations" and constitutes each praxis into a force that is
its own enemy and its own negation as the praxis of the
Other. It is insurmountable not because of its material inertia, but because it is sustained by a multiplicity of dis-

19 Ibid., pp. 381–432.
20 Ibid., pp. 308–47.
21 Ibid., pp. 225–60.

persed praxes "sealed" together by materiality. As long as
this dispersion persists, *each* individual suffers the "common condition"—for instance, pollution, overcrowding, etc.
—as a bond of materiality imposed onto him, through the
mediation of matter, by *all* others. In traffic jams, queues,
crowds or in processes like slumps, inflation, etc., *all* are
always for each individual the external unity of the Others
and each is his own enemy as an Other among others. Each
individual in a series is just "one more Other" and has a
serial behavior, which means that his actions are determined by this and everyone else's otherness, as when he
sells his stock because the others, acting as Others, will
sell, or rushes to the stores to hoard food because the
Others can be expected to do so. Each acts to save himself
from the effects of the foreseeable actions of the others—
there will be a slump; food threatens to be short—and
thereby produces these effects as an Other. The slump or
the food shortage might be prevented only if all acted together for a common purpose. But precisely their situation,
type of external cohesion, self-interest and behavior are
such that their union remains a practical impossibility.
Speculators cannot unite because speculating is in its essence a serial praxis and the stock exchange or food market an institution produced by serial relations and designed
to perpetuate them. The same goes for all so-called "collectives"[22]—markets, services, cities, classes—which are but
the external unity of the praxis of all as Others, the
practico-inert unity of dispersed multiplicity.

Only in determinate historical circumstances, in situations of extreme urgency, when everyone needs everyone
else to act as *one*, can serial alienation and impotence be
overcome and the reign of liberty supersede that of necessity. This is the case when individuals unite into a group
so as to produce freely their practical unity, aiming at a
shared goal through a shared unified praxis. The fusion of
the group is a privileged instant (that of insurrection or

22 Ibid., pp. 306–86.

revolution, for instance) in which history and the destiny of all are really borne by the freedom of fraternal individuals, and in which the possibility of the reign of man manifests itself as the possible meaning of history.

Sartre takes great care to define the circumstances of the emergence of a fused group. Among the conditions he emphasizes are: vital urgency (danger of death, for instance), geographical proximity, previous objective unification (in the face of the common enemy) of the multiplicity into a "collective" (namely, a class) which will be the "matrix" of the group. When the threat which weighs upon each as other among others cannot be removed except by the common action of all, and *the physical and historical circumstances are propitious,* each totalizes all in the same way as they totalize him, in the movement towards a shared goal. The interiorization of number and the accompanying communalization of the object of praxis are not just subjectivist sleight of hand. They describe the more or less daily experience of each of "us"; the factory worker who feels himself one of five thousand or ten thousand other workers is powerless when he is separated from all the others by seriality, by the reign of terror. He naturally asks himself: "Why fight back if nobody else does?" The serial behavior of each worker, as Other in the passive unity of the collective, will take the form of putting himself first. But when, in certain definite situations, the repression which is directed against one or more of these separate Others is seen as an external threat to the vital interests of each, then each himself becomes part of the five thousand or ten thousand in the demand that everywhere each worker "interiorize" their number, and so experience it as the shared force of the shared being of all in shared activity. Each man, by liquidating in and about him seriality and impotent alterity, behaves as he wants all and each to behave. Each becomes the way by which all become themselves and all become the way by which each becomes himself. The necessity of freedom is this praxis of the common individual who recognizes and reflects himself in the

common praxis and common object of all. He both effects
the ongoing totalization and, at the same time, feels himself required as part of the totalization effected about him.
"The group is both the most effective means of controlling
surrounding materiality within the framework of scarcity
and the absolute end which as pure freedom liberates men
from alterity."[23]

Violence

Much could be said about the group seen as sovereignty
and as the original source of juridical power. This raises
the question of the pledge, which is both the affirmation of
the power of each individual over all as each becomes
guarantor of the unity of the group, and demands of all
that they should forbid the relapse of each into serial
alterity. This right exercised by each over all and all over
each tends to replace fear of the enemy or of common
danger—temporarily past—by fear which has been produced
as the free product of the group: by Fraternity-Terror.[24]
It is astonishing to find Marxists rejecting the notion of Terror, of violence both against the Other and against the
"selves" as structures of the revolutionary group, and dismissing these concepts as the product of Sartre's "aesthetic
romanticism." The real romantics—bourgeois romantics—
are those wistful dreamers who think that groups constitute themselves not out of revolt against the necessity of
the practico-inert, as a violent refusal to be subjected to
violence, but as the result of some sort of social contract or
convergence of individual interests. Again, Sartre cannot
be accused of voluntarism; he insists that groups and common action can only be produced in direct struggle the
violence of the enemy. The real voluntarists are those who
go on dreaming of a non-violent transformation of society,
carried out by decree, in accordance with rules established

23 Ibid., p. 639.
24 Ibid., p. 428 et seq.

and accepted in advance by some kind of popular "consensus."

It may seem difficult to accept Hope, Terror, Violence and sovereign Freedom as structures of this kind of group formation if we view these things simply from a tactical point of view in a given situation. But we need only have experienced a strike—even a small strike—or a mass demonstration to realize that these are indeed the "essential structures"[25] of the fused group and hence of the pledged (or statutory) group. A strike is always waged against both the class enemy *and* against fear, which gives birth to betrayal, to the serialized Other, to the scab. Violence against scabs need not necessarily be physical; violence is nonetheless the climate of a mass strike. Non-violent revolution (or even non-violent strikes) is not made possible just because our particular situation rules out the opportunity for armed insurrection. For any transition to socialism, however effected, by whatever kind of mass action, will be a violent rejection of violence—the violence of the class enemy, real or threatened. Hence there will be "sacred unity" and "Terror" in the sense defined above. This violence can perfectly well also be exercised against those within the revolutionary group who advocate armed force. Every militant is well aware that "moral" violence ("moral pressure") against advocates of physical violence is a kind of violence in its turn.

THE METAMORPHOSES OF THE GROUP

Two thirds of the second book of the *Critique*[26] are an attempt to describe the formal laws of the dialectic which will enable us to understand the metamorphoses of the group: the gradual degradation of the fused group into the statutory group and thence into the institutionalized

25 Ibid., p. 429.
26 Ibid., pp. 381–639.

group, which by exercising a monopoly, is able to manipulate serial ensembles from without and thus, eventually, relapse into seriality in its own turn. At this point, we are back where we first started, the cycle is completed, "the basic experience has been accomplished." This does not mean that Sartre is trying to show the circularity of History and the eternal re-emergence of the same structures. His aim is rather to reconstruct and render dialectically intelligible "the ensemble of frames, curves, structures and conditions which make up the *formal milieu* in which the concrete reality of history must necessarily be produced."[27]

In other words, dialectical experience has made intelligible the emergence from individual praxes of all practical ensembles, and their transformation into each other, given that no single one of them has any historical priority vis-à-vis the others. The series, collective, fused group, statutory group, institutionalized group, etc. are not successive stages of historical development but coexist, clash and coalesce as the elementary formal structures (partial totalities and totalizations) of which history is the totalization.

The Revolutionary State

Sartre's descriptions of the metamorphoses of the group have, nevertheless, a very particular contemporary interest. For they schematize the modern historical experience of the formation of states and bureaucracies after periods of revolutionary élan. Sartre refers implicitly (and sometimes explicitly) to the French, Russian, Cuban and Algerian revolutions. It is quite clear that for Sartre the "formal laws of the dialectic" always have inevitably led the fused group—a community which is active and sovereign through and through—to relapse into a diversified, opaque and alienated form of unity. Stalinism was not a more or less accidental deviation. The process by which all past revolutions have ended up in more or less petrified bureaucratic forms,

27 Ibid., p. 637.

even when—as in Yugoslavia—they have made efforts to
fight against this, illustrates dialectical laws which need to
be understood.

For Sartre the fused group represents the elimination of
serial alienation, but this cannot be a lasting elimination in
a world of scarcity and struggle. The fused group exists as
the instant of the revolutionary apocalypse, of full freedom, when totalization is produced everywhere and in everyone, under everyone's sovereignty, when there are no
leaders, no hierarchies, no functions. Every slogan and
initiative is immediately recognized by each individual as a
common slogan and initiative, in the service of a common
goal.

The fused group, in which all men are brothers, is produced as an ongoing unity by a multiplicity of individual
syntheses, all of which share a common goal and in doing
so demand and sustain this unity. "Group unity is immanent in the multiplicity of its syntheses," it "is never that
of a completed totality but that of a totalization under
way." "The intelligibility of the group as praxis is based on
the intelligibility of individual praxis."[28]

Now, in order to realize its goal, the group must necessarily endow itself with inertia. It must safeguard itself
against breakdown by the pledge, by exercising juridical
power over each of its members. It must differentiate itself in order to cope with a diversity of tasks and hence
reorganize itself by creating functions and specialized subgroups, with their own inertia, discipline and hierarchy. It
passes from constituent reason (or dialectic)—that of living
organic individual praxis—to constituted reason, to the
praxis-process of the organization. The unity of group
praxis is then no longer assured by each individual's synthesis of the action of all but by the inertia of an organization and an apparatus. "The group is constructed on the
model of free individual action," "it produces an organic
action although it is not itself a living organism," "it is a

[28] Ibid., p. 432.

machine for producing non-mechanical responses" and "inertia constitutes both its being and its reason for being, as it does with every human product."[29] The specialized subgroups, capable of coping with tasks of increasing complexity and scope, fall into a permanent danger of being out of step with every other subgroup, of being separated and serialized; hence it is necessary to co-ordinate and integrate their activity—to incarnate the unity of the group—by means of a supreme organism, a sovereign (for example, the state or the leader) who controls and monopolizes group function, guaranteeing and reflecting the practical unity of the group, which is already undergoing serialization and petrification. Thus we arrive at the institutionalized group, which is created when "under the pressure of external circumstances, the individual desires to become a thing, pressed against all other things by the unity of a seal; the model of the institutional group will be the forged tool."[30] This is the moment, in other words, of the reification of praxis. A special study would be needed to show the rich contribution this part of the *Critique* could make to a Marxist theory of law and of the state.[31] I will restrict myself to a few brief remarks:

Sartre explicitly rejects "the optimistic and over-hastily formulated notion" of the dictatorship of the proletariat, "the very idea [of which] is absurd, a bastard compromise between the active and sovereign group and passive seriality."[32] He denounces as a mystification "the idea of a diffused popular sovereignty which would incarnate itself in the sovereign." Sovereignty can belong only to organic praxis, whether of the individual or the group. "The state can under no circumstances be considered the product or the expression of the totality of social individuals or even

29 Ibid., p. 544.
30 Ibid., p. 585.
31 Ibid., pp. 581–637. In this connection, see also N. Poulantzas, "L'Préliminaires á l'étude de l'hégémonie dans l'Etat," *Les Temps Modernes,* November and December 1965.
32 *Critique,* p. 630.

of their majority."[33] On the contrary, it appears as a specific group produced by the ruling class to defend its general interests against the conflict of particular interests within the ruling class itself, and to render this general interest acceptable to other classes. In other words, the state is the sovereign group by which the serialized ruling class is guaranteed in its unity *but maintained in its serial dispersion*, manipulated and thwarted in its efforts at regroupment.

The group thus undergoes an inevitable degradation as it becomes increasingly differentiated, and a serialization as each specialized subgroup becomes ignorant of the actions of the other subgroups and divided from them by conflicts of interest. This in turn creates the demand for a retotalization of the unity of partial praxes by a "sovereign." But with the emergence of the sovereign, the unity of the group falls into radical exteriority, for its sovereignty becomes incarnated in a Third Party, the only totalizer of the group, and its members have no more than serial relations between them. Each of them is for the other an Other, they are the same only by the mediation of the sovereign Third. This degradation perhaps evokes Stalinist Russia—or China today, where the unity and truth of the society reside for each member in the political thought of Mao, source of all rights and duties. Now the following thesis is defended by certain Marxists: namely, that the root of alienation is the *natural* division of labor, hence it can be suppressed by a *voluntary* division of labor (or co-operation). But the problem here is to know under just what conditions there can be genuine "voluntary co-operation" and what one means by this term. In a large country, under present material conditions, the rational unity of social praxis can be forged only by *organized* voluntary co-operation, by the formation of subgroups whose task is linked to that of other subgroups which are themselves interlinked by the centralizing group or sovereign. It is evident that this is a society

33 Ibid., p. 609.

whose praxis-process is organized with rigorous rationality on the model of petrified individual praxis, and cannot be totalized by any of the groups' individuals. "Volunteer work"—in the Chinese model, for example—is the product of internalized constraints that individuals impose on themselves and on others (with all the persuasive mildness in which Fraternity-Terror can be clad) in the name of the sovereign. The belief that this generalized rational organization—with the failures and wastages which are the inevitable product of bureaucrats fearing the central authority and distrusting their equals—*is* communism, or the end of alienation, was held in China in 1958, in the heroic epoch of the Communes.

The Fused Group in History

The *Critique*, by contrast, suggests that the only true model of "voluntary co-operation" is the fused group. That the fused group cannot have a durable existence is due to several factors: (1) scarcity and the multiplicity of antagonistic processes in the world; (2) the nature of tools (or means of production), that is to say, the resistance, the inertia and the complexity of the practical field, structured as it is by the available techniques. This inertia and complexity oblige the group to make itself inert and complex in order to be effective and determine within it both specialization and scarcity of productive forces. It should at this point be remembered that, for Marx in Books II and III of *Capital*, communism is distinguished by the end of scarcity, by polytechnicism (the opposite of specialization), which will permit the indefinite permutation of tasks between individuals, and by the abolition of work as "an obligation imposed by poverty and by external goals." The realization of these three conditions still remains difficult for us to imagine, more difficult perhaps than a hundred years ago.

Marxists should therefore not be astonished that the *Critique* suggests that, in the world of scarcity and class struggle, any group which raises itself above alienation and the practico-inert finishes by falling back into it. Can one be a Marxist and believe, even for an instant, that in this hunger-ridden world, ravaged by imperialist wars, by inter-imperialist antagonisms, by the conflicts between the oppressed peoples themselves, a revolutionary group—even supposing that it embraced the totality of the class or people grouped for its liberation—could locally triumph over alienation? Such a belief derives, properly speaking, from the spirit of optimistic utopianism that one finds in certain religious communities. Sartre has provided us with a devastating criticism of just this spirit in *Le Diable et le bon Dieu*.

Of course, the revolutionary Marxist movement can and even must work to limit the ravages caused by the objective tendency towards petrification and serialization in society and in parties, towards the centralization and sclerosis of every apparatus. But this corrective work is necessary just because this objective tendency is a "formal law of the dialectic," and it is possible only if one starts by recognizing the existence of this tendency and the impossibility of suppressing it once and for all in present circumstances.

The work of the philosopher is to raise problems, to show their existence, not to pretend presumptuously to solve them. To turn against him the problems which he poses, and on the pretext that he does not know the answers, to accuse him of nihilism or despairing solipsism is to dispose of problems cheaply and to outlaw philosophy. In fact, most of the criticisms so far addressed by Marxists to Sartre start with *petitio principii* unverified by historical experience. He has been accused of not showing that alienation, scarcity, violence, bureaucracy, the state and so on can be abolished. Under cover of Marxist "science," these critics abandon science and above all the effort to understand history. By contrast, Sartre's enterprise is to give himself (and us) the instruments of dialectical understanding, and thereby the means to pose the question of the possibility of suppressing the inhuman in human history, and of the eventual conditions of its suppressibility. To anticipate the answer to these questions by giving them in advance in the guise of Marxist "science" or to refuse them by announcing that they stem from idealist speculation, is the best way to learn nothing. Such an attitude reveals a singular lack of confidence in Marxism: a fear that the discoveries we might make will shatter our convictions and the depth of our commitment.